CASES IN COMPARATIVE POLITICS
ASIA

CASES IN COMPARATIVE POLITICS ASIA

EDITED BY Lucian W. Pye

Massachusetts Institute of Technology

LITTLE, BROWN AND COMPANY BOSTON

LIBRARY OF CONGRESS CATALOG CARD NO. 70-101306

FIRST PRINTING

Published simultaneously in Canada
by Little, Brown & Company (Canada) Limited

PRINTED IN THE UNITED STATES OF AMERICA

THE CONTRIBUTORS

JOSE VELOSO ABUEVA, Professor and Assistant Dean at the College of Public Administration, University of the Philippines, is Visiting Professor of Political Science at Yale University (1969–70). He is the author of *Focus on the Barrio* and a political biography of Ramon Magsaysay (now in press); a coeditor of *Foundations and Dynamics of Filipino Government and Politics;* and a contributing author of *Public Administration in the Philippines, Political and Administrative Development,* and *Development Administration in Asia.* He has served the Philippine Government as Director of the Administrative Development Staff on Foreign Affairs and as Executive Director of the Congressional Joint Local Government Reform Commission. Professor Abueva received his Ph.D. from the University of Michigan.

HANS H. BAERWALD, Professor of Political Science, University of California (Los Angeles), is on leave during 1969–70 as Director of the Study Center of the University of California and Visiting Professor at International Christian University, Mitaka, Tokyo, Japan. His major publications include *The Purge of Japanese Leaders under the Occupation* and coauthorship of *The American Republic.* He grew up in Japan and has served there intermittently in a variety of capacities for twenty-five years; he received his Ph.D. from the University of California at Berkeley.

HAROLD HINTON is Professor of Political Science and International Affairs at the Institute for Sino-Soviet Studies at the George Washington University. He is the author of a number of writings on Chinese politics and foreign policy, including *Communist China in World Politics* and the forthcoming *China's Turbulent Quest.* Professor Hinton received his Ph.D. from Harvard University.

GENE D. OVERSTREET was, until his death in 1965, associate research professor in the Institute for Sino-Soviet Studies of George Washington

University and visiting associate professor at American University. His undergraduate work was done at Reed College and he received his Ph.D. at Columbia University. Before going to George Washington he taught at Michigan State University and Swarthmore College. From 1953 to 1955 he studied in India on a Ford Foundation Fellowship. He was co-author (with Marshall Windmiller) of *Communism in India* (1959) and he contributed articles on India and communism to several professional journals.

Lucian W. Pye, Professor of Political Science at the Massachusetts Institute of Technology, is Chairman of the Committee on Comparative Politics of the Social Science Research Council. He grew up in North China and has engaged in extensive research in Southeast Asia. Professor Pye is the author of many books and articles on Asian affairs and political development, including *Aspects of Political Development; Politics, Personality and Nation-Building,* and *The Spirit of Chinese Politics.* Professor Pye received his Ph.D. from Yale University.

Ann Ruth Willner is Associate Professor of Political Science at the University of Kansas. She served as an adviser with the Indonesian Ministry of Foreign Affairs and National Planning Bureau. She has contributed articles on Indonesia to a number of journals, including *World Politics, Asian Survey, Human Organization,* and the *New Leader.* She is completing a book on charismatic political leadership, a part of which has been published as *Charismatic Political Leadership: A Theory.* Professor Willner received her Ph.D. from the University of Chicago.

CONTENTS

CASES IN COMPARATIVE POLITICS ASIA

PART I INTRODUCTION

LUCIAN W. PYE

The end of empire and the emergence of new states in Asia and Africa, which have brought so many profound changes to our world, have inevitably affected both the world of scholarship and life in the classroom. For political science the many new nation states in the world have radically altered our universe for analysis, and studying the politics of the diverse Asian and African cultures has brought stimulation and new vitality to our discipline.

Indeed, fundamental changes in politics call for equally fundamental changes in the approaches adopted by the political scientist. Political theory, traditionally the core of political science, can no longer treat only the intellectual traditions in Western political thought. If we are to arrive at truly universal concepts on which to base our discipline, we must make sure that our theories are relevant not only for Western societies, but for all the diverse systems in Asia and Africa as well. Comparative politics is faced with a vital and interesting challenge. Already, appropriate changes have begun to enlarge our vision of the range of political systems.

The initial effort to incorporate the study of Asian politics into the main stream of political science quite properly focused, first, on learning more about the great historical traditions of Asia, and, second, upon exploring contemporary social, economic, and political modernization and development. Very often these two approaches have not been closely integrated. For example, students of Confucian thought and institutions or of Hindu philosophy have concentrated mainly on history and the earlier and more glorious ages of Asia, and have been prone either to think recent events insignificant or to see such events as merely continuations in new guises of old Asian practices. On the other hand, students of political development, have concentrated almost exclusively upon the contemporary scene and upon appropriate ways of categorizing and distinguishing between traditional and modern modes of behavior. Preeminent in this approach is determining the factors that facilitate or inhibit economic growth and nation building, and, consequently, distinctions among the great traditions, which are of the essence for those with historical interests, are largely ignored and casually lumped together in a general abstraction called the "traditional order."

Thus, students of traditional Asian cultures and languages have understandably been little interested in viewing change, except possibly to bemoan it, whereas students of change and development have had little interest in the specific characteristics of Asian cultures, except possibly to bemoan their persistence.

In spite of this difference in emphasis between the two principal approaches to the study of Asian politics, they have one important quality in common. Both have concentrated on the most fundamental historical and sociological processes that underlie politics, and in their different ways each has minimized the actual process of politics itself. We have sometimes confused our descriptions of the social, economic, and cultural bases of politics – crucial as these are – with all that needs to be known of politics in distant societies. We have, consequently, built up a picture of Asian societies as responsive only to the grossest forces of history but lacking in those mechanisms of politics through which people can resolve their conflicts and seek power and influence. In arriving at our first approximations of the nature of Asian political systems we have understandably emphasized what appeared to be the most fundamental and also the most universal determinants of their historical experiences: their great traditions of political thought and the new, powerful feelings of nationalism in response to the Western influence, on the one hand, and the decisive consequences of limited economic development and widespread subsistence agriculture, on the other. Asian societies have thus apparently been activated in the past to an extraordinary degree either by past traditions or by nationalistic passions and the stings of recent humiliations. And under present conditions we are prone to believe that Asian peoples can only be absorbed with achieving economic development in the face of manifest poverty. Their public life thus far has seemed to be no more than a direct response to sociological and economic conditions.

In this picture of Asia we find lacking a representation of those political processes by which men, using wit and imagination, strive competitively to mobilize support and to outmaneuver each other so that some views of the public good will prevail over others and so that some interests will be better served than others. Only when we examine political life in Asia in greater depth will we discover that in these societies politicians are responding to more than just the larger historic forces; they are also obliged to work out power relationships with their political friends and foes. Leaders are not only prisoners of the forces that have previously shaped their national histories; they must also defer to the more intimate forces that guide their personal destinies. Therefore, most Asian leaders feel that they are governed not so much by the diffuse powers of history as by the all too limited support of specific, contemporary constituencies.

In studying American and European politics we have progressed to a stage at which we can seek to put into appropriate balance background considerations and the immediate dynamics of the political process. The time has now arrived for us to strive to do the same in studying Asian politics. We must seek a sounder and more sensitive understanding of day-to-day political life in Asian countries. By tracing through the decision-making activities and by examining in some detail historic examples of these political processes in action, we can hope to identify the most important factors shaping political developments in this most populated part of the world.

It is true that, historically, Asian societies have not possessed as distinctly organized or as explicitly recognized means of expressing political forces as can be found in the modern West. Functions that are performed in the West by political parties and pressure groups have traditionally been fulfilled in Asia by far more informal methods, with the result that political processes there are less conspicuous to the Western eye. The more tradition-bound attitudes common to many Asian peoples have made them appear better prepared to accept the disposition of fate – that is, of social and economic forces. Their leaders have felt no compelling need to organize institutions that could be clearly identified as foci for political pressure and as having responsibility for political decisions. Politics, with its own logic and as a semiautonomous process in which men engage in activities based on their conception of how events can be influenced by human effort, has tended usually to remain relatively obscured in Asian societies.

The difficulty, even at present, of clearly perceiving a pattern in day-to-day political activities in Asia strengthens the impression that these countries do not have politics but rather only histories of social and economic trends. Asian societies are thus frequently considered to be organized without benefit of those arrangements by which men seek to control the social world about them and by which they are, in turn, conditioned. What there is of political life becomes a matter of irrational and automatic response to the impersonal forces of social and political change. Since they are simply the passive recipients of such forces, the Asian peoples and their leaders are viewed all too frequently as incapable of all the complex responses and choices, both rational and prejudicial, which are the essence of politics and which bring out both the dignity and the meanness of man. With the political scene left unstructured and nearly void, any Asian leader who assumes a strong political posture seems merely to be acting out of individual cussedness or isolated utopianism rather than in response to the types of political pressure that confront Western politicians. To discuss the "awakening" of Asia without referring to the details of political relationships would be to risk leaving the impression that until recently Asians were politically unsophisticated and hardly social beings, and that even today they are still less than rational as they seek to solve their problems in a fit of passion, be it Communist or nationalist.

There is no question that the social and economic setting conditions and shapes a society's political life, but to understand how this happens requires hypotheses and data not usually found in examining the general features of a society. Overpopulation, lack of capital, limited technological development, and the like all variously shape the political life of Asian countries, but in precisely what manner remains far from clear. How do the different Asian populations and their leaders perceive these problems? How do they react to them? What role do they assign to rational choice? What do they consider to be rational? Questions such as these must be asked if we are to bridge the gap between hypotheses about the general structure of these societies and the reality of their day-to-day political life. We need propositions that can link the actual behavior of leaders and followers to the larger social and economic realities of Asia. These intermediate propositions become the key to understanding political developments. They also suggest relationships that are critical for policy thinking, since they involve statements about the political response that can be expected to follow from alternative policy choices.

We have clearly reached the stage in our study of Asian political systems at which we must supplement the general social, economic, and historical analyses now available with a more detailed analysis of the everyday political processes. One of the most effective methods for examining the political process in any society is to concentrate on historical events and to notice who the principal actors were, how they interacted with each other, and what they were able to accomplish. In short, the case study approach can provide the drama essential to bringing life to the otherwise relatively impersonal analysis of Asian systems. Case studies can suggest how the larger historical forces are in part transformed into human relationships.

By suggesting that the time is ripe for introducing more case studies into the study of Asian politics we do not intend to belittle in any fashion more general studies; quite the contrary, because any case study can be significant only insofar as it reveals the basic character of a society. Before it was possible to enrich our study of Asian politics with individual case studies we first had to have the solid bases in historical and general social analysis that have been building up in recent years.

Therefore, in arriving at a systematic approach to the comparative study of Asian political systems it is proper that we begin with the grand cultural traditions and see how these contributed in forming the historical communities of Asia. Vital ingredients in all these great traditions were the principal religious and intellectual persuasions of Asia — Buddhism, Hinduism, Taoism, Confucianism, and Islam — which gave strength and form to Asian institutions. For as these great ideologies developed there emerged sophisticated institutions that once dominated the Asian societies. In China, the Confucian order was sustained by an elaborate bureaucratic system of rule. In India, the Hindu states produced a system of law and princely rule that reinforced Hinduism as a social force that bound men to their respective positions in society. In Southeast Asia, Buddhism on the mainland and Islam in the island areas, each in its separate way, influenced the developing secular authorities and shaped the most substantial political institutions that evolved in these traditional cultures.

Once the different patterns of traditional thought and institutional evolution have been distinguished, it is important for comparative analysis to appraise the different forms that contact with the West took in touching the lives of traditional Asian societies. In some areas, the influence was direct, harsh, and complete, whereas in others, it was much more indirect and subtle. Even where colonial rule existed, patterns varied according to the practices adopted by the European powers. Differences also appeared among the institution of direct colonial rule and the more subtle practices of indirect rule as carried out in some Malay states and parts of Indonesia.

In addition to historical interpretations, the systematic comparative analysis of Asian societies requires that we examine the contemporary social and economic determinants of national development in the Asian societies. Although from afar village life may look the same throughout the world, in actuality the differences among village traditions are profound. Similarly, in spite of superficial similarities in the rapid growth of urban life in the various Asian countries, there are, in fact, striking differences; in some cities, such as Rangoon and Djakarta, rapid growth has produced relatively tightly knit subcommunities because the migrants from the countryside have settled as neighbors of people whom they already knew, whereas in other cities, such as Calcutta and Singapore, urban growth has been accompanied by greater anonymity and impersonality.

These differences in historical traditions and in the contemporary realities of social and economic life together have produced different patterns of power and different assumptions about authority and the proper role of government in each of the Asian countries. The fact that most Asian societies today have similar problems in national development does not mean that there are not great differences in the ways in which social and political power is organized and created within their societies or in the ways in which they go about realizing public policy objectives.

In the first decade after World War II most Asian societies were absorbed with their internal problems as they sought to establish modern nation states. For many of these the task was essentially one of taking over the formal structure of government that had been implanted in the society by an alien colonial rule. In other cases, such as China, deep social cleavages appeared as new institutions and ideologies challenged each other to determine how old societies would become modern nations. At the most general level, all Asian societies have been caught up in the tension between contending worldwide ideologies – ranging from Communism to democracy and from republicanism and federalism to various forms of socialism.

In each country, however, the actual development of institutions has been more responsive to local and immediate historical considerations. Each of the Asian countries is now working out for itself appropriate institutions for handling the tasks of modernization and for coping with the contemporary world. These patterns have been greatly influenced by the extraordinary leaders who have dominated the recent Asian scene. In China, the personalities of Mao Tse-tung and Chiang K'ai-shek have shaped the destiny of the largest country in the world far more than most theories of social forces would suggest is possible. Indian development is still heavily indebted to Nehru's guiding influence. In Southeast Asia, Sukarno dominated the Indonesian scene for the first decade of independence, whereas in Burma, U Nu and Ne Win have in their separate ways determined that nation's development.

Once we are prepared to admit the influence of great men on national development, the stage should be set for analyzing their associations and contacts, and we should be ready to examine the actual political process in its particular issues and events. Before turning to the case studies that make up this volume, however, it would be useful to remind ourselves of some of the distinctive characteristics of the principal political systems in Asia. As we have suggested, the value of any case study depends on how sharply it highlights the distinctive qualities of the political system it represents.

In Asia, Japan appears to have the democratic political system that most resembles those found in the more industrial parts of the world. In Japan, the elective process has produced parties which divide along liberal and conservative lines and which seem to touch upon issues comparable to those in recent Western history. Also, Japanese political institutions seem to be solid and relatively entrenched. Yet all these developments are extremely recent. On the surface, the country has a modern political system, many of the basic institutions of contemporary Japan having been implanted during the American occupation after World War II. Beneath the surface, however, many traditional Japanese habits of mind and of practice continue to influence the character of Japanese politics.

In particular, it is striking that in Japan national development has not depended upon one dominant, charismatic personality. Instead, group cohesion and collective sentiments have been of prime importance in moving the country into the modern age. Japanese sensitivity to the need to maintain group cohesion and national consensus has meant that, often, those who had political power have hesitated to act without constant attention to and consultation with minority elements. Basically, the Japanese political process seeks always to incorporate all elements into a national consensus. Japanese party leaders are hesitant to move decisively even when they manifestly have the power or the votes for a clear majority in the Diet, or Parliament. Thus the use of power in Japan is subject to some peculiar constraints, and these have to be understood if one is to appreciate Japanese politics. The case studies by Hans H. Baerwald in this volume admirably illustrate this basic Japanese problem in the use of power.

Although Japan is the leading industrial power in Asia, China has always occupied the center of the Asian stage. The mass of China, both geographically and demographically, with its nearly 800,000,000 people, must ultimately be the central element in any Asian system of states. How China develops and what political system evolves there will indeed influence much of Asia and the rest of the world. The general outlines of Chinese development in the modern era are relatively easy to chart. China possessed probably the most sophisticated and elaborate cultural system in traditional Asia. Before the Europeans arrived the Chinese had achieved great successes, both in organizing society and in developing the arts. The Western influence was thus peculiarly threatening for Chinese society and civilization. Deep attachments to the Confucian order had to be overcome and new adjustments made to the kind of society essential for modern economic and social development. The fall of the empire in 1911 brought an attempt to establish republican institutions. But during the 1910's and 1920's, China floundered in trying to emulate Western institutions as power gravitated to the provinces, where it was grasped by military commanders who conducted elaborate warlord politics.

In 1927, the nationalist movement under the leadership of Chiang K'ai-shek brought the Kuomintang to power in Nanking. A brief period of national reunification followed before the Japanese attacked in Manchuria in 1931 and the major war broke out between China and Japan in 1937. During the war years the Kuomintang lost its ability to govern and to hold the loyalty of the Chinese people. With the Japanese surrender, China was divided between the Nationalists and the Communists. It was the Communists who through guerrilla warfare mobilized the larger segment of the rural population and who succeeded in isolating the Nationalists in the cities.

Finally, in 1949, the Communists came to power, ushering in a new era in which China appeared to be very close to the Soviet Union and wedded to the international Communist movement. During the 1950's, the government in Peking under Mao Tse-tung seemed to be putting together a unified, highly integrated Chinese governmental system. The Communist Party dominated the government and controlled all levels of society. Yet by the end of the 1950's, the Chinese were deeply embroiled in an apparently mad and frantic effort to drive their society ahead more rapidly than it had the capacity to move. The Great Leap Forward, as it was called, taxed the economic and control systems that the Communists had so carefully built up over the previous period. In the early 1960's, the system had to return to more modest levels of performance when it became clear that the Great Leap had failed. Although by then Mao had committed himself to an extreme vision of Communism and a romantic attachment to revolution, power in the party briefly reverted to the hands of those who were more pragmatic in their approach to the problems of government and who were interested mainly in the technical problems of Chinese modernization. Gradually, by the mid-1960's, China seemed again to be straightening out her problems of government, and it looked as though she would be moving ahead once more in economic and social development.

At this stage, however, Mao again plunged the country into an extreme form of activity; this time it was the Great Proletarian Cultural Revolution, which fascinated the whole world when, most dramatically, young student groups appeared all over China organized as the Red Guards. From 1966 through 1968, the Chinese system was torn apart as these young revolutionaries challenged every symbol of past authority. Mao was determined that a romantic vision of revolution should become the one guiding principle for all China. The party apparatus and the bureaucratic structure of government were weakened as purges eliminated those who were identified with the non-Maoist forces.

From observing the Cultural Revolution it became apparent that many signs of order and achievement that had once seemed to characterize Chinese Communism were façades behind which intense political jockeying and competition were going on. Probably the Chinese leaders were never quite so effectively organized as they had appeared to be during the 1950's. The emphasis on Communist doctrine and Communist organization obscured the extent to which Chinese society still reflected regional differences and the extent to which Chinese politics still had to accommodate to such differences. The Cultural Revolution made it possible to see much more clearly how the Communist system operates in China. The case studies by Harold Hinton in this volume are imaginative attempts to penetrate the Bamboo Curtain and to speculate about the critical determinants involving individuals and groups that affect public policies in China today.

In the last fifteen years remarkable changes have appeared in the tone of government in India. The basic structures and forms of administration and authority were well established by the time India gained its independence from the British. During the first years of independence, Nehru dominated and his personality seemed to set the style of Indian performance, both domestically and in foreign affairs. Increasingly, however, it has become apparent that the Indian system of government must in fact reflect all the complexities of Indian society. At the top, and at the center, the Congress Party stands for the great secular tradition of India that emerged from the colonial period; it reflects a commitment to British standards of law and order and to the basic principles of representative government.

The state governments also have been committed to orderly rule, but there the values tend more to be those of traditional India.

Language differences have created divisions in the society that are now fully reflected at all levels of political life. In the north the Hindi language is readily championed by those who see it as the appropriate national tongue, but in the south the people do not speak Hindi, and for them national unity would be better served by the continued use of English. India is thus divided by language, region, and religion and is also split between modernists and traditionalists.

The basic clash in Indian politics is between the forces which would move the country ahead toward economic development and modernization and those which remain more sensitive to the traditional divisions and realities of social organization. Indian public life has been dominated since independence by the overarching structure of the national Congress Party, but, in fact, Indian politics is organized in competing special interest groups and increasingly articulate and the dictates of elections govern the politicians' calculations. Both tradition of Western politics, in which the demands of interest groups and the dictates of elections govern the politicians' calculations. Both national and state leaders are constantly called upon to accommodate and adjust to the conflicting demands of their constituents. The two case studies by Gene D. Overstreet in this volume capture the blend of old and new and the intense clash between competing forces that clearly characterize contemporary Indian politics.

In Southeast Asia all the countries except Thailand experienced colonial rule in one form or another. A complex and unstable blend of Western institutions and traditional practices has resulted. The colonial era brought a freeze to dynamic politics, with foreign rulers dominating the heights of government and the diverse local ethnic and religious communities coming to occupy separate and special niches in loosely structured societies. In the end colonialism produced a consciousness of nationalism strong enough to achieve independence but too weak to realize true nationhood.

In Southeast Asia fundamental social changes are taking place as new elements in each society seek a larger role in public affairs, often increasing national disunity because leaders appeal primarily to their immediate followers, with very few able to speak effectively to all elements of the society. In Vietnam the division goes much deeper than that between Communists and Nationalists, for in that country there are also complex divisions between Catholics and Buddhists, northerners and southerners, Hoa Hao and Cao Dai, as well as between mountain peoples and plains peoples and between Chinese rice merchants and local peasants. In Indonesia are found not only the divisions between the dominant Javanese and the people in the outer islands, but among the Javanese themselves, who are divided according to region and the differences in the intensity of their Islamic religious traditions.

In many respects the political processes in Southeast Asian societies are far less structured and certainly less integrated than in the major countries of Asia. Comparatively, these societies are governed more by ancient social traditions, and the lives of people are more directly exposed to basic economic and social forces.

At the same time within government we find strange contradictions and striking anachronisms. In some offices, and on certain issues, the guiding ideas and basic patterns of behavior are still remarkably close to foreign traditions and reflect the colonial experiences of that society. In other situations, however, one finds that the old traditions have reasserted themselves and that the dominant spirit behind ostensibly modern institutions is essentially an ancient cultural attitude, which may seriously impede the effective modernization of the country.

In the Philippines during the American period constitutional development and the role of the elected politician were emphasized. The basic issues of Filipino politics have a peculiarly American ring: eliminating corruption and graft, electing good and true men to office, and the frustrations in implementing campaign promises. The problem of organizing a national effort at community development, which Jose V. Abueva describes, seems in many ways to be only a step removed from similar recent efforts at organizing antipoverty programs in America. Thus, in this ex-colonial society we are able to find a perplexing mirror in which to examine some basic qualities of American or Western approaches to government.

Elsewhere in Southeast Asia, colonialism brought mainly bureaucratic administrations rather than popular politics. Some of the bureaucracies developed high levels of efficiency; in others the standards were never particularly high. In all, however, the post-independence period has seen a steady trend of accommodating colonial practices to local traditions. Gradually, in Burma, Indonesia, Malaysia, and Vietnam, the colonial institutions of daily rule have given way to practices that reflect, in many cases, the pre-Western traditions of these societies. In most of these countries it is still hard to discern the ultimate pattern of constitutional arrangement. In all, the conflict between Western imports and traditional habits is still going on. At the same time a new institution building seeks to enable these societies to carry on the task of modernization and economic development. The great value of Ann Willner's essay, which concludes this volume, is that it analyzes the ways in which traditional concepts and practices continue to influence institution building in Indonesia.

From this very brief survey of the state of Asian politics, we can sense the extent to which Asian countries are developing complex systems of their own. The organized forces representing different interests and values can in some respects give to these societies much stability. They are also likely to generate tensions and conflicts that may impede the rate of development. Whichever direction they take, Asian societies do have very human processes of political action and interaction and in their politics one can find the same heights of idealism side by side with the same calculations of narrow self-interest that one finds in the politics of any society. The search by Asians for Asian solutions is the fundamental objective of contemporary Asian politics. It is therefore essential for the American student to perceive the realities of these Asian approaches to politics as they have been expressed in concrete situations.

With these general considerations in mind we are now prepared to turn to specific case studies to see how politics operates in selected Asian societies.

PART II JAPAN

Today Japan is the anomaly of Asia. She is the one highly industrial country of Asia, with the third largest economy in the world, yet she has little influence in international affairs and is not thought of as a political force in Asia. Since her defeat in World War II, Japan has been absorbed with her domestic program of democratization and with building a modern economy.

When the American occupation ended, the Japanese continued to be unsure of themselves. The experience of war and defeat and of breathtakingly rapid changes in all aspects of social life had left the Japanese questioning their own feelings of nationalism and wondering about the commitments of their fellow citizens. The miraculous Japanese economic growth failed to provide self-assurance; instead it seemed to make the majority of the Japanese timid about any actions that might disrupt the economy.

In foreign affairs the Japanese government reflected this insecurity by following a policy of "separating politics from economics," by adopting a "low posture" in political matters, that is by avoiding leadership and taking initiatives only when pursuing economic interests. This limited approach to foreign affairs conformed with the pacifistic mood of the Japanese and the revulsion they felt against security and military matters, an attitude that had its roots in the trauma of defeat and occupation.

In the years ahead Japan will no doubt assert herself more and more in foreign affairs and adopt an international stance more in keeping with her economic capabilities. It is, therefore, appropriate to begin with a case study that vividly portrays the links between domestic considerations and foreign policy obligations. In describing the manner in which the Japanese Diet (or Parliament) ratified the treaty normalizing relations with South Korea, Hans H. Baerwald illuminates the difficulties confronting the Japanese as they reluctantly face the need for finding an appropriate international role. His study reveals that it is not so much particular substantive issues that trouble the Japanese as the frustrating lack of a consensus.

Throughout history, the Japanese were a remarkably homogenous people and now they find it is threatening to have to engage in partisan conflicts. Even when one group, such as the Liberal Democratic Party, has the dominant power in the

Diet, there is a general feeling that it should not impose its views on society at large or in any manner push aside the minority. Yet, at the same time, it is clear to most Japanese that allowing the minority to have its way would be intolerable. The strange compromise that the Japanese seem to be working toward will find them ultimately accepting the need for the majority to rule, but allowing this only under conditions that will make the majority appear immoral and the minority cruelly wronged.

In the Diet this peculiarly Japanese approach to partisan politics has focused attention on all minority claims while largely ignoring the claims of the great majority. The author of our second case study examines the dominant party and its method of selecting a leader to rule the country. In this study Hans H. Baerwald illustrates the more traditional Japanese style of coping with factional conflicts and loyalties. He shows that within the dominant Liberal Democratic Party partisan divisions threaten the capacity of the top leaders to assert the full power of the party in much the same fashion as the inter-party divisions within the country as a whole make it difficult for the Japanese government to act effectively on the international scene. Just as in the Diet, the problem the Liberal Democrats seem most disturbed about is the relationship between a clear and decisive majority and a vigorous minority. Minority factions within the Liberal Democratic Party were able to seriously disrupt the leaders' plans and to arouse all manner of tender concern for their sensitivities. Yet in the end no alternative was left but to allow the majority to have its way, but only after making the majority appear to be immoral in doing the inevitable.

These two case studies thus vividly illustrate that behind the larger forces of history there is in fact considerable tension and human drama in Japanese politics. The need to respect the sensitivities of minority, but potentially disruptive, elements does give an appearance of nearly immobile politics to a country that is otherwise one of the most dynamic and rapidly changing in the entire world.

HANS H. BAERWALD

1 Nikkan Kokkai: The Japan-Korea Treaty Diet

BACKGROUND ASPECTS

Relations between Japan and Korea, and between the peoples of both countries, have a long and not altogether amicable history. Since the Japanese left Korea in 1945, Koreans have viewed their erstwhile masters through the memories of thirty-five years of colonial rule (1910–1945), during which their land of the Morning Calm (Korea) was exploited, according to critics of Japanese policy, or economically developed, according to apologists. Concurrently, too many Japanese have succumbed to ethnic prejudice in their dealings with the Korean people, especially in adopting discriminatory attitudes and policies against the Korean minority in Japan.[1]

These mutual antagonisms were further complicated by two related factors. First, official relations between the two countries had been

A generous grant from the Rockefeller Foundation made possible the research for this essay. Japanese names appear in the vernacular style, family name first.

[1] For an extensive background discussion of the basic issues in Japanese-Korean relations, see James W. Morley, *Japan and Korea: America's Allies in the Pacific* (New York: Walker and Company, 1965), *passim*, but especially pp. 54–66.

left in a state of suspension by the Japanese Peace Treaty of 1952. Korea became formally independent of Japan, indeed it had become so at the end of the Pacific War, but no formal diplomatic relations were established at that time. Second, Korea had become two countries after the World War II period – initially because of the military decision to have the surrender of Japanese troops accepted by Russian military forces north of the 38th parallel and by the Americans to the south of that line, a decision subsequently reconfirmed at great cost in the Korean War. As a consequence, when the establishment of formal diplomatic relations between Japan and Korea was considered, the inevitable question that arose was "which Korea?" Few thought it possible to accomplish the diplomatic feat of Japan's reaching an accord with both Koreas simultaneously.

A BRIEF BACKGROUND OF NEGOTIATIONS

Formal and informal contacts between Japan and Korea, primarily with the South but occasionally with the North, gradually culminated in specific negotiations designed to lead to normalized diplomatic relations between Japan and South Korea. These negotiations were tortured both because of the mutual antagonism at the governmental level, especially in the case of Korea so long as Syngman Rhee remained as president (until April 1960), and because of the lack of public consensus in both countries in support of their respective governments' efforts to establish formal diplomatic ties.

Talks between representatives of the Republic of Korea (South) and Japan had actually begun in 1952, but very little substantive progress was made until Chung-Hee Park became president of South Korea in 1962. Even thereafter, substantial opposition to any formal rapprochement with Japan remained a formidable obstacle to negotiations. Demonstrations and riots against the proposed treaty led to stern acts of suppression and to the proclamation of martial law (June 1964).

On the Japanese side, too, considerable popular opposition was presented by the Socialist Party, the major trade union federation SŌHYŌ, and the student movement Zengakuren. If hatred and suspicion of their erstwhile colonial masters motivated the Koreans in their antipathy to the establishment of diplomatic ties with Japan, what can be said about the motives for Japanese opposition? Probably foremost was the fear that by establishing diplomatic relations with South Korea, Japan would be drawn even further into the American network of alliances with the noncommunist powers in northeast Asia, namely South Korea and Taiwan (Formosa). Indeed, Japanese opponents of the treaty were convinced that its conclusion would be one further step toward something they designated "NEATO" (Northeast Asia Treaty Organization). This fear was voiced again and again despite repeated denials by American diplomatic representatives.

Fears were also expressed that the (Japanese) economy would suffer because of Japanese capital finding more lucrative investment returns in the Korean market, thereby reducing the domestic rate of expansion and thereby, from the viewpoint of the trade unions, reducing the number of new jobs. Concurrently, it was feared that various consumer goods made with "cheap" Korean labor would flood the Japanese market and adversely affect the survival capabilities of Japanese manufacturers, especially in the small- and medium-enterprise category.

Beyond these fears some issues of substance separated the negotiators. Because fish is a staple food in both the Japanese and Korean diets, fishing rights in the waters that surround the Japanese islands and the Korean peninsula are vital to both countries. Early in 1952 the government of South Korea had unilaterally proclaimed a line on the high seas, subsequently dubbed the "Rhee Line," delineating a substantial area from which Japanese fishing vessels were to be excluded. Portions of this line extended fifty miles offshore, a rather sizable increase over the more generally accepted three- and twelve-mile concepts of territorial waters under international law. Japanese fishermen who had "violated" the Rhee Line on occasion had been seized and detained by the Koreans.[2]

A second issue of substance — of exponential rather than face value — was the ownership of the island of Takeshima (*Dokdo* in Korean). This island, or small group of islets, located in the Sea of Japan, is uninhabited — indeed, it is less than one-tenth of a square mile in area. Nonetheless, its disposition served as a constant irritant in the negotiations leading to the signing of the treaty. In fact, this issue was not settled in the treaty (nor has it yet been settled), and its irresolution served as a convenient item of reference for those who

[2] The whole matter of fishing rights was ultimately dealt with in the Agreement Concerning Fisheries, which was attached to, but not an integral portion of, the Treaty of Basic Relations between Japan and the Republic of Korea. The English text of this agreement appears in *Contemporary Japan*, XXVIII, No. 3 (May 1966), 678–680.

wished to oppose the treaty, both during its negotiation and during the process of its approval by the Diet (Parliament) in Japan.

Two other issues also slowed the negotiations. One was the whole matter of Japanese properties in Korea and Korean properties in Japan, compensation for which involved endless wrangling over whether the Japanese had "exploited" Korea or had assisted in her economic development. Intimately related to this problem was the extent to which Japan would pay restitution for economic losses sustained by the Koreans while under Japanese rule. Whereas Japan had earlier agreed that she had renounced any property rights her nationals might have had to properties that had been left in Korea at the end of World War II, Korea had insisted on restitution, in part as a symbol of Japan's wrongdoing during the period of colonial rule, but, more important, because the funds would provide South Korea with some much needed development capital. Regarding the latter, the final sum agreed upon was an outright grant of $300,000,000. Other issues on property claims and economic cooperation were included in a second, separate agreement attached to the basic treaty.[3]

The other issue was the status of Korean residents in Japan. Discrimination against Koreans and their offspring has already been mentioned.[4] Many of these unfortunate people had been forcibly brought to Japan as cheap and unskilled labor immediately prior to and during World War II; others had come at the end of the nineteenth century and after the Japanese colonial annexation of Korea in 1910. Many had returned to their homeland in the immediate postwar years, but about 600,000 remained in Japan. Some of those remaining, generally believed to be less than a thousand, struck it rich; but the vast majority found their way into the ranks of unskilled labor or into occupations that were on the gray side of legality. Indeed, a popular Japanese myth is that most of the criminals in Japan are Koreans.

International politics complicated the issue of Korean residents in Japan. For much of the 1950's, the government of South Korea paid little attention to their countrymen in Japan; this attitude changed when substantial numbers of Korean residents in Japan sought repatriation to their homeland, especially since many wished to return to

[3] "Agreement Concerning Property Claims and Economic Cooperation," *ibid.*, 681–684.
[4] Richard H. Mitchell, *The Korean Minority in Japan* (Berkeley and Los Angeles: University of California Press, 1967), *passim*, but especially Chaps. VIII-XI.

North Korea through a voluntary repatriation program adopted by the Japanese government. This upset the government of South Korea both because of the adverse propaganda (all Koreans should look to the Republic of Korea as their true homeland) and because any dealings by any country, especially Japan, with North Korea might adversely affect South Korea's claim to be the only "true" government of Korea. This issue was serious enough to bring the whole process of negotiation to a halt during 1959 and 1960. As finally worked out in another agreement attached to the basic treaty, the Japanese agreed to grant "the right of permanent residence in Japan to any *Republic of Korea national*" meeting certain specifications.[5] The key wording involves recognizing special status for those Koreans living in Japan who claim allegiance to South Korea, but leaves undetermined the status of other Koreans, that is, those looking to the North.

Each of these issues – fishing rights, the disposition of Takeshima, property claims and economic restitution, and the status of Koreans residing in Japan – had consumed years of negotiation between the governments of Japan and the Republic of Korea. In fact, more than thirteen years transpired between the earliest talks (February 1952) and the final signing of the draft treaty and its attached agreements (June 1965). In both countries, but especially in Korea, the treaty had caused substantial political turmoil.

The treaty itself, however, is a rather simple document in contrast to the attached agreements. Article I[6] calls for establishing diplomatic and consular relations, including the exchange of ambassadors. Article II confirms that all treaties and agreements made between the empires of Japan and Korea prior to August 22, 1910, are void. Article III is the key clause: "It is confirmed that the government of the Republic of Korea is the only lawful government in Korea as specified in the Resolution 195 (III) of the United Nations General Assembly." This clause settled the basic question: which of the two Koreas did Japan recognize as the legitimate one? Articles IV through VII were noncontroversial.

A significant milestone in Japanese-Korean relations had been reached, but it was not the end of controversy. Both governments had to formally approve the treaty (and its attached agreements) be-

[5] "Agreement Concerning the Legal Status and Treatment of the South Korean Residents in Japan," *Contemporary Japan, op. cit.,* 685–686. The italics are added.

[6] The full text of the treaty is attached as an appendix to this essay.

fore it could come into force. In the Korean case, the National Assembly's action was speedy and none too elegant. On the Japanese side, the proponents and opponents of the treaty readied themselves for a battle that would test anew the viability of parliamentarism in Japan.

THE DIET AND THE TREATY

According to the Japanese Constitution, it is the Diet that is the "highest organ of state power" and the "sole law-making organ of the state."[7] Treaties must be approved by the Diet in order to become the law of the land.[8]

Once the arduous negotiations between Japan and Korea had been successfully concluded, the next stage in the treaty's final ratification was its approval by the Diet. This institution, consisting of two chambers (the House of Representatives and the House of Councillors), confronts an occasionally hostile and often unsympathetic public. Depending on the observer's ideological orientation, it is viewed either as a rubber stamp that does "the government's" or "the Establishment's" bidding or, conversely, as the scene of unsightly shenanigans by those who wish to obstruct the orderly process of government.

Legislatures throughout the world have not had a good press in recent years, but this is especially true of the Japanese Diet. In part, criticism of this parliament reflects the inordinate attention given to lapses of decorum that occasionally occur in the Diet's proceedings. During the fracas over the Diet's approval of the Revised United States-Japan Security Pact in the spring of 1960, some of the demonstrators against that treaty indicated their dismay with the institution by urinating and defecating against the main doors of the structure — doors through which only the Emperor may enter.[9] These critics forget, of course, that it is their representatives, elected in free elections, who sit in the Diet and who in turn select Japan's executive, the prime minister and his cabinet ministers, a majority of whom themselves must be members of the Diet.

Channeling popular attitudes and selecting candidates for the Diet

[7] See Article 41, *The Constitution of Japan* (Toyko: The National Diet of Japan, 1960), p. 11.

[8] See Article 61, *The Constitution of Japan, ibid.*, p. 15.

[9] For a full discussion of that crisis, see George R. Packard III, *Protest in Tokyo, The Security Treaty Crisis of 1960* (Princeton: Princeton University Press, 1966).

and other representative institutions are Japan's political parties. Critics of the Diet as a representative body often complain that the electoral contests are unequal because "the Establishment" – that is, the leaders of the *zaikai* (financial-commerical-industrial community), the senior civil servants (bureaucrats), and the leaders of the government party (the Jiyu-Minshu-To, or Liberal Democratic Party) – has inordinate economic and social power. Furthermore, the critics argue, the Japanese voter, particularly in rural areas, is still relatively unsophisticated; and they find proof of this in the consistent majorities that the conservatives in the Liberal Democratic Party (hereafter LDP) have been given in rural constituencies.

Each of these criticisms contains valid elements, but the attitudes create a climate of distrust of the parliamentary process that goes well beyond what might be needed to correct some of the Diet's shortcomings. Part of the trouble is that few Japanese are really concerned about the inner workings of their parliament. Those who are well informed are to be found principally among the journalists (of press, radio, and television), who often are more interested in gossip than in any coherent analysis. Furthermore, many of these close observers use outworn shibboleths of how parliaments should work as yardsticks against which to measure the performance of the Diet. Resultant public attitudes can be compared to the American scene were Congress to be viewed through the prism of high school civics texts written prior to World War II.

Japanese political scientists, who might be expected to play a corrective role, are on the whole not much help in assisting the public to understand how the Diet arrives at a decision. It is just not considered terribly chic or avant-garde to concern oneself with the Diet. After all, would this not mean being engaged in institutional analysis, than which there is presumably nothing more old-fashioned? Furthermore, it would also mean that an academician might come into personal contact with a member of the Diet – and even worse, with one who is an LDPer (conservative) – and thereby lose his privileged virginity, which he has hitherto protected by studiously avoiding any encounter with members of the governing power structure. A chasm between the "intellectual" and "political" communities is only gradually being bridged.

Any academician in Japan must constantly be aware of the possibility that one who is known to have access to those "in power" may easily lose status with his peers, who may decide that he has "sold out." Finally, even should a Japanese political scientist be interested in exploring the decision-making processes of the Diet, he would probably be confronted with two almost insurmountable obstacles. First, he would be met with a good deal of hostility and suspicion by the conservative Dietmen in whose hands power lies. Second, because of the heavy teaching load that is his unhappy lot, he would be confronted with extreme difficulty in finding time to observe proceedings at first hand. As a consequence, our understanding of the Diet, the role that it plays in Japanese politics, and the manner in which decisions are made are still in their infancy.

The tale that follows concerns the Diet's approval of one specific piece of legislation as seen through the eyes of a foreigner. A *gaijin* (literally "outsider," a word more accurate in its implications than is "foreigner") is in a privileged position in certain respects. He does not have to fear (or hope for) loss of his virginity in Japanese politics, because he forever remains on the outside. He also has curiosity value and can provide members of the Diet with diversion during some of the interminable sessions when proceedings have come to a standstill — at which point there might be time for questions over a cup of tea or coffee in the Dietmen's dining room.[10]

THE FIFTIETH SPECIAL DIET IS CONVENED

In mid-September, 1965, Prime Minister Satō and his cabinet, after determining that the necessary groundwork had been laid, decided to convoke an extraordinary session of the Diet.[11] An agreement had been reached with the parties of the opposition (the Japan Socialist Party, the Democratic-Socialist Party, and the Komeito[12]) that the session was to last seventy days. Such an agreement is a normal prelude to the opening of any session and though formally

[10] Observation of proceedings and interviews with Dietmen were checked for accuracy with members of the Japanese press assigned to cover the Diet. Their assistance, which was given unstintingly and at some inconvenience to themselves, is gratefully acknowledged. They taught me much, but they also made me aware, normally with gentleness and good humor, how much there still remained to learn.

[11] The cabinet has this power under Article 53. See *The Constitution of Japan, op, cit.,* p. 13.

[12] The Komeito, usually translated as the "Clean Government Party," is the political wing of the Soka Gakkai, a neo-Buddhist religious organization that at the time of the Fiftieth Special Diet had representatives in the House of Councillors, but none in the much more powerful House of Representatives. Another element of the opposition, the Japan Communist Party, was not consulted.

undertaken by the speaker of the House of Representatives and president of the House of Councillors,[13] it is in reality made by representatives of the major parties, usually their secretary-generals.

Agreement on the length of the Fiftieth Special Diet was virtually the last formal decision made during that session between the Liberal Democrats (representing the government) and the Socialists (representing the major element of the opposition). Observers had been freely predicting that a parliamentary session convened to approve the Japan-Korea Treaty would be among the stormiest to take place since the end of World War II. To the degree that Prime Minister Satō and his Liberal Democratic Party colleagues were committed to the treaty's approval, to that same degree were Chairman Sasaki and his Socialist Party comrades committed to blocking its passage.

These commitments by the major parties had been made at prior party conventions. For the LDP and its leader Prime Minister Satō, the stakes involved more than mere ratification of the treaty. As the governing party, it had to anticipate how serious delays in the treaty's approval might affect other government proposals, including, for example, the Diet's approval of some much-needed supplementary appropriations to the budget. In addition, the manner or style in which the treaty was approved could well have repercussions on the political future of those individuals in the LDP who had either hitched their wagon to the current Prime Minister's star or, conversely, who hoped that their own ambitions would best be served by observing the fray from the sidelines. We must emphasize that the LDP — even though its representatives could be expected to vote as a bloc — consists of a number of factions among which tension and rivalry are continuously present, one of the elements of which is disagreement over the degree to which the LDP should use its preponderant majority[14] in the Diet

[13] See Article 20, Paragraph 2, *Rules of the House of Representatives* (Tokyo: The National Diet of Japan, 1960), pp. 68–69.

[14] The distribution of seats in the Fiftieth Special Diet was as follows:

	House of Representatives	*House of Councillors*
LDP	283	137
Socialist	145	74
Democratic-Socialist	23	7
Communist	4	4
Komeito	––	20
Independent	2	7
Vacant	10	1
	467	250

to ram through legislation that is known to be anathema to the opposition. Over the years, some LDPers had been loath to push the negotiations with Korea regarding the Normalization Treaty too hard for fear that the parliamentary process would suffer when the time came for the Diet to approve the treaty. Indeed, such fears were voiced to me by members of the LDP who were antagonistic to Prime Minister Satō's leadership.

For the Japan Socialists (JSP) and their Chairman Sasaki, the stakes were equally high. The party leadership had made a compact with its supporters that the treaty would be opposed to the fullest extent possible. However, because the JSP is as factionalized as the LDP, party positions are arrived at only after serious intraparty squabbling. Inevitably, such decisions are thereafter difficult to alter so that the party's leadership has precious little room for maneuver in the give and take normally associated with the parliamentary process. Indeed, any welching or "selling-out" by the party's leadership on promises made at a party convention could lead to the replacement of one set of party leaders by another. Since leaders of the JSP are as loath to lose power as those of any other political party, the prospect of being supplanted by rivals is a powerful sanction.

THE LEGISLATIVE PROCESS

October 5, 1965, was the date selected for convoking the Fiftieth Special Diet, the major business of which was to be approval of the Japan-Korea Normalization Treaty. For a variety of reasons, including the facts that October 7 was the fifth anniversary of the assassination of Asanuma Inejiro,[15] which required that memorials be read eulogizing his services as a parliamentarian, and that a weekend intervened, the Emperor did not appear until October 11 to read his rescript officially opening the session. A delay of six days — almost a week — had fallen into the hands of the opposition, a fortuitous opening in its tactics of dalliance.

Work on the treaty itself did not really begin before October 25,

[15] Asanuma was knifed to death by a mentally sick young man on the stage of the Hibiya Public Hall, one of Tokyo's largest. He was secretary-general of the Japan Socialist Party at the time. The assassination was witnessed by millions of television viewers as well as by the large audience in the hall itself. His assassin belonged to an ultraright terrorist group.

on which date the House of Representatives Special Committee on the Japan-Korea Treaty held its opening session. In the intervening two weeks, there had been lengthy discussions as to whether the treaty, the attached agreements, and domestic legislation should be handled in one package by a special committee or whether they should be considered separately by the existing standing committees. Were the latter alternative to have been utilized, the Agreement Concerning Fisheries, for example, would have been assigned to the Committee on Agriculture, Forestry, and Fishery.[16]

Once this issue had been settled in favor of the special committee-one package approach, there was the matter of selecting a chairman; Ando Kaku finally agreed to serve in this capacity.[17] Serious difficulties both inside and outside the Diet were expected to arise during the approval proceedings. Hence, the chairmanship of the Special Committee, while conferring upon whoever was selected considerable publicity (a commodity of substantial value to any Dietman), might also involve a fracas that would subject a principal to bodily harm.

Ando's appointment had the further benefit of building up factional support for the treaty inside the LDP because of his membership in one of the factions (the one that had been led by Kōno Ichirō) that had been most bitterly opposed to Satō's becoming president of the party and thus Prime Minister of Japan. Kōno had been Satō's principal rival, and therefore it was possible that some members of his faction might not give their full support to the parliamentary maneuvering that would be necessary for treaty approval.

Not only the chairman but also the other members of the Special Committee had to be selected. For transparent reasons of delay the Socialists experienced extreme difficulty in locating representatives in their ranks who were willing to serve on the committee. Had the existing standing committees been utilized, this element of delay could have been eliminated, but the LDP leadership feared that some of the standing committees to which portions of the treaty might be

[16] See Article 92, *Rules of the House of Representatives, op. cit.*, pp. 82–85. The subject-matter committee system is a post-World War II innovation in Diet procedure and represents possibly the most crucial aspect of American congressional practice to be grafted onto the basically English parliamentary practices of the prewar Diet.

[17] Ando was a veteran parliamentarian, having been elected five times. He was then a member of the Mori faction, which had been one of the subgroupings in the faction led until his death by LDP stalwart Kōno Ichirō, best known in America as the cabinet minister who was in charge of the Olympics held in Japan in 1964.

assigned would not prove altogether reliable in doing the government's bidding.[18] Almost a month had passed since the special session opened and all that had been accomplished was to begin the committee stage of deliberations.

A deadline began to loom with ever-increasing intensity on the horizon of the LDP leadership's calculations. If the House of Representatives were to pass the treaty by November 13, one calendar month of the session's seventy days would remain. Assuming that this deadline could be met, the Diet's approval of the treaty would be assured regardless of the fate dealt it by the House of Councillors. Under Articles 60 and 61 of the Constitution, on matters pertaining to the budget and treaties, the decision of the House of Representatives is final providing that its action has been taken one month prior to the agreed-upon end of the session.

Nineteen days remained, if this deadline were to be met, for the LDP to push the treaty through the Special Committee and get it considered and acted upon in plenary session. Deliberations within the committee were not of a very high order. Government spokesmen, mostly cabinet ministers, either could not or would not answer some pointed questions posed by the Socialists relative to unsettled issues such as the disposition of Takeshima, the actual status of the Rhee Line in connection with the Agreement Concerning Fisheries, or fine points in the Agreement Concerning Property Claims and Economic Cooperation. Both the manner in which the questions were asked and the responses they elicited from seemingly very tired or arrogant officials could be taken as evidence that one and all were merely going through the expected motions. For the LDP, each question and answer consumed precious time, of which the Socialists, of course, were well aware. The sooner the committee proceedings could be ended, the more easily the Prime Minister and his supporters could breathe.

Uppermost in the minds of participants and observers was the question of when and under what circumstances the committee would end its deliberations and vote to send the treaty to the plenary session of the House of Representatives, where the next act of the drama

[18] The existing standing committees in the House of Representatives were less of a problem to the LDP than those in the House of Councillors. In the latter house, some of the standing committees were chaired by Socialists who by virtue of their power could impede proceedings.

was to transpire. On Saturday morning, November 6, Fujieda Sensuke,[19] a former minister of state in charge of the Defense Agency, was recognized by Chairman Ando. No one really heard the content of Mr. Fujieda's motion because of the noise level in the Committee Room. Indeed, the transcript of committee proceedings had to be completed after the conclusion of the Fiftieth Special Diet Session, an unusually creative approach to the matter of verbatim transcripts.[20]

In defense of this LDP maneuver, it must be recognized that no one could foretell how long the Socialists might continue to stall committee proceedings by asking yet another series of questions. Prime Minister Satō was quoted as having stated that Japan had been debating the treaty for fourteen years and that all questions had been thoroughly aired. His impatience was understandable, but might also be viewed as indicative of his feelings on parliamentary politics in general. If committee hearings are intended to assist the public and its representatives in understanding more fully the legislation under consideration, this objective was not achieved.

Be that as it may, the committee's style of approval and referral of the treaty and related agreements to the full House (which, with the help of printer's ink, was the substance of Mr. Fujieda's unheard motion) was irregular and had unfortunate repercussions. To the opposition it was proof positive that the normal Diet machinery for determining a day's agenda and related procedural matters had completely broken down. To them, the Special Committee's final motion and its approval by standing vote at a moment when everyone was on his feet and pandemonium reigned seemed merely the last in a series of loosely construed parliamentary maneuvers that had begun

[19] Fujieda, another senior LDPer (six terms), is a member of LDP Vice-President Kawashima Shōjirō's faction. His being called upon to make the motion was not accidental, since he is also the brother of Funada Naka, the then Speaker of the House of Representatives.

[20] The Special Committee record for November 6, 1965, was not printed until August 3, 1966. See House of Representatives Fiftieth District Session, "Nihon-Koku to Dai-Kanmin-Koku to no Joyaku oyobi Kyotei nado ni kansuru Tokubetsu Iinkai Giroku" (Transcript of the Special Committee concerning the Treaty and Other Agreements between Japan and Korea), p. 24. Members of the Diet Secretariat had been extremely gracious about providing me with copies of the *Kampo* (*Diet Record*), but the transcript of the Special Committee's proceedings for November 6 could not be provided. It was only after the intervention of a personal friend who was a Dietman's administrative assistant that a copy of the record cited here was made available. The transcript is replete with the words *choshu funō* ("impossible to hear").

with a forced vote to hear the advice of three "experts" — all of whom had predictably testified on behalf of the treaty's approval.[21]

Over the balance of the weekend of November 6, House of Representatives Speaker Funada attempted to establish some semblance of regularity in Diet proceedings preparatory to the plenary session. These efforts included marathon meetings among government and opposition party leaders. In the end Speaker Funada found it necessary to convene the plenary session on his own authority on Tuesday, November 9.[22] Four days remained for the deadline to be met.

By convening the plenary session on his own authority, Speaker Funada had bypassed normal procedure, which involves having the day's agenda agreed upon by the House Management (Steering) Committee (Giin Unei Iinkai) which in turn usually respects the decisions of each party's Diet Strategy Committee (Kokkai Taisaku Iinkai).[23] In certain difficult interparty situations, it is also not unusual for the secretary-generals of the major parties to confer or, if necessary, for the supreme leaders of the parties (president for the LDP, chairman for the Socialists and Democratic-Socialists) to do so.

There are risks in going up the ladders of the party hierarchies. A lack of agreement at a Himalayan height always carries with it the possibility that the whole parliamentary process may no longer be viable. In order to avoid such a crisis it might then be necessary for one or more of the principals to resign their government and/or party posts. Furthermore, for such negotiations to occur — regardless of the risks involved — the individuals must first agree to meet, which in this instance was clearly impossible.

When it had become clear that Speaker Funada would convene the

[21] *Ibid.*, Special Committee Transcript for November 4, 1965. The three experts who testified were Professor Tamura Kosaku of Kokushikan University and political critics Mitarai Tatsuo and Utsumi Teizo.

[22] Article 55, Paragraph 2 of *The Diet Law* (Tokyo: The National Diet of Japan, 1960), p. 37, states: "In case the president [speaker] deems it urgent, he may call a plenary sitting by notifying merely the date and time of such sitting to the members of the House." (The foregoing is the official translation.)

[23] The language in the *Diet Law* (Article 55-II) is permissive: "The president [speaker] may consult with the chairman of the Committee on House Management and Proceedings Conference. . . ." However, this permissive language is somewhat misleading. In the vast majority of basic decisions affecting the agenda, a good deal of prior negotiations both within the parties (in their Diet strategy committees) and among them (in the House Management Committee) has taken place. A complete breakdown in this part of the Diet's internal decision-making machinery occurred over the weekend of November 6. See *ibid.*, p. 37.

plenary session on his own authority, the possibility arose that no Socialists would participate in the deliberations. Presumably, a boycott of Diet proceedings by the Socialists would embarrass the LDP in the eyes of the public and might make it reconsider some of its more forceful parliamentary maneuvers. On the other hand, while the Socialists were considering this tactic, some of their leaders argued that if they absented themselves, their public supporters might interpret this behavior as a failure of nerve — giving up the battle before it had actually been lost.

Instead of the boycott, the Socialists decided to continue their tactics of delay and procrastination. The former included demanding a vote by open ballot at every opportunity.[24] An "open vote" necessitates casting ballots (white for, blue against) into separate urns placed on the rostrum below the speaker's chair.[25] This style of voting lends itself to *gyuho senjutsu* (literally, "cow-walking"), or snail's-pace tactics, which involves simply standing in, and thus blocking, the passageway between the speaker's raised dais and the rostrum on which the waiting ballot boxes rest, slowing the vote almost to a standstill. In the House of Representatives it is the opposition whose roll is called first, so that it is easy for some of their sturdier members to keep all others from the goal of depositing their ballots. It is virtually impossible under these conditions for anyone to cast his vote without a good deal of pushing and shoving, which raises tempers and on occasion leads to a real brawl.

In the House of Councillors, where the opposition votes last, members resort to such devices as examining the beautifully ornate woodwork in the Chamber; forgetting ballots at their desks, a lapse of memory that necessitates a second trip; or simply chatting with a colleague. Periodically, the presiding officer will intone *"tōhyō onegaishimasu"* ("please vote"). In either house a vote normally completed in fifteen or twenty minutes can in this way consume two hours or more. Patience, self-restraint, and other virtues are tested to the extreme.

As a further delaying device, the Socialists embarked on a series of non-confidence motions against various cabinet ministers. These mo-

[24] Paragraph 2, Article 151, *Rules of the House of Representatives*, states: "In case the speaker finds it difficult to ascertain whether the standing members are in the majority or not, or when one-fifth or more of the members present have taken exception to this declaration, he shall put the matter to a vote by open ballot." *Ibid.*, p. 95.

[25] Articles 152 and 153, *Rules of the House of Representatives*, *ibid.*, p. 95.

tions had the triple advantage of enjoying preferential status over all other agenda items (by custom rather than by law); of entailing time-consuming debate; and of requiring a minimum of three official votes, for each of which an open ballot could be demanded.

During the final vote on the non-confidence motion against Foreign Minister Shiina Etsusaburō, that gentleman found it necessary (for compelling reasons of his own) to depart from the Chamber. He did so, with the chief parliamentarian's permission, but after the Diet Chamber had been locked — a step always taken at the beginning of each official vote in order to avoid double voting. Diet protocol demands that the individual against whom a non-confidence motion is being debated and voted upon be present in the Chamber. On the other hand, Diet rules forbid anyone to enter while a vote is being taken. A noisy, totally uncontrolled floor debate ensued. How could a vote on a motion of non-confidence be completed against an individual who was not present and how could he be made to be present when no one is admitted — or even readmitted — until a vote has been completed? To the despair of the LDPers and the delight of the opposition the plenary session had to be recessed.

After frantic huddles in caucus and committee rooms, private members' offices, the dining room, and the lobbies, the Speaker managed to reconvene the session later that same evening. A new vote on the motion of non-confidence against Foreign Minister Shiina was conducted without incident. Nonetheless, about eight precious hours had been lost.

Throughout that same night (Tuesday, November 9) and all the next day, the plenary session dragged on with other motions of non-confidence being presented by the Socialist minority against other cabinet ministers and then voted down, after debate, by the LDP majority. By Wednesday evening (the 10th), as nerve endings became raw, lack of sleep exacerbated the prevailing tension despite the forming of relay teams (three for the LDP and two for the Socialists) to render unnecessary the presence of everyone in the Chamber at the same time.[26] In this maneuver some unpublicized agreement between the major antagonists was notable: there was no effort on the part of the Socialists to have all their troops on the floor when only two-

[26] Flower-like badges of different colors identify the separate teams and add a touch of color to an otherwise somber spectacle.

thirds of the Liberal Democrats were present; such a move could have brought representation between the government and its opposition up to near parity and a snap vote favorable to the Socialists would then have become a far-out possibility. Priorities, however, exhibit a force of their own, and the exigencies of sleep thus promoted a gentlemanly rapprochement.

By the evening of Wednesday the 10th, members of the House had been in almost continuous session – except for some brief recesses – for nearly thirty hours. Socialist tactics of delay seemed to be accomplishing their purpose and were creating a deepening sense of despair among the government's representatives. A mood of lassitude became noticeable among the LDPers, who were further discouraged because their leader, Prime Minister Satō, had decided to go home to sleep. Newspapermen caught grumbling comments about Satō crawling into his own comfortable *futon* (quilts) while the rank and file had to catch catnaps at their desks or on sofas in the lobby or, in a few instances, on cots in their offices across the street.[27]

By the next morning (November 11), the only business that the House had been able to consider was the opposition's series of non-confidence motions against certain cabinet ministers – and several more remained on the agenda. No debate on the treaty itself had yet taken place. Clearly the government was confronting a crisis, for if there was no change in tactics, the November 13 deadline would be lost under the shuffling feet of the somnambulant cow-walkers. In the midst of the debate on a motion of non-confidence against Justice Minister Ishii Mitsujirō,[28] a recess was called.

Shortly after 11:00 that evening, some twelve hours after the recess began, the session was reconvened. No substantive business was enacted; the agenda of the day was simply carried over to the meeting scheduled to begin shortly after midnight – a move directed to keep the legislative machinery in motion from one calendar day to the next.[29]

[27] According to Article 211, *Rules of the House of Representatives,* "The members shall respect the dignity of the House." *Ibid.*, p. 104.

[28] Ishii subsequently became speaker of the House of Representatives (in January 1966).

[29] According to Article 113, *Rules of the House of Representatives,* "When any bill or matter on the agenda was not taken up or its consideration was not finished on the appointed day, the speaker shall place it again on the agenda for another day." *Ibid.*, p. 89.

A MIDNIGHT SESSION: "PEARL HARBOR" REVISITED

All was calm on the surface as Speaker Funada took his seat as the midnight session began. However, within some fifty seconds (at 00:18, Friday, November 12) the House of Representatives approved the Japan-Korea Normalization Treaty, attached agreements, and related domestic legislation.[30] It was all over. A Japanese newspaper friend subsequently observed to me that the government had employed "Pearl Harbor tactics," that is, a sneak attack.

The entire sequence of events leading to this midnight session will undoubtedly remain shrouded in mystery for some time. Dissident Socialists made dark allegations against their party leaders to the effect that they had accepted substantial quantities of legal tender from the LDP in order that the rank and file would be unprepared for the government's sudden move.[31] On one point, and one point only, there is certainty — the LDP's leadership had been quietly busy during Thursday's recess after concluding that the time had come to act.

Among the prime movers, the principal figures apparently were Tanaka Kakuei (LDP Secretary-General and, at the time, one of Prime Minister Satō's most trusted lieutenants); Speaker Funada; Vice-Speaker Tanaka Isaji; and, possibly most crucial of all, Kaya Okinori, a close associate of former Prime Minister Kishi, a senior Liberal Democrat and chief of the party's Japan-Korea Treaty strategy committee. Undoubtedly, Prime Minister Satō, in his capacity as LDP president, was also involved in the decision to act, but his role as Diet strategist appears to have been limited. Together they decided that the hour to break the logjam had arrived. How this feat was to be accomplished was left to one of the ranking members of the LDP's Diet strategy committee, Tamura Hajime.[32]

Consulting only with himself, Mr. Tamura gathered three groups of LDP representatives whose seats on the floor were near the front of

[30] *Kampō Gōgai* (Diet Record Extra), November 12, 1965, p. 159. The Record indicates that the session began at 00:18 and ended at 00:19.

[31] Members of the LDP strategy committee do have a slush fund, which is not fully audited. It is alleged that in mah-jongg games senior Liberal Democrats see to it that their Socialist friends are allowed to win. In this fashion, yen can change hands freely.

[32] Mr. Tamura belongs to the Murakami faction, which was led by former LDP Vice-President Ohno Bamboku until his death. The other wing of the "Ohno" faction came to be led by Speaker Funada.

the Chamber.[33] Two of the groups were first- or second-term representatives (in the Diet, junior representatives sit to the front of the Chamber), the third group consisting of the parliamentary vice-ministers, most of whom are second or third termers. They were selected both for their ready access to the speaker's rostrum and for their comparatively youthful physiques. Each group was put into a separate caucus or committee room behind locked doors to receive its instructions. Surprise would be achieved by means of a feint. Everyone would enter the Chamber quietly but quickly and take his seat in a calm and dignified fashion, befitting his rank and station. To do otherwise would be to alert the opposition that something other than the left-over agenda item from the previous day — the motion of non-confidence against Justice Minister Ishii — would be up for consideration.

Their stratagem worked so well that not only the opposition but also the more senior Liberal Democrats sitting toward the rear of the Chamber were fooled — the latter being heard to make a variety of uncomplimentary remarks about their own leadership's indifference to their welfare. It was, after all, the third midnight session to which they were being subjected.

As soon as calm had settled over the Chamber (the Socialists, sensing that the LDP might act, had initially rushed to surround the speaker's chair and thereby to obstruct the session, but had sheepishly returned to their seats when they noticed the serene dignity of the government party's representatives) and everyone was seated at his desk, Speaker Funada entered and took his seat. As he was doing so, each of the three groups of LDPers rushed to its predetermined post to protect the Speaker.[34]

Simultaneously, the Speaker intoned that the order of the day's agenda was altered. Item one had been continuation of debate on the non-confidence motion against Justice Minister Ishii. Items two through

[33] Details of this story were initially learned during a lengthy interview with Mr. Tamura on December 4, 1965. Mr. Tamura was extremely gracious in reviewing the whole episode. He remarked that part of his motivation for actively participating in the passage of the treaty lay in earlier having been among those within the LDP who had opposed the rapprochement with South Korea alone. He asserted that he wanted to get the approval over with as quickly as possible so that the task of toppling Prime Minister Satō could be begun. (This reasoning is somewhat obscure.)

[34] Please see chart of House of Representatives, which is based on a rough sketch drawn by Mr. Tamura during the interview on December 4, 1965. This story was subsequently confirmed in a number of interviews with Japanese newspapermen assigned to cover the Diet.

CHAMBER OF THE HOUSE OF REPRESENTATIVES

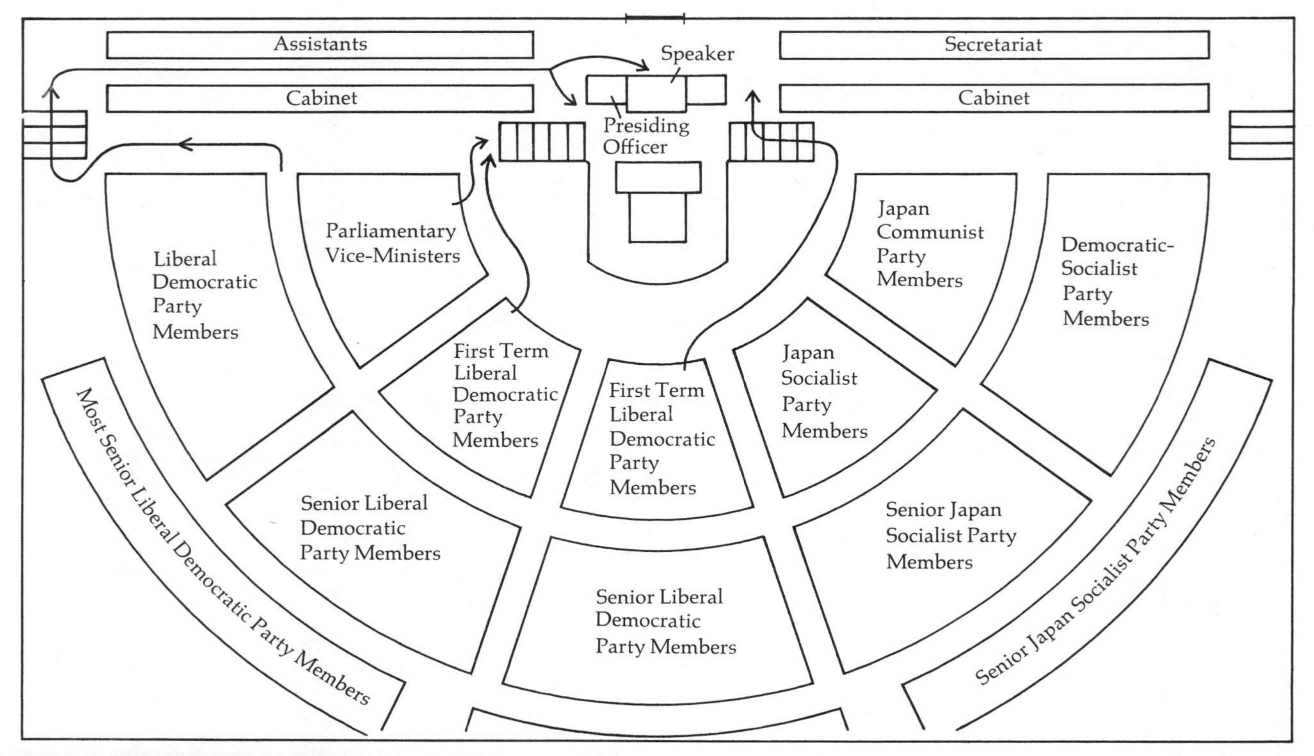

five concerned the treaty and its attached agreements. The Speaker moved to replace item one by items two through five, which motion was approved by a "standing vote" (by this time everyone was on his feet). He thereupon moved that items two through five be considered together, that the report of the chairman of the Special Committee be dispensed with, and that those in favor of items two through five indicate their approval by standing.[35] Afterward, the opposition asserted that no one really heard the Speaker's motions because of the bedlam in the Chamber. Nonetheless, the Diet Record reflects official approval, and that is, after all, what counts.

It was, as Mr. Tamura subsequently reflected, a once-in-a-lifetime operation. In its execution surprise, speed, and lack of physical violence — all conditions laid down by the LDP's directorate — had been observed to the letter. Contributing to the element of surprise was the fact that an item on the previous day's agenda had been left hanging in suspended animation. The Socialists had not foreseen that the non-confidence motion against Mr. Ishii would not be dealt with prior to the treaty's consideration; their strategists had not done their homework, because the Speaker does have the power to alter the agenda.[36] Technically speaking, he may do so only after consulting the House, but obviously such consultation would have eliminated the element of surprise. It was argued in defense of the move that with the overwhelming majority of seats held by the LDP, Speaker Funada's motion would have been upheld; hence, a formal vote was superfluous.

Approval of the Japan-Korea Normalization Treaty and its attached agreements had been accomplished by the House of Representatives, and it had taken place within the deadline, indeed with almost forty-eight hours to spare.

THE COUNCILLORS ACT

In one sense, the decision by the House of Representatives approving the treaty could be viewed as final. Constitutionally, the

[35] *Kampō Gōgai* (Diet Record Extra), November 12, 1965, p. 159. Technically speaking, item two (the treaty) was moved for approval separately from items three through five (the attached agreements).

[36] According to Article 112, *Rules of the House of Representatives, op. cit.*, p. 89, "When the speaker deems it necessary . . . he may alter the order in the agenda, or add new items to it *after consulting the House* without debate" (emphasis added).

treaty had been approved regardless of what action the Diet's second chamber, the House of Councillors, might take. As we have seen, so long as one calendar month of a Diet's session remained after approval of a treaty by the House of Representatives (and Mr. Tamura's maneuver had assured this), approval by the House of Councillors was not really required. A decision by the councillors approving the treaty would be merely redundant. A decision disapproving the treaty — a virtual impossibility because of the LDP majority — would have no force. Nonetheless, a repetition of the drama that had transpired in the House of Representatives was acted out.

Why this further step was considered necessary is difficult to determine. A partial explanation lies in the ambiguous position of the House of Councillors, which has not managed to carve a distinctive niche for itself in Japan's postwar parliamentary politics. "Since it does exist, it must do something" — a statement made to me by a number of Japanese observers — may well be the best answer that can be provided. The councillors could not be baldly ignored.

For the government, approval in the House of Councillors was a challenge. Conceivably, positive action accomplished with decorum might undo some of the damage to parliamentarism that had been done in the House of Representatives. Furthermore, such action by the councillors might be used to buttress the government's case that there did exist widespread support for the treaty. On the other hand, it was one more opportunity for the opposition to embarrass the government.

What did happen was an almost exact repetition of the decision-making process in the House of Representatives. A special committee was established to handle the treaty and related agreements in one package. This committee, in addition to holding hearings in the Diet, went out to the outlying cities of Fukuoka and Osaka as well as to Tokyo itself in order to hear testimony from the public and to explain the contents of the treaty. Socialist members of the Special Committee also devoted much time to questioning the Prime Minister and his cabinet ministers about the "forced vote" approval at the final House of Representatives session.

Once again, the Special Committee's deliberations ended in a debacle. The transcript indicates that LDP Councillor Ueki Mitsunori rose and managed to say, "Chairman . . . ." This is followed by a notation to the effect that many are speaking, that the Chamber is in an uproar and that it is impossible to hear.[37] There is then the further notation that motions cutting off debate, to approve the treaty, and to approve the attached agreements are all carried. Unfortunately, in his initial press conference, held within minutes after the committee meeting, Mr. Ueki said that he had simply moved to cut off debate. A couple of hours later, presumably after party headquarters had passed the word to him, he called a second press conference in which he corrected his initial report and brought it into conformity with the transcript.

Another minor point of procedure at variance with that of the House of Representatives was that for the final vote in the plenary session the Socialist and Komeito councillors as well as several Independents absented themselves from the Chamber. Approval of the treaty by those bothering to attend was therefore recorded as unanimous.[38] The councillors, too, had acted and had done so almost two days prior to the expiration of the Fiftieth Diet Session.

REFLECTIONS AND TENTATIVE CONCLUSIONS

The Diet had made a decision. Henceforth the Treaty on Basic Relations between Japan and Korea and its attached agreements would be part of the law of the land. To be sure, Diet members had not covered themselves with laurels in their dedication to parliamentarism. The high-handed tactics employed by the Liberal Democrats were counterbalanced by the obstructionist tactics the Socialists had resorted to. Both parties' activities would appear equally difficult to countenance. Although this reaction, voiced by observers both domestic and foreign, is understandable, a number of factors must be considered in order to set the process of treaty approval into a somewhat broader perspective.

First and foremost, what has been described here as having taken place in the Diet is only one instance of a vast number of cases that might have been used to illustrate the inner workings of this parliament. Second, the legislation being considered was the most controver-

[37] *Sangiin Nikkan Joyaku Nado Tokubetsu Iinkai Kaigiroku Dai Ju-Gō* (House of Councillors Special Committee on the Japan-Korea Treaty, etc.), No. 10, p. 19.

[38] *Kampō Gōgai* (Diet Record Extra), December 11, 1965, p. 251. The Record notes, "White Ballots: 136," "Blue Ballots: None."

sial that had confronted the Diet since the approval of the revised United States-Japan Security Pact of 1960. Third, the confrontation between the governing conservatives (LDP) and their opponents (principally the JSP) had been an unequal contest from the start, because of the former's almost two-thirds majority in both chambers. Fourth, the powers of the presiding officers, both of the special committees and of the plenary sessions, are so substantial in matters of agenda and time allotted for debate that the opposition is almost forced to resort to questionable tactics such as snail's-pace voting or relatively meaningless motions of non-confidence in order to make itself seen, if not heard. In contrast to the American Congress, in which a well-organized minority has an almost limitless arsenal of parliamentary tactics with which to delay the will of a disjointed majority, an opposition minority in Japan has few parliamentary devices to effect a holding action against the majority.

Beyond the foregoing, the substance of the treaty itself must be considered. The fact remains that it is foreign policy questions rather than domestic issues that have been the source of the greatest division between the government and its opposition in postwar Japan. It would be as if in the United States the Congress had been confronted with a whole series of Tonkin Bay resolutions rather than the syndrome of malaise associated with the urban-ethnic minorities-civil rights crises that have wracked the American body politic since the early 1960's.

Furthermore, whereas in the United States only a small percentage of individuals are so alienated from political processes and procedures that they are willing to challenge the "rules of the game," in Japan this percentage is considerably larger. Just how large the group that distrusts parliamentary politics in Japan really is, is a question on which views differ markedly. It is clear that among both Liberal Democrats and Socialists there are individuals who are willing to press the Diet and its procedures to the very limits of its survival capacity.

The Diet did survive even if public confidence in it was at least temporarily shaken. One may wonder how often this parliamentary institution and its processes can be subjected to the kind of treatment it received during the Japan-Korea Treaty approval process. It had been known by one and all that the reestablishment of relations with Korea, or rather South Korea, would be controversial. Hence, the government knew that by concluding the negotiation with the

Republic of Korea the political system might well be stretched to the breaking point. Yet, once these decisions had been made, there was no easy way to change directions. From the LDP's point of view, not only its capacity to govern, but also its commitment to honor international agreements previously concluded, would have been seriously, possibly irreparably, damaged had the treaty not been approved by the Diet.

Similarly, the JSP had made a compact with its supporters at home, and possibly abroad (for example, North Korea and China), to oppose the treaty with every means at its disposal. It too had placed its honor on the line. Under such circumstances, it is perhaps easier to empathize with the participants in the legislative struggle. At the very least, one can understand why compromise between the government and its opposition was difficult to achieve. There simply was no room for it, or at least so little that commitments to parliamentarism would have had to be considerably stronger than they were.

This element of commitment to parliamentarism brings us to a discussion of one more variable in the equation: the internal structure of Japan's major political parties. It so happened that both the LDP and the JSP were controlled by their more militant elements during that session of the Diet. Prime Minister Satō belongs to that wing of his party (the LDP) which is willing to introduce and to push policies or programs that are known to be anathema to the opposition. In this, he followed in the footsteps of his older brother Kishi, who had been prime minister during the crisis over the Security Pact in 1960. Likewise, Chairman Sasaki Kozo of the JSP was, at least verbally, a leader of that wing of the Socialist movement which espoused Marxist dogmas and was willing to establish close ties with the Chinese Communists when even the Japanese Communists were beginning to have reservations about Peking. Thus, to an already explosive issue, the treaty itself, was added the factor that groups of individuals who were least likely to seek any form of accommodation with each other were in control of the major parties.

Passage of the treaty by the Diet might well have been far less destructive of parliamentarism had power been in different hands. During the years that Prime Minister Ikeda governed Japan and controlled the LDP (July 1960–October 1964) and Chairman Kawakami Jōtarō led the Socialists, the Diet functioned relatively smoothly. Had these individuals and their supporters within the major parties still been in control, a rather different scenario than the one presented here might have been written.

Such a theory is, by its nature, difficult to prove; however, Ōhira Masayoshi, one of former Prime Minister Ikeda's principal lieutenants has tried and his thoughts go to the heart of parliamentarism in Japan.[39] It is his contention that after the difficulties in the Special Committee in the House of Representatives, the LDP should have approached the Socialists with the suggestion that the Diet session be extended for about ten days in return for their limiting the level of their obstructionism. Had such an agreement been accepted, the LDP might have been able to approve the treaty without the midnight travesty of the final session, and the JSP could have been assured of a face-saving argument with its supporters.

Mr. Ōhira's compromise would not have avoided all difficulties, a point he is more than willing to concede, but it represents an emphasis on the matter of parliamentary tactics that greatly differs from that displayed by Mr. Satō and his supporters. Their basic position was that inasmuch as the Japanese people had given the LDP a majority of seats in the Diet the party should exercise its power to overwhelm the opposition. Furthermore, they tended to believe that the JSP was so "un-Japanese" in its policy orientations that it could, and probably should, be ignored with impunity. Finally, for the LDP militants, there was great danger in the viewpoint expressed by Mr. Ōhira in that it could all too readily lead to a kind of immobilism. This view was forcefully expressed by one of Mr. Satō's most trusted supporters, Fukuda Takeo, when he asserted that "Prime Minister Ikeda was the worst prime minister of the worst cabinet of the worst government in the world."[40]

Thus, it is not just the volatility of an issue (such as the treaty) or the disagreement over foreign policy between the LDP and the JSP, but also the specific coalition of individuals and groups who are in control of Japan's major parties, which must be considered in assessing the manner of the Diet's approval of the Japan-Korea Treaty.

[39] The following is based on an interview with Ōhira Masayoshi, former Foreign Minister of Japan, in his Diet office, November 26, 1965.

[40] Quoted from an interview with Fukuda Takeo at his home, July 9, 1963. At the time, Mr. Ikeda was prime minister and Mr. Fukuda, though a senior member of the LDP, was neither a cabinet minister nor an important party official.

Decision-making within the framework of parliamentary politics is a delicate art. It is especially difficult in a society where deep fissures still exist, despite the best efforts of the Japan Travel Bureau to depict it as serenely dedicated to cultivating the tea ceremony and the art of flower arrangement. The Diet would not have been true to its representative function, especially in Japanese-Korean relations, had it not reflected some of the underlying tensions that still persist within the Japanese body politic.

APPENDIX

The Japan-Korea Treaty

THE TREATY ON BASIC RELATIONS BETWEEN JAPAN AND THE REPUBLIC OF KOREA WITH AGREEMENTS AND PROTOCOLS SIGNED AT TOKYO, JUNE 22, 1965 (INSTRUMENTS OF RATIFICATION EXCHANGED AT SEOUL ON DECEMBER 18, 1965)

Japan and the Republic of Korea,

Considering the historical background of relationship between their peoples and their mutual desire for good neighborliness and for the normalization of their relations on the basis of the principle of mutual respect for sovereignty;

Recognizing the importance of their close cooperation in conformity with the principles of the Charter of the United Nations to the promotion of their mutual welfare and common interests and to the maintenance of international peace and security; and

Recalling the relevant provisions of the Treaty of Peace with Japan signed at the city of San Francisco on September 8, 1951 and the Resolution 195 (III) adopted by the United Nations General Assembly on December 12, 1948;

Have resolved to conclude the present Treaty on Basic Relations and have accordingly appointed as their Plenipotentiaries,

Japan:

Etsusaburo Shiina, Minister for Foreign Affairs of Japan
Shinichi Takasugi

The Republic of Korea:

Tong Won Lee, Minister of Foreign Affairs of the Republic of Korea
Dong Jo Kim, Ambassador Extraordinary and Plenipotentiary of the Republic of Korea

Who, having communicated to each other their full powers found to be in good and due form, have agreed upon the following articles:

ARTICLE I

Diplomatic and consular relations shall be established between the High Contracting Parties. The High Contracting Parties shall exchange diplomatic envoys with the Ambassadorial rank without delay. The High Contracting Parties will also establish consulates at locations to be agreed upon by the two Governments.

ARTICLE II

It is confirmed that all treaties or agreements concluded between the Empire of Japan and the Empire of Korea on or before August 22, 1910 are already null and void.

ARTICLE III

It is confirmed that the Government of the Republic of Korea is the only lawful Government in Korea as specified in the Resolution 195 (III) of the United Nations General Assembly.

ARTICLE IV

(a) The High Contracting Parties will be guided by the principles of the Charter of the United Nations in their mutual relations.

(b) The High Contracting Parties will cooperate in conformity with the principles of the Charter of the United Nations in promoting their mutual welfare and common interests.

ARTICLE V

The High Contracting Parties will enter into negotiations at the earliest practicable date for the conclusion of treaties or agreements to place their trading, maritime and other commercial relations on a stable and friendly basis.

ARTICLE VI

The High Contracting Parties will enter into negotiations at the earliest practicable date for the conclusion of an agreement relating to civil air transport.

ARTICLE VII

The present Treaty shall be ratified. The instruments of ratification shall be exchanged at Seoul as soon as possible. The present Treaty shall enter into force as from the date on which the instruments of ratification are exchanged.

IN WITNESS WHEREOF, the respective Plenipotentiaries have signed the present Treaty and have affixed thereto their seals.

DONE in duplicate at Tokyo, this twenty-second day of June of the year one thousand nine hundred and sixty-five in the Japanese, Korean, and English languages, each text being equally authentic. In case of any divergence of interpretation, the English text shall prevail.

FOR JAPAN:
Etsusaburo Shiina
Shinichi Takasugi

FOR THE REPUBLIC OF KOREA:
Tong Won Lee
Dong Jo Kim

AGREEMENT CONCERNING FISHERIES
(Unofficial translation of the gist of the agreements)

Japan and the Republic of Korea are desirous of maintaining a maximum and lasting productivity of fishery resources in waters of mutual interest.

The two countries recognize and believe that the preservation of fishery resources in the said waters as well as the rational development and expansion of the resources will contribute to the interests of both countries.

The principle of the freedom of the high seas will be respected by the two countries in all cases except those stipulated in the agreement.

The two countries are desirous of the high seas to be respected to avoid disputes in fishing operations resulting from the complicated nature of such operations due to the geographic proximity of the two countries.

The following articles have been agreed upon with the hope that the two countries will cooperate with each other in expanding their respective fishing industries.

ARTICLE I

1. Waters within 12 nautical miles off the base lines of each nation shall be designated their exclusive fishing waters.

If either nation wishes to draw the demarcation line designating its exclusive fishing zone in a straight line, it shall obtain the consent of the other nation.

2. Neither nation shall raise objections if one nation declares its exclusive fishing zone off limits to the fishing vessels of the other nation.

3. Areas where the exclusive fishing zones of the two nations overlap shall be divided in two by straight lines joining the ends of the overlapping areas with the midpoints of straight lines drawn across the areas at their widest points.

ARTICLE II

The two nations shall establish a joint control zone.

ARTICLE III

Pending the completion of exhaustive scientific surveys for ensuring maximum and lasting productivity of fish resources in joint restrictive zones, dragnet fishing, surrounding net fishing and mackerel fishing by fishing boats of over 60 tons shall be governed by temporary regulatory measures to be set forth in documents attached to this agreement.

ARTICLE IV

1. The authority for policing (including the right to halt and inspect vessels) and exercising court jurisdiction in waters outside the exclusive fishing zones shall be exercised by the nation to which the fishing boat belongs.

2. Both nations shall extend appropriate guidance and supervision to ensure that the temporary regulatory measures are faithfully observed by their peo-

ples and fishing boats. Violations shall be handled with domestic measures including appropriate penalties.

ARTICLE V

Joint surveys shall be conducted on fishery resources in waters to be established outside the joint control zones.

The extent of the areas where the surveys shall be conducted and the details of the surveys shall be determined through consultations by the two nations on the basis of the recommendations to be made by the joint fishery committee to be referred to in Article VI.

ARTICLE VI

A joint fishery committee shall be established and maintained to attain the objective set forth in this agreement.

ARTICLE VII

1. The committee shall perform the following tasks:

(a) To make recommendations to the two contracting parties regarding the scientific research to be made for the purpose of studying fishery resources in the joint control zones on regulatory measures to be taken on the basis of the findings of research.

(b) To make recommendations to the two parties on the boundaries of sea areas, the resources of which are to be studied jointly by the two parties.

(c) To deliberate on matters related to the temporary regulating measures for fishing when the need arises and to make recommendations to the two parties on measures to be taken based on the results of the deliberations.

2. Omitted.

3. Governments of the two contracting parties shall respect recommendations made by the committee as much as possible.

ARTICLE VIII

The two contracting parties shall take measures which they deem appropriate to have persons and fishing vessels of their own nationalities observe the international practices concerning voyages, to seek safe operations by fishing vessels belonging to them, to maintain order among operating fishing vessels and to achieve smooth and speedy settlement of incidents between their fishing boats on the seas.

ARTICLE IX

1. Attempts shall be made to solve disputes arising between the two contracting parties over interpretation and execution of the agreement first through diplomatic channels.

2. Disputes which cannot be settled under the preceding provision shall be referred to the Mediation Committee composed of two members, each of whom is to be appointed by the Government of each contracting country, and another member whose appointment is to be agreed on by the two members.

The third member, however, must not be a person belonging to either of the two contracting parties.

3. In case any of the Governments of the two contracting parties fails to appoint a member within the prescribed time or in case agreement is not reached on the third Mediation Committee member or on the country the third member belongs to within the prescribed time, the Mediation Committee shall be composed of two members to be appointed by Governments of two countries, each of whom is to be named within 30 days by one of the two contracting parties and a third member to be appointed by the government of a country which is to be named by the two governments through consultations.

4. The Governments of the two contracting parties shall obey the decisions to be made by the Mediation Committee under the provisions of this article.

ARTICLE X

The agreement shall be effective for five years. After that, it shall remain effective for a further one-year period from the day when either of the contracting parties informs the other of its intention to abrogate the agreement.

Agreed Minutes on the Japan-ROK Fishery Agreement

(a) The yearly haul of mackerel in the joint control waters by trawl nets, surrounding nets and boats of more than 60 tons shall be set at a total 150,000 tons with a 10 per cent leeway above and below this figure.

Each Government shall be ready to control the number or size of a fleet of fishing boats so as to keep the total catch down to 165,000 tons or less whenever the catch appears certain to exceed the basic quantity of 150,000 tons.

(b) Each Government shall designate landing ports for ships of its own nationality which have caught fish in joint control waters subject to temporary regulatory measures as regards fishing.

Provisional Restrictive Measures: Control and Violations

(a) The authorized Government employee aboard an inspection vessel of either of the parties shall notify the counterpart of the other party of violations of the said restrictive measures, immediately after he has discovered what he believes to be obvious and definite cases of such violations.

The Government of the other party after being informed of the violation, shall respect the notice in exercising his patrolling rights and disciplining the violator.

(b) Concerning the temporary measures, each Government shall provide as many facilities as possible for the authorized official of the other party to check the enforcement of such measures on its territories, should such a request be received.

(c) Each Government, when the other party asks for its employee to inspect the actual control of its fishing boats and this request is considered reasonable, shall agree to take him aboard the inspection ship which engages in such a mission.

Notes in Regard to Fishery Cooperation

The Governments of Japan and the Republic of Korea, in order to develop and improve their fishery industries, will extend their utmost cooperation in technological and economic aspects, including:

1. The exchange of fishery information and technique.
2. The exchange of fishery experts and engineers.

Agreement Concerning Property Claims and Economic Cooperation

Japan and the Republic of Korea have entered into agreement in the hope of settling problems concerning property of the two countries and their nationals and the propery claims between the two countries and their nationals as follows:

ARTICLE I

1. Japan will supply to the Republic of Korea free of charge:

(a) Japanese products and services valued at $300 million, equivalent to ¥108,000 million at present rate of exchange, over a period of 10 years from the date when this agreement comes into effect. The products and services will be supplied each year within the limit of $30 million, which is equivalent to ¥10,800 million at the present rate of exchange. If the supply does not reach the above amount, the balance will be added to the amount of products and services to be supplied in the following year. However, the amount of products and services to be supplied each year may be increased or decreased according to an agreement between the two signatory countries.

Japan will provide the ROK with long-term and low-interest loans up to $200 million, equivalent to ¥72,000 million at the present rate of exchange over a period of 10 years from the date when this agreement comes into effect. The loans will be used for the procurement by South Koreans of Japanese products and services required by the ROK Government for the execution of projects that will be decided under an arrangement to be concluded in accordance with Item 3 of Article I.

The loans will be provided from the funds of Japan's Overseas Economic Cooperation Fund and the Japanese Government will take the necessary steps to enable the Overseas Economic Cooperation Fund to secure the funds required to provide the loans in an equal amount annually.

The above-mentioned supply of products, services and loans must be conducive to the economic development of South Korea.

2. The two countries will establish a joint committee, composed of representatives of the Governments of the two countries, as a consultative organ which will be authorized to make recommendations regarding the problems related to the enforcement of provisions of this article.

3. The two countries will conclude arrangements necessary for the execution of provisions of this article.

ARTICLE II

1. The two signatory countries confirm that the problems concerning the property, rights and interests between the two countries and their peoples and the property claims between the two countries and their peoples have been fully and finally settled, including those stipulated under Paragraph (a) of Article IV of the Peace Treaty with Japan signed in San Francisco on Sept. 8, 1951.

2. The provisions of this article will not have effect on the following (excluding those covered by the special measures taken by the two countries up to the signing of this agreement).

(a) Property, rights and interests of nationals of either of the two signatory nations who have resided in the other signatory nation between Aug. 15, 1947 and the date when the agreement was signed.

(b) The property, rights and interests of either of the two signatory nations and its people which have been obtained through normal contacts after Aug. 15, 1945 or have come under the jurisdiction of the other signatory nation.

3. No claim can be made regarding the property, rights and interests of either of the two signatory nations and its people which are under the jurisdiction of the other signatory nation on the date this agreement is signed. This also applies to the property claim held by either of the two signatory nations and its people against the other signatory nation and its people if such a claim is caused before the agreement is signed.

ARTICLE III

1. Any dispute between the two signatory nations concerning the interpretation and enforcement of the agreement shall be settled first through diplomatic channels.

2. Any dispute which cannot be settled by the provisions of Item 1 shall be referred to a mediation committee. The committee will be organized by three mediators, one each from the signatory nations who will be appointed by either of the Governments of the two countries within 30 days from the date when either of the Governments of the two countries received an official document calling for mediation in the dispute and another mediator selected by the two mediators within 30 days after the expiration of the first 30-day period or one who will be appointed by the Government of a third country selected by the two mediators within the 30-day period. However, a third mediator shall not be a national of either of the two signatory nations.

3. If the Government of either of the two signatory nations fails to appoint a mediator within the specified period or if no agreement is reached regarding the third mediator or the third country within the specified period, the mediation committee shall be composed of three mediators, one each from two countries selected by the signatory nations within a 30-day period and another to be appointed by a third country selected by the two countries through consultations.

4. The two signatory nations shall abide by the decisions made by the mediation committee stipulated in this Article IV.

This agreement must be ratified. The ratification instruments should be exchanged in Seoul as soon as possible. This agreement comes into force on the date when the ratification instruments are exchanged.

(The First Protocol, concerning the extension of $300 million in outright grants to South Korea by Japan, is omitted.)

Second Protocol

ARTICLE I

The Republic of Korea shall make installment repayments without interest and within the next 10-year period after the protocol goes into effect as follows on the Japanese credit of $45,729,398 which has been confirmed as the unsettled amount under the open accounts between Japan and the Republic of Korea under the documents exchanged between the two countries on April 22, 1961.

The amount of the first through the ninth annual installment repayments: $4,573,000.

The amount of the tenth annual installment repayment: $4,572,398.08.

ARTICLE II

Should there be a request from the Republic of Korea over the annual installment repayment described in the foregoing article, the amount of products and services as well as the amount of supply set for that year which are prescribed under section (a), Item 1 of Article I of the Agreement is reduced by an equivalent amount to that requested by the Republic of Korea in spite of the provisions of the same section (a), Item 1 of Article I and, when this reduction takes place as requested, it is then taken to mean that the annual installment repayment has been completed to the amount of products and services provided as stipulated in the amount which is equivalent to the amount requested by the Republic of Korea.

ARTICLE III

The Republic of Korea shall make the first annual installment repayment for the Japanese credit described in Article I on the day the protocol becomes effective. The subsequent payments that begin with the second installment repayment shall be made annually before the same date as the first repayment is made in the first year.

ARTICLE IV

The request of the Republic of Korea as described in Article II of the protocol is to be made, considering the practice of the Japanese financial administration, before October 1 of the year previous to the beginning of the Japanese fiscal year to which the date of the repayment belongs under the stipulation of the foregoing Article. However, the request affecting the first repayment and the second repayment shall be made on the day when the protocol becomes legally effective.

ARTICLE V

The request of the Republic of Korea shall be made on a portion or the whole of the annual installment repayment described in Article I of the Protocol.

ARTICLE VI

When the request by the Republic of Korea is not made before the date set forth under the provisions of Article IV and when the repayments set under the provisions of Article III are not made on a portion or the whole of the repayment amount by the date set under Article III, it shall then be taken to mean that the Republic of Korea has made the request on a portion or the whole of the installment repayment under the provisions of Article II.

Notes on the Japan-South Korea Joint Committee to be Established in Accordance with the Agreement on Claims and Economic Cooperation

It is hereby confirmed that the Joint Japan-South Korea Committee will be established according to the following terms:

1. The committee shall be located in Japan.
2. The committee shall be composed of members assigned by both countries, including one representative each and several deputy representatives.
3. The committee shall be summoned at the request of either of the two Governments.
4. The committee shall hold consultations and make recommendations on the following matters whenever requested:

(a) Approval of plans, contracts and payment procedures as related to the implementation of the outright grant to South Korea by Japan.

(b) Review of the implementation of Item 1, Article I of the Agreement on Claims and Economic Cooperation (including the computation of the amount of grant and credits extended at appropriate times).

Notes on Commercial Credits

1. It is expected that the nationals of Japan will extend commercial credits on a non-governmental basis exceeding $300 million to the Government or the nationals of the Republic of Korea. The extension of the said loans will be expedited and facilitated in accordance with the relevant laws and regulations in Japan.

2. The said loans will include those for fishery cooperation, which are expected to amount to $90 million, and another $30 million for the export of vessels to the Republic of Korea, to which the Japanese Government will give as much favorable consideration as possible.

Notes on the Extension of Long-Term Credits by Overseas Economic Cooperation Fund

1. The loans stipulated in Article I, 1 (b) of the Agreement will be implemented on loan contracts and agreements on a project basis to be concluded between the Republic of Korea Government and the Japanese Overseas Economic Cooperation Fund.

2. The two Governments agree that the following conditions will be included in the contracts and plans.

(a) The loans will be extended in equal amounts every year as far as practicable.

(b) The repayment period of the principal will be 20 years, including a seven-year period of grace beginning six months after the project goes into effect. The interest will be 3.5 per cent per annum.

(c) Repayment of the principal will be made on an annual basis in equal amounts.

(d) The repayment of the principal and interest will be made in convertible Japanese yen.

3. The repayment period of the loans may be extended by agreement between the two countries if such extensions become necessary in consideration of the financial situation in the two countries and the landing position of the Overseas Economic Cooperation Fund.

4. Both countries will hold annual consultations to agree on loan projects and implementation plans presented by the Republic of Korea.

Proceedings Related to the Settlement of Property Claims and Economic Cooperation

The Korean delegation, in regard to Article II of the agreement on property claims and economic cooperation, expressed their wish for special consideration by the Japanese Government in dealing with the properties that belonged to their people who had left Japan after the state of war ceased to exist at the end of World War II and before the date of Aug. 15, 1947. The Japanese side assured them that the wish would be closely studied.

It was confirmed also that the problems on properties, rights, and interests and also the claims issue between the two countries and their peoples of which solution is prescribed completely and solved finally in Article I of the agreement, included all the claims listed in the "List of Korean's Claims to Japan" presented during the Japan-Korea normalization talks. Any assertion based on the said list is null and void.

Both sides also confirmed that the claim rights of both countries and their peoples of which solution is prescribed completely and solved finally in Article I of the agreement, included all damage claims of Japanese fishing boats that are captured and seized by the Korean authorities prior to the signing of the agreement; the Japanese side would not be in a state to make claims to the Korean Government in these cases.

The Korean delegation in regard to Clause 1, Article II of the First Protocol of the agreement, expressed their wish to be granted US$150 million worth of raw materials other than capital goods, thus ensuring sufficient domestic funds required to carry on the various projects with the grants and credits extended by Japan in accordance with Clause 1, Article I of the agreement.

Agreement Concerning the Legal Status and Treatment of the South Korean Residents in Japan

Whereas, Japan and the Republic of Korea consider the long-time special contacts of Korean residents with Japanese society to have developed out of the many years of their residence in Japan;

Whereas, both parties recognize as beneficial to the furtherance of friendly relationship between the two countries or the two peoples for Japan to provide Korean residents with the means to enjoy a stable life under the Japanese social order;

Japan and the Republic of Korea have, therefore, agreed on the following provisions:

ARTICLE I

1. The Japanese Government shall grant the right of permanent residence in Japan to any Republic of Korea national meeting any of the following specifications upon application for the same right according to the prescribed procedure within five years after the present agreement goes into effect.

(a) Those who have been residing in Japan since before August 15, 1945 and have continued to do so up to the time of application.

(b) Direct descendants of Korean nationals specified in (a) who were born after August 16, 1945 or who are to be born within five years after the coming into force of the present agreement and who will have continued to reside in Japan up to the time of application.

2. The Japanese Government shall grant permanent residential rights to any offspring born in Japan more than five years after the present agreement goes into effect to Koreans already enjoying the same rights under Article I when applications are made for the same rights according to the prescribed procedure within 60 days after their birth.

ARTICLE II

1. The Japanese Government shall comply with the Republic of Korea Government's request for consultations whenever made any time within 25 years after the present agreement goes into effect regarding the residence in Japan of direct descendants of Korean nationals entitled to permanent residential rights under Article I.

ARTICLE III

Those Korean nationals entitled to the right of permanent residence in Japan under Article I shall not be subjected to deportation from Japan except when any of their acts, committed after the present agreement goes into effect, falls within the following categories:

(a) Those who have been sentenced to prison terms or subjected to any severer punitive action on charges of insurrection or for crimes relating to foreign aggression.

(b) Those who have been sentenced to imprisonment or subjected to any other severer forms of penalty for offenses affecting Japan's diplomatic interests or for criminal offenses which involve a foreign head of state, foreign diplomatic personnel or their property and are injurious to Japan's diplomatic interests.

(c) Those who have been sentenced to penal servitude or imprisonment of more than three years for the breach of any laws or ordinances controlling narcotic transactions aimed at profit making (excepting the case where such sentences are suspended) as well as those who have been convicted more than three times for the same offense.

(However, those convicted for a third time for a narcotic offense committed before the coming into force of the present agreement will become deportable if and when convicted of two additional repeated offenses.)

(d) Those who have been sentenced to imprisonment or penal servitude of more than seven years for the breach of any Japanese laws or ordinances.

ARTICLE IV

The Japanese Government shall give appropriate consideration to the following matters:

(a) Matters concerning the education, livelihood protection and national health insurance coverage in Japan of those Korean nationals entitled or eligible to permanent residence in Japan under Article I.

(b) Matters concerning the taking out of Japan of properties in kind as well as in cash by any Korean nationals returning from Japan to the Republic of Korea by waiving their wish for continued residence in Japan.

Agreement Concerning Cultural Assets and Cultural Cooperation

ARTICLE I

The Governments of Japan and the Republic of Korea shall extend as much efforts as possible for the promotion of cultural relations between the peoples of the two countries.

ARTICLE II

The Japanese Government will transfer to the Government of the Republic of Korea, within six months after this agreement comes into force, all cultural properties listed in the attached document through methods agreed between the two Governments.

ARTICLE III

The Governments of both countries will provide the peoples of each country with opportunities to study cultural properties in possession of art galleries, museums and libraries and other academic and cultural facilities in their respective countries.

The attached document, which is part of the agreement, lists the following cultural properties to be transferred to the Republic of Korea:

Ninety articles of ceramic ware; 84 items of anthropological data; two stone objects of art; 163 historical documents, and 20 telecommunication articles.

Notes on the Peaceful Disposition of Disputes between the Two Countries

The Governments of both countries agree to settle disputes arising between Japan and South Korea through diplomatic channels, provided they are specified otherwise in the agreements between the two countries.

In case the disputes cannot be settled by such channels, the two countries agree to settle the disputes through mediation based on procedures agreed upon between the two countries.

(Note: these notes are understood as referring to the dispute over Takeshima Island.)

SELECTED BIBLIOGRAPHY

Ikematsu Fumio. "The ROK-Japan Treaty and Political Parties." *Contemporary Japan,* Vol. XXVIII, No. 3 (May 1966), pp. 494–519. An "establishment" view, written by a senior Japanese journalist.

Langdon, Frank. *Politics in Japan.* Boston: Little, Brown, 1967. Chapter IV, "Making Political Demands," Chapter V, "Choosing Policies and Politicians," and Chapter VI, "Governmental Processes" are especially valuable.

Morley, James William. *Japan and Korea: America's Allies in the Pacific.* New York: Walker, 1965. A comprehensive treatment of basic background information.

Scalapino, Robert A. and Junnosuke Masumi. *Parties and Politics in Contemporary Japan.* Berkeley: University of California Press, 1962. Unfortunately, somewhat out of date, but still an excellent introduction to the Japanese party system.

Tsuneishi, Warren. *Japanese Political Style: An Introduction to the Government and Politics of Modern Japan.* New York: Harper and Row, 1966. Chapter V, "The National Diet: Functions, Organization, Representation" and Chapter VI, "The National Diet in Action" provide a broader perspective on decision-making in the Diet.

Ward, Robert E. *Japan's Political System.* Englewood Cliffs, N.J.: Prentice-Hall, 1967. The best brief introduction to contemporary Japanese government and politics.

HANS H. BAERWALD

2 Tento-Mura: At the Making of a Cabinet

In the courtyard of the prime minister's official residence the tents of the newspapers and radio and television networks were once again assembled. Each tent had its own time-honored vantage point and was elaborately equipped with the various medias' stock-in-trade, inevitably including extra telephone lines. The erection of the *tento-mura,* or "tent village," signaled, as it had since the 1920's, another shift of personnel at the apex of Japan's executive branch, the cabinet.

The tento-mura is no longer absolutely necessary, because in the early 1960's a spacious annex was completed to house the press corps assigned to cover the cabinet. Nonetheless a cabinet reshuffle would not be complete, so I was told, without the tents, which represent continuity and tradition, important to the Japanese despite their headlong rush into modernity. In the past the tents were highly functional; the newly appointed ministers would be driven through the area, and a well-placed tent might give one of the reporters a split-second edge over his competitors in relaying their names to his editor.

Research for this case study was made possible by a generous grant from the Rockefeller Foundation, for whose assistance I am deeply grateful.

During a number of cabinet reorganizations my friends in the Japanese newspaper world have permitted me to be with them in the tent village and the neighboring Press Club[1] in order to observe the proceedings. Most of the following story of the making of a cabinet in Japan is based on personal observation and is to that extent impressionistic and particularistic.

THE POLITICAL PARTY MATRIX

The Liberal Democratic Party (LDP)[2] has governed Japan since 1955. Indeed, if the LDP's direct antecedents are included, it has controlled the executive branch since the end of World War II with the exception of a brief interregnum in 1947–48 of a coalition cabinet – first under the Socialist Katayama Tetsu, then under the Democrat Ashida Hitoshi, as prime ministers.

"Liberal" and "Democrat" are misleading as descriptions of the LDP. Its "liberalism" is more classical than contemporary, and its dedication to "democracy" is ambiguous and ambivalent. The LDP is, above all else, an organization that has been remarkably successful in electing candidates to public office. So successful has it been that in the four elections for the House of Representatives that have taken place in the last decade, it has consistently captured nearly two-thirds of the available seats.

[1] The Japanese press clubs are extremely exclusive organizations. It is not sufficient to be accredited by one's newspaper or network to cover the cabinet or the Diet or one of the ministries or a party headquarters. In addition, one must be formally invited by one's colleagues who are in the "Club," which in turn regulates the activities of its members. A "scoop" is virtually unknown, since the Club exercises restraints the violation of which can lead to suspension or even expulsion, so that a newspaperman may find himself in the unenviable position of being assigned to cover the prime minister's office but not being able to fulfill his assignment because of not being in the Club. No foreign newspaperman has been allowed to join any of the clubs, which has led to considerable frustration. The Japanese respond with the assertion that most foreigners do not know the Japanese language sufficiently well to benefit (generally true) from membership and might therefore misinterpret remarks made during a press conference (possibly valid). As a consequence, most news about Japanese domestic politics is filtered through articles that appear in the vernacular press or are broadcast over radio and television, thus precluding most independent news-gathering by foreigners, which in turn has led to rather pallid and superficial reporting.

[2] In Japanese the LDP is known as the *Jiyu-Minshu-Tō*, frequently abbreviated to *Jimintō*. It has an impressively modern party headquarters, one short block from the Diet, employing hundreds of party workers.

TABLE 1 LDP STRENGTH IN HOUSE OF REPRESENTATIVES, 1958–1968

Election	*Total seats*	*Seats won by LDP*	%
May 22, 1958	467	287	61.4
Nov. 11, 1960	467	296	63.3
Oct. 21, 1963	467	283	61.4
Jan. 29, 1967	486	277	56.9

Source: Jichishō Senkyō-kyoku (Autonomy Ministry Election Bureau), *Shugiin Giin Sōsenkyō Kekka Shirabe* (Report of the House of Representatives General Election), Tokyo, 1967, pp. 13–14.

On the surface, the party presents a façade of unity of structure and purpose, and one might well suppose that the task of forming a cabinet would be relatively simple for the party president, who, so long as the LDP enjoys its substantial majority in the Diet, doubles as prime minister of the cabinet. Since the Constitution stipulates that a majority of the ministers must be members of the Diet – indeed all except two[3] of those appointed to the December, 1966 cabinet were M.P.'s at the time of their appointment – the pool of talent from which the selections are to be made is relatively small, so that one could expect that the prime minister's task would be primarily to find "the right man for the right job." Though the latter is an oft-heard slogan, and is occasionally honored, other factors do complicate the decision-making process.

Foremost among the complications is the existence of factions inside the party. These groups are so significant that it is virtually impossible to comprehend Japanese politics without at least a brief review of their origins and of the functions they perform.

Among the reasons generally cited for the existence of factionalism in the LDP, the most obvious, though gradually becoming less significant, is the duality implicit in the party's name. The party is a fusion of two major strands, plus a number of minor ones, in the

[3] Fujiyama Aiichirō and Miyazawa Kiichi. Fujiyama was one of Japan's richest men at the time of his appointment as Foreign Minister in the first Kishi cabinet (1957). Miyazawa had been a member of the House of Councillors, but was not a member of either house at the time of his appointment as minister in charge of the Economic Planning Agency in the December 1966 Satō cabinet. Miyazawa, one of the brightest stars in the LDP, intended to run for a seat in the House of Representatives in the forthcoming election and hoped that a ministerial appointment would assist him in winning. His hopes were fulfilled. (Please see Appendix for basic data on the individuals who are mentioned.)

development of Japanese party politics after World War II – the Liberal Party and the Democratic (also occasionally named "Progressive") Party. This dual ancestry still stretches internal LDP unity to the breaking point on occasion, a fact which is partially explained by the friction inherent in the combination of two groups, each with its own distinct loyalties, but which is exacerbated in Japan by the fierce devotion accorded the primary group.

A second factor that has contributed its share to the growth of factionalism in the LDP is that some of the party leaders were temporarily removed from public office by the purge of militarists, ultranationalists, and their allies during the occupation,[4] whereas other leaders came to the fore during the same period. Indeed, the return of the "purgees" from political limbo contributed substantially to a temporary split in the Liberal Party in 1951. This factor is on the verge of losing its importance as the group of "old purgees" gradually becomes extinct.

A third factor, closely related to the purgee versus non-purgee split, is the competition between those in the party whose careers have been primarily in electoral politics (whether at the local, prefectural, or national level) and those who entered politics after a career in the governmental bureaucracy. In Japanese the former are called the *Tōjin-ha* (politicians' group) and the latter, the *Kanryō-ha,* which since 1957 has dominated the LDP under the successive prime ministerships of Kishi Nobusuke, Ikeda Hayato, and Satō Eisaku, all of whom were career bureaucrats prior to their entry into politics. The Tōjin-ha has not managed to return to the dominance it exercised under Prime Ministers Hatoyama Ichirō and Ishibashi Tanzan, both of whom were ex-purgees; nor are its current prospects for leadership of the caliber enjoyed by Kōno Ichirō or Ohno Bamboku, both of whom died in the early 1960's. Nonetheless, the conflict implicit in the different approaches to politics taken by the "politicians" and the "bureaucrats" continues to add its bit to factional strife.

Japan's electoral district system for the House of Representatives is the fourth factor contributing to factionalism. Representatives are elected from three-, four-, or five-member constituencies. Inasmuch as several candidates from the same party vie for the allegiance of the

[4] For further details, see Hans H. Baerwald, *The Purge of Japanese Leaders Under the Occupation* (Berkeley: University of California Press, 1959).

voters, and because each voter can write the name of only one candidate on his ballot (the names are prominently displayed so that the voter is not required to remember how to write his choice providing he can read, which more than 99 per cent of the Japanese are able to do), there is considerable – often excruciating – conflict between candidates from the same party. In the Kanagawa First District (Yokohama and its suburbs), the following pattern resulted from the 1963 election:[5]

Fujiyama Aiichirō	LDP	126,415
Moji Ryō	Democratic-Socialist	107,855
Noma Chiyozo	Socialist	104,530
Oide Shun	Socialist	101,241
Okazaki Kazuo	LDP	92,711

Since it was a four-man district at the time (a fifth seat was added in the reapportionment that went into effect in the 1967 election), the second LDP candidate, Okazaki (a former ambassador to the United Nations), was defeated. Yet he and Fujiyama could both have been elected had their campaign managers been able to cooperate in dividing up territorial strengths. A shift of 10,000 LDP votes would have sufficed for Okazaki to beat the second Socialist candidate, Oide, still leaving Fujiyama with a comfortable margin at the top of the list. However, Okazaki belonged to Prime Minister Satō's faction, whereas Fujiyama is the leader of his own faction and has entertained hopes of becoming prime minister. The electoral system itself can thus be seen as promoting factional infighting rather than cooperation among candidates of the same party in the same district.

Funds to conduct these electoral campaigns – and, in particular, the collection and disbursement of such funds – also contribute to divisiveness in the LDP. As in most political systems in which there is a relationship between financial resources and "electability," Japanese candidates find their electoral expenses mounting with each successive campaign. (A few candidates are so well established that they do not have to conduct elaborate campaigns to be elected, but their number is small and growing smaller.) An endorsed LDP candidate can normally count on receiving about half his campaign kitty from the party itself. The balance must come from somewhere else,

[5] Jichishō Senkyō-kyoku (Autonomy Ministry Election Bureau), *Shugiin Giin Sōsenkyō Kekka Shirabe* (Report of the House of Representatives General Election) (Tokyo, 1964), p. 167.

frequently one of the factional leaders, who are able to become leaders precisely because of their ability to raise funds. The larger the number of successful candidates a faction leader (called *oyabun,* or "boss") can support, the greater his power within the national party, especially manifest at party conventions. Both the oyabun and the candidates are confronted with difficult choices; for example, an aspiring freshman candidate may attempt to receive financial assistance from two or three faction leaders, increasing his chances of winning but at the same time incurring the risk of being labeled "unreliable." Therefore, despite its necessity, the disbursement of funds — not only at election time but also to keep constituents happy between contests — contributes its share to perpetuating factionalism.

Electing the party's president and (so long as the LDP controls a majority of seats in the Diet) the prime minister of the country is a sixth factor perpetuating factionalism. Which faction supported what candidate for the ultimate prize, and at what stage of the deliberations, are considerations that weigh heavily in the rise and fall of factions and their oyabun, each of whom is playing his role precisely because he is dreaming of one day capturing the prize of supreme party leader and chief executive of Japan for himself. Once again a different element of the system, in this instance that of electing the party's president in a national convention (presumably by secret ballot, though knowledgeable observers usually know who voted for whom), contributes its share to the persistence of factionalism in the LDP.

One additional element among the factors contributing to factionalism that requires brief mention — that of ideology, or at least differences over policy. It is a marginal factor, however, and cannot be taken too seriously in explaining the existence of factions. The LDP encompasses a wide spectrum of viewpoints — for example, from advocacy of the immediate recognition of Red China to undying devotion to Formosa — and, on occasion, such divergent policies do enter into party infighting. However, policy disputes are normally counters in the elaborate chess game (or game of *shogi* or *go,* in the Japanese context) the factional leaders play with each other rather than a basis for factionalism. LDPers are pragmatists rather than ideologues, which latter role they are perfectly willing to let their principal opponents, the Socialists, play to the hilt.

Obviously, each of the factors cited could be elaborated upon at much greater length, but even this cursory examination provides some indication of the kind of organization the LDP is. It is not one tightly knit, monolithic party, but rather an association, or coalition, of factions that has somehow managed to survive as an entity for more than a decade. It often gives the appearance of coming apart at the seams only to be stitched back together at the last minute, if for no other reason than that a permanent rip might provide an opening for the Socialists to come to power. This prospect alarms LDPers not only for ideological reasons but, perhaps more realistically, also for the practical one that longed-for cabinet posts would then no longer be within the realm of possibility.

BACKGROUND OF THE 1966 CABINETS

Prime Minister Satō undertook two full-scale reorganizations of his cabinet during 1966. Of the two, the latter, that of December, was far more significant than the former; but politics being a seamless web (unless interrupted by revolution), the two will be considered part of one continuous process.

Satō Eisaku had become president of the LDP and prime minister of Japan on November 9, 1964. His immediate predecessor, the late Prime Minister Ikeda Hayato, had been forced to retire prematurely for medical reasons (the diagnosis, terminal cancer). Ikeda had just been reelected to a third two-year term during the previous summer at a stormy LDP convention in which he had won on the first ballot by only four votes more than the absolute majority of voting delegates (a total of 238). His principal rival had been Satō, who had received the support of 160 delegates.

No one, least of all the business community, which foots the bill for party conventions, wanted to have a second expensive gathering within a four-month period. Ikeda, as the retiring party leader, together with his immediate associates, thus decided to transfer the reins of power by means of "talks" (*hanashiai*) among the principals.[6] The choice was basically between Satō, who epitomized the LDP's bureaucratic group (Kanryō-ha), and Kōno Ichirō, who represented the careerist politicians (Tōjin-ha). For a variety of complex reasons, perhaps principally the fact that Satō had the support of the big business community to a far greater extent than did Kōno, it was he who became prime minister.

[6] For further details, see Baerwald, "Japan: The Politics of Transition," *Asian Survey*, January 1965, pp. 33–42.

Satō at first moved very cautiously in adjusting personnel within the cabinet.[7] Indeed, he retained the entire Ikeda cabinet with one major exception: he replaced Suzuki Zenko as chief cabinet secretary with one of his own long-time loyal associates, Hashimoto Tomisaburō.[8]

By the summer of 1966 Satō had managed to consolidate his position as leader of the party. In the interim, to be sure, he had undertaken some shifts in the cabinet, but he had not basically altered the factional balance that had existed in the last Ikeda cabinet. Most important, he had managed to have the Diet approve the treaty normalizing diplomatic relations between Japan and the Republic of Korea.

Satō could therefore look forward with some confidence to two crucial political events that were in the offing. The first was another party convention that would determine whether he would be reelected for another two-year term as president of his party. The second was a general election, the timing of which was flexible, although it had to take place prior to October of 1967.[9]

Prime Minister Satō's position was both strong and weak, depending upon which elements of his situation were emphasized. Those who saw him as having a secure base of power could cite his leadership in getting the Diet to approve the Japan-Korea Treaty — a major legislative achievement, even if it had placed great strains on the parliamentary process.[10] He also had the advantage of being the leader of the numerically largest faction so that no one was sufficiently strong to challenge him. Three major leaders — former Prime Minister Ikeda, former Vice-President Ohno Bamboku, and former Tōjin-ha strongman Kōno Ichirō — had all died within the previous two years.

Each had been a leader of one of the important factions in the LDP and each of their factions was faced with varying degrees of internal

[7] The prime minister has the power to appoint and dismiss cabinet ministers. Article 68, *The Constitution of Japan* (Tokyo: The National Diet of Japan, 1960), p. 16.

[8] The post of chief cabinet secretary (of ministerial rank) combines the functions of principal administrative assistant (e.g., the role performed by Sherman Adams for President Eisenhower) with that of official press secretary. It is a post that requires constant and close collaboration with the prime minister and is normally filled by a member of the latter's own faction. Thus, Suzuki was an Ikeda man, whereas Hashimoto was one of the most senior members of Satō's faction.

[9] Members of the House of Representatives are elected for four-year terms. However, the House can be dissolved and a general election called for prior to the expiration of the four years. Article 45, *The Constitution of Japan, op. cit.*

[10] For additional details, please see the companion case study, "Nikkan Kokkai," pp. 19–45.

turmoil. Ohno's group split relatively quickly into the Funada[11] and Murakami[12] factions, Kōno's later into the Mori[13] and Nakasone[14] factions, with only Ikeda's managing to survive as an entity under the astute guidance of Maeo Shigesaburō.[15] By the summer of 1966 Satō had gone far toward consolidating his support within the LDP with the help of his older brother Kishi and the latter's close associate Fukuda Takeo. Table 2 will afford some insight into the relative strengths of the various factions at that time.

TABLE 2 FACTIONS IN THE LDP (1966)

Faction	*Members in House of Representatives*	*Members in House of Councillors*	*Total*
Satō	44	52	96
Fukuda (Kishi)	20	0	20
Miki	36	10	46
Kawashima	18	0	18
Ishii	14	10	24
Funada (ex-Ohno)	12 } +3	9	35
Murakami (Ohno)	11 }		
Maeo (ex-Ikeda)	47	15	62
ex-Kōno	44	14	58
Fujiyama	18	11	29
Minor and Independent	20	0	20

Source: *Kokkai Binran* (Diet Handbook), Tokyo: Nihon Seikei Shimbun Shuppan-bu, September 1966, pp. 324–330.

These figures should be considered as indicating factional strength for comparison only, not as absolute or final in any way or even at

[11] Funada Naka's career was capped by the speakership of the House of Representatives in the mid-1960's. Basic biographical data have been taken from *Shugiin Yōran* (Otsu), *House of Representatives Directory* (B) (Tokyo: Okurashō Insatsukyoku [Finance Ministry Printing Bureau], 1964 and 1967).

[12] Murakami Isamu had served as minister of Postal Services and minister of Construction.

[13] Mori Kiyoshi's most senior post was minister of state in charge of the Prime Minister's Office.

[14] Nakasone Yasuhirō, one of the youngest men ever to become a cabinet minister, was Minister of Transportation in 1968.

[15] Maeo Shigesaburō, a long-time Finance Ministry official, served three terms as LDP secretary-general under Ikeda and has also been Minister of International Trade and Industry.

any time. Each newspaper or other analysis, correct in its own way, is slightly different from every other – primarily a reflection of some LDPers' shifting factional allegiances. With this qualification in mind, we can reasonably view Table 2 as an accurate reduction of the situation that prevailed in the summer and fall of 1966. More crucial, Satō's coalition not only encompassed the Fukuda (Kishi) faction, but also had the support of most of the Miki,[16] Kawashima,[17] Ishii,[18] and Murakami factions. Of the major groupings, only the allegiance of the Maeo (ex-Ikeda), ex-Kōno, and Fujiyama factions was in doubt.

These doubts were reflected in shifts in personnel that the Prime Minister made in the last week of July. Maeo was moved from chairman of the party's Executive Board (*Sōmu-Kaichō*) to the less significant post of minister in charge of the Hokkaido Development Agency. Second, Aiichi Kiichi replaced Hashimoto as chief cabinet secretary. Both were Satō lieutenants, but the shift was viewed as indicative of troubles brewing inside the Satō faction, one group being led by Hori Shigeru, the other by Tanaka Kakuei. Satō's faction is so large that some of his followers do not have easy access to their leader, especially while he is serving as prime minister, so that there is a built-in tendency for the faction to splinter into subgroups. In this connection, disagreement is widespread about the optimum size of a faction. A large faction (more than forty members in the House of Representatives) aids its leader by providing him with votes when and if he decides to run for party president. On the other hand, it also requires that the faction leader provide payoffs to his factional supporters (for example, a cabinet appointment or the chairmanship of a standing committee in the Diet) and limitations do exist on the rewards that can be given. Since the amount of patronage is limited, the larger the faction is the larger also is the number of those whose aspirations must be disappointed. Internal friction within the faction is then difficult to avoid.

Critics of Satō also seized on two disastrous cabinet appointments in the July reshuffle. The first was Arafune Seijurō, whose tenure as minister of transportation was extremely short-lived (less than three months). Arafune was one of the senior *kobun* (followers) of LDP Vice-President Kawashima, but even though he had served for seven

[16] Miki Takeo served as Foreign Minister until the fall of 1968.
[17] Kawashima Shōjirō is currently again Vice-President of the LDP.
[18] Ishii Mitsujirō was Speaker of the House of Representatives until the summer of 1969.

terms as an M.P., he had never had a ministerial appointment. (Normally, a member of the House of Representatives becomes eligible for consideration after five terms.) Some of his friends in the newspaper world had carefully inserted articles about his being considered for a high post or had otherwise alluded to him in their columns, as part of a campaign to put pressure on his faction leader Kawashima to in turn put pressure on Satō.[19] This elaborate campaign succeeded in its immediate aim, but unexpectedly backfired when some of Arafune's subsequent activities as transportation minister could not stand the limelight's glare when it continued to shine upon him. For example, shortly after acceding to the post, he changed the schedule of an express train to include a stop at a small town whose location had nothing to recommend it as an express train stop other than that it was in the heart of his own constituency. The joy created among his constituents was somewhat offset by the anguish of his Ministry of Transportation bureaucratic subordinates, who were quick to notify their friends in the media. More serious was his private secretary's message to corporate leaders of industries having contracts with the Transportation Ministry that they were expected to become members of the Minister's "support organization" (that is, financial contributors to his political campaigns). Though such a relationship between a minister and industries in his field of activity are not uncommon, the message was apparently unacceptably blatant in this instance. Arafune, as a Tōjin-ha (politicians' group) product, also had the misfortune of being caught by the antagonism that is felt by bureaucrats in the established ministries for superiors who come from outside their ranks. Such feelings of condescension can be overcome by a minister with finesse and force of personality, but Arafune, although known as a "nice guy," lacked both these essential qualities. His retirement from the cabinet subsequently affected relations between Satō and Kawashima, who indicated his displeasure by declining to serve as vice-president of the LDP for the greater part of 1967.

The second appointment that created consternation was that of Kambayashiyama Eikichi as minister of state in charge of the Defense Agency. Directorship of the agency has not been one of the more prestigious cabinet posts, partly because Defense is still an agency rather than a full-fledged ministry — reflecting in turn the negative

[19] Information based on personal interviews with Japanese newsmen in June and July, 1966.

feelings of most Japanese toward military matters since the end of World War II. Nonetheless, many of the press corps members assigned to cover the July 1966 cabinet reshuffle expressed to me their surprise and dismay when it first became known that Kambayashiyama had been designated. His career in the House of Representatives had not been distinguished; though elected seven times, his principal achievement was the chairmanship of a special committee on the problems of the coal industry. Observers generally agreed that his selection was based on having been reelected the requisite number of times and on having been a loyal retainer in Satō's own faction. He too almost immediately became embroiled in some shenanigans that created adverse publicity for his oyabun; for example, a special parade, including elements from Japan's Self-Defense Forces, was held in his honor in his constituency (located in Kagoshima at the southern end of Kyushu). It was a minor incident and would probably have been overlooked had it not been for the opinion of the media editors that Kambayashiyama was unqualified and that Satō himself was to be rebuked for having made such a laughable appointment. Despite public criticism he remained as director of the Defense Agency almost to the time of the December reshuffle, which further exacerbated feelings between Satō and some of Kawashima's supporters, who claimed that their man (Arafune) had been readily dismissed whereas Satō's man (Kambayashiyama) had been allowed to remain.

Each of these cases of ministerial maladroitness would have escaped becoming a cause célèbre had it not been for the general mood of disaffection with the LDP, Prime Minister Satō, and his cabinet. If Satō's position inside the LDP seemed secure, such was not true with the public at large. From having had the support of close to 50 per cent of the public, according to an opinion poll conducted shortly after he became prime minister in 1964, Satō's support had dipped well below 30 per cent, according to polls conducted during the late summer of 1966.

A series of scandals involving LDPers helped shake the public's confidence. The first involved Tanaka Shōji, who was indicted for intimidation and extortion. Though a minor figure in the LDP, he had exercised considerable power as chairman of the House of Representatives Audit Committee — a post that allowed him to make life miserable for colleagues whose probity had come into question.

A second concerned the Kyowa Seitō, a sugar trust. The scandal involved excessively large governmental loans on watered collateral made by Agriculture and Forestry Ministry banks to a company that had, in turn, made sizable political donations despite ostensibly being in straitened financial circumstances. It also implicated former Minister of Agriculture and Forestry Shigemasa Seishi, an LDP representative of substantial seniority and a staunch Satō supporter.

Third, the so-called "Ban-no-kon" scandals broke. Bananas ("ba") from Taiwan, *nori* ("no," laver, or dried seaweed, a delicacy) from Korea, and *konyaku* ("kon," a vegetable product from which the spaghetti-like substance in sukiyaki is made) from China – were all products involving import licenses, which were found to have been granted to a favored few who in turn were alleged to have made the requisite political donations.

Each scandal by itself would not have been terribly serious, but together they added up to what the newspapers came to call the *kuroi Kiri* (black mist) which had settled like a blanket of smog over Prime Minister Satō and his cabinet.

THE DECEMBER 1966 LDP CONVENTION

As the "Black Mist" enveloped the LDP, some of its leaders began to assess the extent of their allegiance to Satō. Cautious probes were made among some of those within the party who wondered whether the time had come to try to overthrow Satō as their president. Part of the motivation was undoubtedly the desire for personal power, but in addition a growing number of LDPers were motivated by fear that unless a new leader took over the direction of the party, the LDP might conceivably face defeat in the upcoming general election.

Satō's opponents embarked on a two-part strategy. As a first step, they would try to deny Satō an absolute majority on the first ballot at the convention by supporting former Foreign Minister Fujiyama. The organizers of this "anti-main stream" coalition, however, recognized that the amorphousness of their solidarity and of their efforts threatened the success of the venture. Their assessment proved to be correct.

The second element of their strategy was more sophisticated. It involved a careful calculation of the kind of support (that is, which delegates) Satō would receive in the convention which would grant him a victory on the first ballot. Delegates to the LDP convention consist of three groups: first, all LDP members of the House of Representatives; second, all who are members of the House of Councillors; and third, one delegate from each of the forty-six prefectural LDP federations.[20] The LDP is clearly dominated by those of its members who are in the Diet. As shown in Table 2, Satō could be expected to have strong support from within that group of delegates who were members of the House of Councillors (52 of 121 were generally listed as being members of his faction and he could count on at least half the others – those from the Ishii, Miki, and ex-Ohno groups). It was also generally believed that he enjoyed the support of a majority of the prefectural delegates. These two groups of delegates plus those from the House of Representatives who were friendly would be more than sufficient to provide him with the necessary simple majority of delegates required to win the party presidency.[21]

Satō's opponents were willing to concede all this. What they hoped for nevertheless was that a substantial number of delegates from the House of Representatives would vote against Satō at the convention and could then be relied upon to vote against Satō for prime minister, an election that would take place in the House of Representatives.[22] Assuming other elements of the plan fell into place, it might then be possible, so its proponents argued, to have Satō as president of the LDP, but to deny him the prime ministership of the government.

The latter scenario was based on the following considerations. First, a general election for the House of Representatives was in the offing, probably to take place in early 1967 (it did on January 29). Second, under the new apportionment, the House would consist of 486 members, which meant that 239 votes would be the minimum needed to win the prime ministership. Third, assuming that the LDP would not do well in the forthcoming election because of the "Black Mist," a defection of some 50 or so anti-Satō LDPers – but possibly an even larger number – might be able to form a coalition

[20] Article 26, "The Constitution of the Liberal Democratic Party" and Article 3, "The Rules of the Election of the President of the [Liberal-Democratic] Party," in Political Party Research Institute, *Political Japan: the Liberal-Democratic Party* (Tokyo: World Policy Research Institute, 1966), pp. 101–102, 114. Prefectural party federations are allowed to have four delegates, but each federation is accorded only one vote.

[21] Article 11, "The Rules of the Election of the President of the Party," *ibid.*, p. 115.

[22] Article 67, *The Constitution of Japan, op. cit.*, p. 16.

cabinet with certain opposition party representatives and thereby elect their own man as prime minister. If the LDP elected 275 representatives, and 50 of them defected, Satō would be left with only 225 votes, less than an absolute majority.

However, proponents of the plan had to face up to some substantial problems in putting together their own majority. Again, assuming 50 LDPers would join such a venture, from where would the balance of the 189 votes come? About 30 might come from the Democratic-Socialists, a centrist group that had split off from the Socialist Party over the twin issues of the United States-Japan Security Pact and "parliamentarism" (both of which the Democratic-Socialists supported but the former of which the Socialists had opposed in 1960). A new group, the *Komeitō* (affiliated with the neo-Buddhist *Sōka Gakkai*, or Value Creation Society), might be able to elect between 25 and 30 representatives, and they too might be prevailed upon to join such a coalition. The most difficult nut to crack would be the Socialist Party, because of the long-standing animosity between it and the LDP.

But the Socialist Party too had its internal splits, principally between its far-out Marxist dogmatists and its more moderate ideologues. The former, who at the time constituted the Socialist Party's main stream under the leadership of Sasaki Kōzo, would probably not join. However, the moderates might. It would depend upon which wing of the party did better in the election. Even assuming that the moderate Socialists were to win about 100 of the 160-plus seats that the Socialists anticipated, more than 50 LDP dissident votes would be needed to gain the necessary 239. The scenario had serious statistical gaps, which its proponents recognized. They also conceded that a necessary precondition would be formal splits within both the Liberal Democratic and Socialist parties, and neither of these was as yet even a mathematical probability. No party regular in either camp would be anxious to court a split just before an election, for which funds from party headquarters were an absolute necessity.

In planning for the LDP convention the key variable that entered into the calculations of Satō's opponents was how many anti-Satō votes could be mustered. Fujiyama and his supporters hoped for 100 as a minimum and 150 as a maximum; Satō's forces hoped that their man would receive the support of at least two-thirds of the delegates. Neither group achieved its goal.

Satō's supporters were shocked that their leader had received less

TABLE 3 RESULTS OF THE DECEMBER 1966 LDP PRESIDENTIAL ELECTION

Satō	289
Fujiyama	89
Maeo	47
Nadao	11
Others	14
Blank Ballots	9
Total	459

than 300 votes, the number that would have brought him close to the two-thirds support they had sought. Contributing to this result was the unanticipated defection of eleven delegates to Nadao Hirokichi, a former Minister of Education and Minister of Welfare who apparently received the support of a substantial group of the Ishii faction to which he belonged but which had been considered part of the Satō coalition. Had the eleven votes cast for Nadao stayed firm for Satō, he would have achieved the anticipated 300 ballots.

Satō's opponents also did not fare as well as they had hoped. Fujiyama's 89 votes fell far short of the hoped-for 150, and there was considerable consternation that he had not even been able to muster 100 votes. Part of this was attributable to the fact that a majority of the old Ikeda faction had cast its ballots for their new leader Maeo rather than for either Satō or Fujiyama. One gathered that this move was dictated by the need to prove to outsiders that the old Ikeda faction had internal solidarity, and that support for either of the major candidates might have led to an irreparable split within the faction.

Nonetheless, Satō had won a clear-cut victory, and he could now turn to the formation of a new cabinet. The anti-main stream centering around Fujiyama and the so-called non-main stream, or neutralists, centering around the old Ikeda faction (Maeo's own leanings remained ambiguous throughout the proceedings, hence the need to use the circumlocution of "old Ikeda faction") were forced to shelve their plan to supplant Satō. Commentators called upon the newly reelected president to provide evidence that he deserved the role of leader by forming a cabinet worthy of the nation's trust. Ideally, this plea meant that he should give precedence to the shibboleth of the "right man for the right job" and disregard "personalities," which meant factional consideration. With Satō's convention victory the basic decision in the making of the new cabinet had been made. There was no longer any doubt as to who would be prime minister.

THE MAKING OF THE DECEMBER 1966 CABINET

Prime Minister Satō immediately turned to restructuring his cabinet, the first stage of which involved filling senior posts in the LDP. Party regulations require that these senior posts be filled after a presidential election,[23] including those of vice-president, chairman of the Executive Board (*Sōmu Kai-chō*), chairman of the Policy Board (*Seisaku Chōsa Kai-chō*, commonly abbreviated to *Seichō Kai-chō*), secretary-general, chairman of the National Organization Committee, chairman of the Finance Committee, chairman of the Party Discipline Committee, and chairman of the Diet Policy Committee. Of these positions, the vice-presidency, the secretary-generalship, and the chairmanships of the Executive and Policy boards are of greater significance than the others listed primarily because an appointment to one of these posts is generally equivalent, if not superior in prestige, to a ministership. As a consequence, the general background and factional affiliations of these appointees are normally an indication of the overall orientation of ministerial appointments that can be expected, especially since some of the top party leaders frequently assist the prime minister in making his cabinet.

As we have seen, Vice-President Kawashima had decided to submit to Satō his resignation from that post. Rumors about his move had been circulating during the autumn — principally because of the Arafune affair. In addition, Kawashima was said to have felt "some sense of personal responsibility" (which sounds and is taken much more seriously in Japan than the English phraseology implies) for the low state to which the LDP had fallen in the public opinion polls as a result of the "Black Mist" scandals.

"Would the Vice-President again accept the vice-presidency after the party convention?" "What attitude might the Vice-President assume vis-à-vis Satō?" "Was he considering joining those within the party

[23] Article 82, Paragraph 2, "The Constitution of the Liberal Democratic Party," *op. cit.*, p. 110.

who were seeking to oust Satō?" To each of these questions, Kawashima either did not respond or would launch into a highly ambiguous analysis (at least, so it sounded to this listener) of the overall political situation.[24] As it turned out, Kawashima did not reaccept the vice-presidency until the subsequent cabinet reshuffle in November 1967, so that the post of vice-president was kept vacant. For Satō to have filled it with someone else would have been a serious affront to Kawashima, possibly forcing him into the camp of the anti-mainstreamers, a risk that was apparently not worth taking. Hence, the easiest solution was adopted, one that is permitted under party regulations.[25]

As party secretary-general — in most instances the most crucial party post (next to the party presidency, of course) — Satō selected Fukuda Takeo, one of the most intellectually brilliant (his educational career had been a series of "firsts"), tough-minded, and, hence, occasionally abrasive leaders in the LDP. His selection in one sense was unusual in that he was the oyabun of his own faction, rather than a follower in Satō's faction. The more usual pattern was for the secretary-generalship to be filled by one of the president's own, most loyal followers. Indeed, until the December convention, Tanaka Kakuei, a trusted Satō lieutenant, had been serving in the post. However, Tanaka (like Kawashima) held "responsibility" for the LDP's decline, and the anti-Tanaka group inside Satō's faction felt that he had been in the limelight far too long in any case. (Tanaka had been Finance Minister in the Ikeda cabinet and had been one of the principal go-betweens in the transfer of power from Ikeda to Satō, a role he could play because of his close friendship with former Foreign Minister Ōhira Masayoshi, a senior Ikeda lieutenant). On the other hand, with Fukuda as secretary-general, Satō was able to widen his base of support by bringing another faction into the center of his coalition. Furthermore, Fukuda's co-leader in his faction was none other than Satō's older brother, former Prime Minister Kishi, whose

[24]This discussion took place late in the evening of November 2, 1966, at Kawashima's home, to which I had been taken by one of my newspaper friends who belonged to that small coterie of newsmen who were members of his inner circle. The questions as cited in the text are rendered in an excessively direct (and thus un-Japanese) fashion for the sake of clarity. A literal translation into English would be practically meaningless.

[25] Article 5, "The Constitution of the Liberal Democratic Party," is permissive: "There may be appointed a vice-president in the party." *Op. cit.*, p. 98.

cooperation was considered necessary in view of the forthcoming general election, which was an important factor in all personnel decisions at this time.

For the other two principal party posts Satō played it safe. The Executive Board chairmanship went to Shiina Etsusaburō, a Kawashima faction member whose stature in the party had risen sharply as a result of his steady leadership as Foreign Minister, an appointment about whose wisdom many had expressed doubts at the time it was made. As Executive Board chairman he could serve as a crucial link with the Kawashima faction, thereby strengthening those somewhat frayed bonds. Nishimura Naomi was Satō's choice for chairman of the Policy Board. He epitomized the best in the Satō faction, having been reelected seven times and having had prior service as director-general of the Defense Agency. In addition, it was generally agreed that he was a neutralist between the warring groups inside the Satō faction and one whose loyalty to Satō himself was unquestioned.[26]

The general outline of the new Satō administration was beginning to take shape. All three party appointees were Tokyo (Imperial) University Law Faculty graduates who had had distinguished careers in the government bureaucracy — Fukuda in the Finance Ministry, Shiina in the Ministry of Commerce and Industry (now named Ministry of International Trade and Industry), and Nishimura in the Home Ministry. They epitomized the LDP Establishment under Satō — safe, tested, senior (all were in their sixties), and with lengthy careers in government service.

These same considerations seem to have guided Satō in the cabinet appointments he turned to as his next task. A prime minister will often consult his fellow official party leaders to assist him in making these decisions, but in this instance it was reported that he ran a basically one-man show, with possibly only the outgoing and incoming

[26] The remaining significant party posts were filled as follows: Chairman of the National Organization Committee, Tsuji Kanichi (elected eight times, with no factional affiliation and no ministerial appointment, experienced as chairman of House of Representatives standing committees); Chairman of Public Relations Committee, Hasegawa Takashi (elected six times, Finance Ministry bureaucrat, and member of the Satō faction); Chairman of the Party Discipline Committee, Saitō Noboru (the sole member of the House of Councillors in a top party post, former Minister of Transportation, and member of the Satō faction); and Chairman of the Diet Policy Committee, Sasaki Hideyo (elected six times, past chairman of the House of Representatives Rules Committee — thus knowledgeable in the fine art of parliamentary maneuver — and member of the old Ikeda faction).

TABLE 4 THE DECEMBER 1966 SATŌ CABINET

Post	*Minister*	*Faction*	*Age*	*Terms in Diet*	*Education*	*Prior career*
Prime Minister	Satō Eisaku	Satō	65	7	Tokyo Law	Transportation Ministry bureaucrat
Justice Minister	Tanaka Isaji	Ishii	60	9	Ritsumeikan	Lawyer
Foreign Minister	Miki Takeo	Miki	59	11	Meiji	Parliamentarian
Finance Minister	Mizuta Mikio	ex-Ohno	61	9	Kyoto Law	Businessman
Education Minister	Kennoki Toshihirō	ex-Kōno	65	3[a]	Tokyo Law	Education Ministry bureaucrat
Welfare Minister	Bō Hideo	Fukuda	62	6	Tokyo Law	Newspaperman
Agriculture-Forestry Minister	Kuraishi Tadao	Fukuda	66	8	Hosei Law	Businessman, author
International Trade and Industry Minister	Kanno Watarō	Miki	71	6	Kyoto Economics	Professor
Transportation Minister	Ōhashi Takeo	ex-Ikeda (Satō?)	67	7	Tokyo Law	Postal Ministry bureaucrat
Labor Minister	Hayakawa Takashi	Miki	50	8	Tokyo Law	Home Ministry bureaucrat
Construction Minister	Nishimura Eiichi	Satō	69	6	Tohoku Engineering	Transportation Ministry bureaucrat
Postal Minister	Kobayashi Takeji	Satō	67	3[a]	Tokyo Law	Postal Ministry bureaucrat
Autonomy Minister	Fujieda Sensuke	Kawashima	59	6	Tokyo Law	Home Ministry bureaucrat
Administrative Management Agency	Matsudaira Isao	Ishii	59	3[a]	Waseda	Corporation executive
Hokkaido Development Agency; Atomic Energy Commission; Science & Technology Agency	Nikaidō Susumu	Satō	57	6	U.S.C.	Navy official (civilian)
Economic Planning Agency	Miyazawa Kiichi	ex-Ikeda	47	(2)[a]	Tokyo Law	Parliamentarian
Defense Agency	Masuda Kaneshichi	Satō	68	7	Kyoto Law	Newspaperman
Chief Cabinet Secretary	Fukunaga Kenji	ex-Ikeda (Satō?)	56	7	Tokyo Law	Parliamentarian
Director-General, Prime Minister's Office	Tsukahara Toshio	Satō	56	7	Tokyo Literary	Newspaperman

[a]Members of the House of Councillors whose terms are six years. Miyazawa had served for two terms, but had not run for reelection and hence was not a member of the Diet, since he was planning to run for a seat in the house of Representatives.

secretary-generals, Tanaka and Fukuda (and through the latter, former Prime Minister Kishi), acting as his confidants.

Satō had quite clearly reflected the prevailing factional balance inside his party in making his cabinet appointments. His own factional followers had received six posts, actually eight if the two former Ikeda lieutenants, Ōhashi and Fukunaga, who were generally believed to have become Satō kobun (followers) in the period after Ikeda's death, are included — or almost half the available posts. Miki's faction had received three, Fukuda's and Ishii's two each, and the others one apiece, with the major exception of Fujiyama's group, which received none; the convention contest had not been forgotten.

The foregoing presupposes that each of the ministerial posts is of equal prestige and importance; however, though this is formally true, some ministerial posts are more equal than others. Little consensus exists on the exact pecking order, but the first division generally includes Finance, Foreign Affairs, and Justice, with the role of the others being fluid and dependent on the significance of the individual who holds the portfolio (for example, while Kōno served as minister of Agriculture and Forestry, it was a prestigious post) or on whether the jurisdiction of the ministry includes a (sometimes temporarily) significant set of problems (for instance, the fact that an election was in the offing meant that the Autonomy Ministry, which oversees the electoral process, was a more crucial portfolio than usual, so that the Kawashima faction was pleased to have one of their men hold it).

The cabinet also reflected Satō's dominance in another fashion. None of the other major factional leaders, with Miki as the sole exception, was an appointee. Kawashima's absence has been explained. Fujiyama's presence would have been surprising in view of his having contested Satō's presidential aspirations, and similar reasons probably explain Maeo's absence. Ishii had managed to place two of his kobun in the cabinet — a disproportionate number for his factions size (see Table 2) — and had apparently been promised the speakership of the House of Representatives, a post he assumed after the January 1967 Diet election. However, none of the new leaders of the old Ohno and Kōno factions was present. To be sure, of the other factional leaders, Fukuda had been installed as secretary-general, but the absence of such a large group of factional leaders from cabinet posts not only reflected Satō's dominance but also the possibility that he was being deserted by his peers pending the results of the forthcoming general election.

It was, as the newsmen observed, a cabinet that was going to fly on one set of engines, and ideologically these engines were all on the starboard wing. This judgment rested on an ambiguous distinction of general tendencies within the LDP as between the "old" and the "new" right. On China policy, for example, the former leaned toward Chiang, whereas the latter favored an expansion of trade with the mainland. On relations with the United States, the "old" tended to be more in favor of continuing close ties, whereas the "new" desired Japan to expand its independence in international affairs, or at least lessen its subservience to America. Domestically, the "old" tended to advocate tactics of confrontation with the opposition socialists, whereas the "new" sought for areas of consensus.

Of generally certified members of the "new" right, there were really only two in the cabinet – Miki and Miyazawa. Miki had been a member of that small group of LDPers who in the spring of 1960 had abstained on the vote approving the revised United States-Japan Security Pact and had subsequently helped to topple Kishi from the prime ministership. He had also entered the LDP after an early postwar period during which he was affiliated with some minor parties that had espoused policies more progressive than those pursued by the Liberal Party, the major precursor of the LDP. However, Miki's past progressive tendencies had been overshadowed by his more recent actions. As party secretary-general, he had been instrumental in the transfer of power from Ikeda to Satō at the cost of a split in his own faction with his co-leader Matsumura Kenzō, who believed that Kōno should have received the mantle because of his espousal of "new right" politics. Hence, Miki's dedication to the more liberal wing of the LDP was questioned, credence being given to the belief that his aspiration was to succeed the Prime Minister, with the latter's blessing.

Miyazawa's case also contained ambiguities. There was little question about his identification with the "new right." Nonetheless, some of his factional colleagues were reported to have been critical of his willingness to join a cabinet so heavily dominated by the more conservative wing of the LDP. As we have mentioned, however, Miyazawa intended to be a candidate for the House of Representatives in the upcoming election. His chances for winning presumably would be improved by being a cabinet minister, since Japanese voters are believed to respond affirmatively to candidates who hold prestigious appointments. His decision to accept a cabinet post therefore was understandable even if his reputation as a member of the "new right" might thereby be (temporarily?) tarnished, especially among his peers in the old Ikeda faction.

By and large, the other ministers all tended to be associated with the "old right," though this label is highly ambiguous. Some of the observers were surprised, though, at the relatively small number of career bureaucrats (seven: Satō, Kennoki, Ōhashi, Hayakawa, Nishimura, Kobayashi, Fujieda) who had been appointed, considering Satō's own career as an official in the Transportation Ministry, the absolute dominance of ex-bureaucrats in the top party posts, and the general belief that ex-bureaucrats were safer and more reliable by comparison to *Tōjin* (politicians). We must recall that Satō was probably still smarting over the criticism he had incurred because of the Arafune and Kambayashiyama cases and was desirous of not opening himself up to any further scandals. (Japanese bureaucrats have a deserved reputation for honesty and competence.)

On the other hand, even if the group of nonbureaucrats was large, nearly all the newly appointed ministers had held ministerial appointments before. Miki had been Minister of International Trade and Industry in the outgoing cabinet and had held previous ministerial appointments; Tanaka had been Vice-Speaker of the House of Representatives; Mizuta had had a prior term as Minister of Finance in one of the Ikeda cabinets; Bō had been Parliamentary Vice-Minister of Finance; Kuraishi had had several terms as Minister of Labor under Prime Ministers Hatoyama and Kishi; Kanno previously had been Minister in charge of the Economic Planning Agency; Nikaidō had been Parliamentary Vice-Minister of Labor; Miyazawa had served as Director-General of the Economic Planning Agency in the Ikeda cabinet; Masuda had held numerous ministerial portfolios — Chief Cabinet Secretary, Transportation, Labor, Construction, as well as having been Governor of Fukushima Prefecture; Fukunaga had been one of Prime Minister Yoshida's chief cabinet secretaries as well as Labor Minister in one of the Ikeda cabinets; and Tsukahara had been a parliamentary vice-minister of construction.

Hence, of the non-career bureaucrats, only Matsudaira had never held a cabinet or sub-cabinet post. He was not without executive experience, however, having risen through the ranks in Mitsubishi Shōji (Trading) Company and affiliated enterprises to the post of managing director.

It was a cabinet of tested men who could be relied on to perform their tasks well and without risk of creating embarrassment. Conversely, there was little infusion of new blood or of new ideas. The evidence suggests that Prime Minister Satō's principal consideration – aside from the requirements imposed by the need to maintain his coalition of factional support – was to form a cabinet with which he could go to the polls. Risk-taking was not on his agenda.

A new cabinet had been formed.[27] It only remained for the new ministerial appointees to don their formal attire (striped pants and morning coats) and go to the Imperial Palace for the formal attestation.[28] A group photograph would appear in all the media and there would be endless speculation as to why some had smiled whereas others appeared to have inadvertently swallowed some *wasabi* (a very hot horseradish whose ingestion shocks the sinus). The tent village would be quickly dismantled until a repetition of the performance – with a slightly different cast of characters – took place.

POSTSCRIPT

Politics had not come to an end with the formation of the cabinet. Its creation represented only one set of decisions – important, to be sure, because the individuals selected would hold an impressive share of power until they were replaced – in the endless drama of Japanese politics.

A general election was in the offing and its results would help to determine how long each of the ministers would serve.

In the preceding pages I have tried to tell the story of one example of this decision-making process, primarily as seen through the eyes

[27] The whole process – party convention (held December 1), selection of principal party leaders (completed December 2), and formation of the cabinet on December 3 (the individual appointees arrived at the Prime Minister's official residence between 4:15 and 5:30 P.M. to receive the news from Satō, and the attestation ceremony at the Palace took place at 7:30 P.M.) – had encompassed not quite three days.

[28] Article 7, *The Constitution of Japan, op. cit.*, p. 5, states: "The Emperor, with the advice and approval of the cabinet, shall perform the following acts in matters of state on behalf of the people: . . . Attestation of the appointment and dismissal of ministers of state. . . ."

of those who have been close observers over a number of years — the Japanese reporters. It is their perspective rather than one imported by a foreigner that has guided the construction of this case study.

In conclusion, I will hazard a few generalizations about cabinet formation in Japan. First and foremost, it is the prime minister, in his capacity as president of his party, who is the most significant decision-maker. Once Prime Minister Satō had survived the convention contest and had won, it was he who had the final say. To be sure, he did receive the counsel of others; for example, both the outgoing Secretary-General of the party Tanaka Kakuei and his successor Fukuda Takeo were closeted with Satō in the official residence, but they acted as assistants rather than as prime movers. Satō's pre-eminence reflected both his dominance and the uncertainty of some of the other party leaders on the desirability of being too closely identified with Satō so long as the "Black Mist" fogged the scene. By contrast, other prime ministers had reportedly brought rival factional leaders much more closely into the making of personnel decisions.

Nonetheless, a second — and, in certain respects, countervailing — factor also existed, that which was provided by the factions inside the LDP. Satō's power was impressive, but he could not avoid giving recognition to the balance of forces that prevailed in the LDP. He did exclude all his factional rivals from the cabinet, excepting Miki of course, but he could not exclude all representatives from other factions. He was able to pick individuals whose loyalties to their own faction were not so strong as to impede their loyalty to him. This judgment would have to be refined in individual cases, but to do so would require an in-depth analysis of the exact position within a faction that each of the selected ministers occupied. It is a judgment based on perception rather than carefully collated empirical evidence.

If the balancing of factional representation has been stressed here, it is because this may well be the critical variable, and will probably remain so until factions disappear from the LDP. Their demise is ardently desired by many Japanese, primarily because they consider the influence of factionalism to be both irrational and pernicious. Their existence allegedly impedes the desired goal of placing the right man in the right slot. On the other hand, factions do perform a valuable role in tempering the absolute authority of the prime minister. So long as the LDP continues to overwhelm the parties of the opposition, which are thereby reduced to being onlookers rather than participants in the policy-making process, the only groups that can (and do) act as alternative centers of real power are the factions. It is the contests between the factions that determine the allocation of cabinet seats and, ultimately, the overall direction that the Japanese government will pursue in its policies. Factions may not be the most obvious device for rational government, and their reasons for supporting one or another individual for a high post or this or that policy alternative may be based upon a desire for power rather than for "what is good for Japan" (a favorite theme of the senior bureaucrats), but without them Japanese politics would be far less open than it is. The principal losers in such a closed system would be the Japanese people.

APPENDIX

Dramatis Personae

Name	*Year of birth*	*University education*	*Career prior to entering politics*	*Electoral district*	*Times elected (incl. 1/29/67)*	*Faction*	*Prior posts*	*Portfolio in 12/66 cabinet or (current significance)*
Aiichi Kiichi	1907	Tokyo Law	Finance Ministry bureaucrat	Miyagi 1	1 (H.C.) 5 (H.R.)	Satō	Min. Educ., Justice, Int'l. Trade & Industry, Econ. Plan. Agcy. Chief Cab. Sec.	(One of key Satō lieut.) (Foreign Minister)
Arafune Seijurō	1907	Meiji	businessman	Saitama 3	8	Kawashima	Min. Transp.	—
Bō Hideo	1904	Tokyo Law	newspaperman	Wakayama 1	7	Fukuda	Parl. Vice-Min., Finance, LDP Policy Bd. Deputy Chrmn.	Welfare
Fujieda Sensuke	1907	Tokyo Law	Home Min. bur.	Gumma 1	7	Kawashima	Dir. Gen'l. P.M.'s Ofc., Defense, Transp.	Autonomy (Home)
Fujiyama Aiichirō	1897	Keio	Corp. exec., Pres., Japan Ch. of Comm.	Kanagawa 1	4	Fujiyama	Foreign Min., EPA Min.	(contender, LDP pres., 1966)
Fukuda Takeo	1905	Tokyo Law	Finance Min. bur.	Gumma 3	7	Fukuda	Agr. & For. Min., Finance Min.	Finance Minister
Fukunaga Kenji	1910	Tokyo Law	parliamentarian	Saitama 1	8	ex-Ikeda (Satō)	Chief Cab. Sec., Labor Min., LDP Exec. Bd. Chrmn.	(Chief Cab. Sec. deceased)
Funada Naka	1895	Tokyo Law	parl.	Tochigi 1	12	ex-Ohno (Funada)	Speaker, H.R. 1964–65	(leader, half of former Ohno faction)
Hashimoto Tomisaburō	1901	Waseda Politics	newsp'mn.	Ibaragi 1	8	Satō	Chief Cab. Sec., Constr. Min.	(one of Satō senior factional lieut.)
Hatoyama Ichirō	1883	Tokyo Law	parl.	Tokyo 1	14	—	Prime Min. 1954–56	(deceased)

Hayakawa Takashi	1916	Tokyo Law	Home Min. bur.	Wakayama 2	9	Miki	Autonomy Min.	Labor
Hori Shigeru	1901	Chuō Econ.	newsp'mn.	Saga	9	Satō	Min. Labor, Welfare, Agr. & For., Chief Cab. Sec.	(leader, subgroup in Satō faction)
Ikeda Hayato	1899	Kyoto Law	Finance Min. bur.	Hiroshima 2	7	Ikeda	Prime Min. 1960–64	(deceased)
Ishibashi Tanzan	1884	Waseda Lit.	author, publisher	Shizuoka 2	5	—	Prime Min. 1956–57	(now in priv. life, active in Sino-Japanese & Russo-Japanese relations)
Ishii Mitsujirō	1889	Tokyo Coll. of Commerce	newsp'mn.	Fukuoka 3	9	Ishii	Min. Justice, Int'l. Trade & Ind., Min. Comm.	(Speaker, H.R. 1967–)
Kambayashiyama Eikichi	1903	Nihon Law	parl.	Kagoshima 1	8	Satō	Min. Def. Agcy.	—
Kanno Watarō	1895	Kyoto Econ.	prof. of econ.	Osaka 1	7	Miki	Econ. Plan. Agcy.	Int'l. Trade & Ind.
Kawashima Shōjirō	1890	Senshu Econ.	newsp'mn.	Chiba 1	13	Kawashima	Autonomy (Home) Min., Admin. Mgt. Agcy. Min.	(V.P. LDP, 1960's)
Kennoki Toshihiro	1901	Tokyo Law	Educ. Min. bur.	Fukuoka	3 (H.C.)	ex-Kōno	Vice-Min. Educ.	educ.
Kishi Nobusuke	1896	Tokyo Law	Commerce & Ind. Min. bur.	Yamaguchi 2	7	Fukuda	Prime Min. 1957–60	(Influential as Satō's older brother)
Kobayashi Takeji	1899	Tokyo Law	Postal Min. bur.	Shizuoka	3 (H.C.)	Satō	Gov., Shizuoka Pref., Min. Welfare	Post and tele-commun.
Kōno Ichirō	1898	Waseda Politics	newsp'mn.	Kanagawa 3	11	Kōno	Agr. & For. Min., contender for Prime Min., early 1960's	(deceased)
Kuraishi Tadao	1900	Hōsei Law, London	author, parl.	Nagano 1	9	Fukuda	Labor Min., Chrmn. Special ILO Comm.	Agr. & For.

APPENDIX (continued)

Name	*Year of birth*	*University education*	*Career prior to entering politics*	*Electoral district*	*Times elected (incl. 1/29/67)*	*Faction*	*Prior posts*	*Portfolio in 12/66 cabinet or (current significance)*
Maeo Shigesaburō	1905	Kyoto Law	Finance Min. bur.	Kyoto 2	8	ex-Ikeda (Maeo)	Int'l. Trade & Ind. Min., Chief Cab. Sec.	(leader old Ikeda faction)
Masuda Kaneshichi	1898	Kyoto Law	newsp'mn.	Nagano 4	8	Satō	Chief Cab. Sec., Transp. Min., Labor Min., Constr. Min., LDP Sec. Gen'l.	Def. Agcy.
Matsudaira Isao	1907	Waseda Commerce	corp. exec. (Mitsubishi)	Fukushima	3 (H.C.)	Ishii	—	Admin. Mgt. Agcy.
Matsumura Kenzō	1883	Waseda Politics	parl.	Toyama 2	13	Independent	Min. Welfare, Agr. & For., Educ.	(former co-leader, Miki-Matsumura faction, which split over Miki's support of Satō)
Miki Takeo	1910	Meiji	parl.	Tokushima 1	12	Miki	Int'l. Trade & Ind. Min., Transp. Min., EPA, AEC	Foreign Affairs
Miyazawa Kiichi	1919	Tokyo Law	Finance Min. bur.	Hiroshima 3	2 (H.C.) 1 (H.R.)	ex-Ikeda	Parl. Vice-Min., Educ., EPA Min.	Econ. Plan. Agcy.
Mizuta Mikio	1905	Kyoto Law	bus'mn.	Chiba 3	10	ex-Ohno	Int'l. Trade & Ind. Min., Finance Min., LDP Policy Bd. Chrmn.	Finance
Mori Kiyoshi	1915	Kyoto Science	corp. exec.	Chiba 3	7	ex-Kōno (Mori)	Dir. Gen'l. Prime Min. Ofc.	(leader, wing of old Kōno faction after split, 12/66.
Murakami Isamu	1902	Waseda	parl.	Oita 1	10	ex-Ohno (Murakami)	Constr., Postal Min.	(leader, half of old Ohno faction)
Nadao Hirokichi	1899	Tokyo Law	Home Min. bur.	Hiroshima 1	7	Ishii	Min. Educ., Min. Welfare	(LDP pres., contestant in 12/66 convention)

Nakasone Yasuhirō	1918	Tokyo Law	author, parl.	Gumma 3	9	ex-Kōno (Nakasone)	Science & Technology Agcy. Min.	(leader, wing of ex-Kōno faction after 12/66 split)
Nikaidō Susumu	1909	USC M.A.	Navy bur., For. Min. official	Kagoshima 3	7	Satō	Parl. Vice-Min., Labor, LDP Dep. Sec. Gen'l.	Hokkaido dev., AEC, Science & Technology Agcy.
Nishimura Eiichi	1897	Tohoku Engineer.	Transp. Min. bur.	Oita 2	7	Satō	Vice-Min. Transp., Welfare Min.	Constr.
Nishimura Naomi	1905	Tokyo Law	Home Min. bur.	Shizuoka 1	8	Satō	Defense Agcy. Min.	(LDP Policy Bd. Chrmn.)
Ohashi Takeo	1904	Tokyo Law	Postal Min. bur.	Shimane	8	ex-Ikeda (Satō)	Justice Min., Labor Min.	Transp.
Ohira Masayoshi	1910	Tokyo Coll. of Commerce	Finance Min. bur.	Kagawa 2	7	ex-Ikeda (Maeo)	Foreign Min., Chief Cab. Sec.	(leader in old Ikeda faction
Ohno Bamboku	1890	Meiji, Waseda	parl.	Gifu 1	13	Ohno	LDP V.P.	(deceased)
Satō Eisaku	1901	Tokyo Law	Transp. Min. bur.	Yamaguchi 2	7	Satō	Const. Min., LDP Sec. Gen'l., Int'l. Min., Chief Cab. Sec.	Prime Min.
Shigemasa Seishi	1897	Tokyo Law	Agr. & For. Min. bur.	Hiroshima 3	5	ex-Kōno (Mori)	Min. Agr. & For.	(co-leader with Mori, wing of old Kōno faction)
Shiina Etsusaburō	1898	Tokyo Law	Commerce & Ind. bur.	Iwate 2	5	Kawashima	Chief Cab. Sec., Int'l. Trade & Ind. Min., Foreign Min.	(LDP Exec. Bd. Chrmn.)
Suzuki Zenko	1911	School of Agr. & For.	Fisheries official	Iwate 1	9	ex-Ikeda (Maeo)	Postal Min., Welfare Min., Chief Cab. Sec.	(one of senior members, Maeo faction)
Tanaka Isaji	1906	Ritsumeikan	parl., lawyer	Kyoto 1	10	Ishii	Vice-Speaker H.R., Autonomy Min.	Justice
Tanaka Kakuei	1918	Chuo Coll. of Engr.	businessman	Miigata 3	9	Satō	Postal Min., Finance Min., Sec. Gen'l. LDP	LDP Sec. Gen'l.
Tsukahara Toshio	1910	Tokyo Lit.	newsp'mn.	Ibaragi 2	8	Satō	Parl. Vice-Min., Constr.	Dir. Gen'l. Prime Min. Ofc.

SELECTED BIBLIOGRAPHY

Fukui Haruhiro. *The Japanese Liberal-Democratic Party and Policy-Making.* Berkeley: University of California Press, 1969. A carefully researched and detailed study focusing on the factors that influence the making of decisions in the LDP.

Leiserson, Michael. "Factions and Coalitions in One-Party Japan: An Interpretation Based on the Theory of Games." *American Political Science Review,* Vol. LXII (September 1968), pp. 770–787. A highly imaginative application of coalition theory to the inner workings of the LDP.

Scalapino, Robert A. and Junnosuki Masumi. *Parties and Politics in Contemporary Japan.* (Please see selected bibliography for "Nikkan Kokkai.")

Thayer, Nathaniel B. *How the Conservatives Rule Japan.* Princeton: Princeton University Press, 1969. The only book-length study of the Liberal-Democratic Party; it is based on extensive and intensive interviews with leading LDP politicians.

Watanabe, Tsuneo. *Habatsu: Nihon Hoshuto no Bunseki* (*Factions: An Analysis of the Japanese Conservative Party*). Tokyo: Kobundo Frontier Books, 1964. An indispensable study by one of Japan's most insightful and knowledgeable journalists.

World Policy Research Institute. *Political Japan: The Liberal-Democratic Party.* Tokyo: Political Party Research Institute, 1966. This study was prepared under the auspices of the LDP to help introduce the party to the English-reading public. It contains brief biographical sketches of key LDP leaders, the "Constitution" of the LDP, as well as lists of all LDP Cabinets between 1955 and 1966.

PART III COMMUNIST CHINA

It might seem that personality, a decisive factor in a democratic and parliamentary country such as Japan, should not be so important in a revolutionary society such as Communist China. Should not ideology and party discipline make all discussion of personal sentiments and associations irrelevant in analyzing developments behind the Bamboo Curtain? Ruling some 800,000,000 people and seeking to change one of the oldest cultures in the world, can the top elite in Peking permit itself any partisan conflicts?

The truth is that professional China-watchers were long impressed with the solidarity of the Chinese regime and the monolithic qualities of the Chinese Communist Party. They have increasingly discovered over the years, though, that even in revolutionary China personal relationships can readily determine historical developments and that behind the curtain of monolithic unity was a great deal of maneuvering and factional conflict. It was, however, the Cultural Revolution and the revelations of the wall posters of the various contending Red Guard factions that brought to public attention the amount and intensity of inner politics among the top leaders of Communist China.

Government and politics within Communist China remain, for the most part, a great mystery to both the outside world and the masses of Chinese citizens. Never in history has so complex and large a ruling system operated so much in private. Public announcements reveal the conclusions arrived at in national meetings and high-level conferences that nobody knew were in session. Years later we find that dramatic events were transpiring when all seemed to be placid on the surface in Peking.

Yet for years Western specialists have been following Chinese developments and learning how to evaluate all possible clues. Although working with incomplete information, and confronted with a massive propaganda effort that seeks to obscure the actual workings of politics in China, these China specialists have been able to piece together gradually the actual story of Chinese politics and government; it is a story of ideological beliefs, rational calculations, and personal ambitions intimately linked.

Above all, contemporary China's story is also that of Mao Tse-tung – the ambitions and illusions, the calculations and prejudices, and the romantic, revolutionary vision of this greatest figure on the current Asian scene. In our first case study of Chinese politics, Harold Hinton traces the considerations that led Mao to initiate the Cultural Revolution, attempting to ensure that revolutionary ardor would endure in succeeding generations of Chinese youth. The dream of perpetual revolution and the heroic expression of human willpower clash dramatically with the forces of orderly and systematic planning and administration.

The second case study is about the events following the Cultural Revolution and illustrates the close ties between domestic Chinese developments and foreign policy considerations. By carefully reviewing the revelations that came out of the Cultural Revolution and the charges and countercharges of the various Red Guard factions, Harold Hinton suggests how Chinese politics has recently revolved about the most fundamental issues of who should control what activities and what regions of the country. His is thus a study of the intense struggles that will determine Communist evolution in China. Although the issues may be described as theoretical or ideological, in fact they are deeply immersed in reality. More particularly, policy choices are not just abstract matters but literally life and death issues for the participants.

The limited information we have about Communist China means that we must rely on disciplined speculation and interpretation. In this sense the China specialist does practice a form of analysis that is different from that of ordinary political scientists. Specialists may differ in their interpretations and, although they may arrive at a consensus about the main outlines of recent developments no one can be dogmatic about details. Thus in these two case studies the reader will find masterfully blended the factual accounting and speculative interpretation that is the art of analyzing Chinese politics. In seeking to fill out the gaps in our knowledge about actual developments, Harold Hinton has advanced hypotheses that represent his best judgments of what must have happened. More important, however, than the factually accurate details of his interpretations is the general picture he presents of plausible ways in which Chinese leaders may think through their problems, perceive their predicaments, and balance their alternative choices.

HAROLD HINTON

3 The Beginning of the Cultural Revolution

ELITE TENSIONS IN CHINESE POLITICS

The varying responses within the Communist world to the Soviet invasion of Czechoslovakia – all but a handful of ruling parties being opposed to it – reminded us of the great difference in interest and attitude between a Communist Party that is in power and one that is not. Similarly, a party generally changes when it comes to power; pragmatic and bureaucratic preoccupations replace idealistic and revolutionary ones. Leaders who cling to the latter, those in the Soviet party often being referred to as "Old Bolsheviks," usually give way or go down in time before others who have espoused the former.

The experience of the Communist Party of China (CPC) has displayed some significant and interesting variations from this pattern. For complex historical reasons, its ascent to power was unusually long and stormy (it occupied approximately the quarter-century preceding 1949) and occurred in relative isolation from both the political control and the bureaucratizing influence of the Soviet Union. The last decade of the CPC's rise was spent under the unchallenged leadership of a man of unusually dynamic personality who was fully aware that his party was the first in the underdeveloped world to come to power primarily through unassisted revolutionary warfare, and that his country was traditionally accustomed to claiming a leading role in the world. For Mao Tse-tung, it would have been ideologically and politically unthinkable for China, once Communist, to confine itself to pragmatic nation building along orthodox Stalinist lines; he may also have reasoned that China lacked the economic resources to succeed in such an endeavor. By no means all Mao's colleagues agreed with his Old Bolshevik views, however. The differences began to become noticeable and serious about 1955, a year of difficulties in agriculture and Sino-Soviet relations, but they did not become unmanageable until 1965. Three major groups or schools may be distinguished.

Mao and his school, which consists mainly of party ideologists and propagandists, in effect insist on carrying into the period of "socialist construction" (since 1949) their version of the attitudes and strategies prevalent during the "socialist revolution" (before 1949) and on projecting these, rather than pragmatic techniques of nation building, as the "model" that the CPC offers to the developing world for its imitation. They have cultivated a psychology of "uninterrupted revolution," or "revolutionary romanticism," emphasizing the peasantry and therefore agriculture, as the road to greatness for China. They believe in the spontaneous goodness and rightness of the masses, provided the latter are enlightened by the charisma of Mao's leadership and by his "thought" and are mobilized by suitable propaganda appeals (in reality, slogans) to their revolutionary enthusiasm. They are convinced of manual labor's ideological and educational value and its special value for members of the elite as a means of keeping in touch with the masses. They stress egalitarianism (among individuals and classes) and uniformity (among individuals and regions), which are to be achieved and maintained ideologically, namely, through a universal and enthusiastic acceptance of the "thought of Mao Tse-tung." They see the army as a highly politicized "nation in arms" and, if in that condition, as an excellent model and energizer for the populace as a whole, into which they try to inject what is sometimes called a "guerrilla" mentality.

The second school, whose principal adherents are or were highly placed in the Communist Party apparatus, believe, in essence, that the tasks and responsibilities of the era of "socialist construction" call for approaches different from, and basically more pragmatic than, those of the era of "socialist revolution." They show more enthusiasm for orthodox Marxism-Leninism than for the "thought of Mao Tse-tung," and they prefer established Leninist methods of "democratic centralism," including genuine majority rule in policy-making bodies, to Mao's tendency to exalt his own "cult of personality." They want the party organization to overshadow not only the leader, Mao, but also the masses, whose instincts they tend to distrust. Compared with the uniformity on an ideological basis favored by Mao, they have tolerated and encouraged that centrally devised policies and procedures be adapted to local conditions, instead of insisting on uniformity, in the belief that the party organization could prevent any resulting centrifugal tendencies from getting out of hand. They prefer to see the armed forces motivated and controlled by orthodox, Leninist-Stalinist, ideological and organizational methods, rather than by the "thought of Mao Tse-tung," and it is unlikely that they share Mao's enthusiasm for the army as a model for Chinese society.

The third school, whose main supporters are in the governmental bureaucracy, the security services, and to some extent the armed forces, have an essentially administrative orientation. They aspire to orderly development, without too heavy an admixture of either the "thought of Mao Tse-tung" or party controls, in politics, economics, military matters, and foreign relations. Perhaps because of a nationalistic preference for the Chinese-minded Mao over the more Soviet-oriented party apparatus, this group, and notably its principal leader Premier Chou En-lai, on the whole have sided with Mao and indeed appear to have provided him with his crucial margin of support.

The evidence we have suggests that these tendencies and differences have carried over into foreign policy, but less than might be expected. This impression probably results only in part from the natural tendency for intra-elite debates on foreign policy to be kept secret more than those on domestic policy; it also results in, and is warranted by, the fact that the three schools, despite their differences, feel that they have more in common with each other than with any foreign elite, including that of the Soviet Union.

The circumstances under which the differences between Mao's school and the leaders of the party apparatus, who for convenience will be given the somewhat too dramatic label "opposition," became significant are not easy to determine. Their emergence seems to have been muted and delayed by the regime's involvement in the Korean

War and its dependence, in this context, on Soviet aid and support and therefore on the towering personality of Stalin. His death in early 1953 removed a powerful pressure in China to conform, for long at any rate, to the Soviet developmental model and enhanced Mao Tse-tung's political stature at home and abroad. The CPC, nevertheless, was already committed to an essentially Soviet-style First Five Year Plan.

During the three years following Stalin's death, Mao increasingly departed from the Soviet model in ways whose rationale has already been indicated, whereas the opposition preferred to deviate in its own direction. In 1956, taking advantage of Khrushchev's attack on Stalin's memory, the opposition quietly undertook to set some limits on Mao's authority and to prune somewhat his luxuriant "cult of personality." Unable to dominate dependably the central policy-making machinery of the party, Mao struck back through the party's propaganda apparatus, which he did control. His first major move was the Hundred Flowers Campaign, which was apparently intended to steal a march both on the opposition and on the Soviet leadership by showing that in China free public discussion would evoke overwhelming popular support not only for the regime as a whole but for Mao in particular. But when the campaign finally got under way in the spring of 1957, after a slow start and under another label, it proved that Mao had miscalculated badly; many devastating criticisms were expressed both of the regime and of him. Badly shaken for a time, Mao adjusted his thinking and policies in a direction more radical than ever and responded with his most dramatic initiative to date, the celebrated Great Leap Forward, which was adopted by the central party leadership over the opposition's reservations in a way that is still not entirely clear. One of the arguments that Mao used, both with his colleagues and with the public, was that the Great Leap Forward was needed to enable China to play its proper part in a worldwide drama that Mao, taking his cue from the Soviet space and missile triumphs of 1957, described as the "East wind" (the "socialist camp" and its allies) prevailing over the "West wind" (the "imperialist camp" and its allies). The Leap was meant through both Mao's propaganda techniques and the opposition's organizational methods, to maximize the exploitation and therefore the output of rural labor by means of the "people's communes," so as to raise China rapidly to a higher level of ideological status ("communism"), political consciousness, and national power.

By late 1958, it was clear that, although the regime was in no political position to admit that the Leap had failed, such extensive adjustments in it were required as to make a readjustment of the party leadership appropriate if not essential. Contrary to later charges from Maoist sources, it was apparently with something approaching common consent that a new basis for leadership and policy making was devised. Mao turned over one of his two major positions, that of Chairman of the Chinese People's Republic (or chief of state) to Liu Shao-ch'i, the senior member of the opposition, and agreed to become much less active in domestic policy, especially economic policy. He retained the leading voice in foreign policy, however, and was greatly helped here by Khrushchev, who soon made himself almost as obnoxious to the opposition – by withdrawing economic and military aid in 1959–60, for example – as to Mao himself. On this basis a modified version of the Great Leap Forward remained in effect for the time being.

In mid-1959, the pragmatically minded Defense Minister, P'eng Te-huai, temporarily brought the two major schools together by attacking even the modified version of the Leap and the policy compromise that underlay it. The basic gap between the schools, however, was soon widened as the economic crisis of 1960–61, caused mainly by the Leap, proved P'eng to have been right and evoked from sources outside the top leadership criticisms of Mao and the Leap and defenses of P'eng with which the opposition seems to have come increasingly to sympathize in private. At the same time, beginning in early 1961, the opposition leadership put into effect a set of reforms, emphasizing greater economic incentives for the peasants and greater freedom for intellectuals and technicians than had been permitted during the reaction following the failure of the Hundred Flowers Campaign. This program produced an economic recovery so rapid that its effects began to be felt early in 1962. In this context, by most rational calculations, Mao Tse-tung appeared obsolescent if not obsolete, even though he had achieved some significant successes in his struggle against Khrushchev. But nothing that had happened had convinced Mao of the essential wrongness, as distinct from the tactical inexpediency, of his fundamental philosophy and strategy.

It has already been argued that personalities, as well as ideas and issues, have been important in Chinese elite politics; we will therefore briefly examine the major personalities.

On the Maoist side, one must take note of a kind of court around Mao that has eulogized him to an incredible degree and apparently also idolizes him with a fervor that it finds compatible with a self-serving use of his coattails for personal advancement. Among this group are some leading propagandists like Ch'en Po-ta, although other propagandists increasingly have sided with the opposition. More important than these is the shadowy figure, K'ang Sheng, an intraparty maneuverer par excellence who apparently manages to combine in full the two characteristics of worship and flattery of Mao with personal opportunism. He seems to have long aspired to succeed Liu Shao-ch'i, de facto if not de jure, as the leading figure in the party apparatus. At some uncertain time K'ang evidently formed a political alliance with Mao's third and current wife, Chiang Ching, another self-serving fanatic who happens to come from the same province as K'ang (Shantung). She was excluded, by a vote of the Central Committee, from taking part in politics when she married Mao in 1939 and therefore has a vested interest in doing whatever may be necessary to remove this ban. She and K'ang have evidently done their best to inflame Mao's mind against Liu Shao-ch'i as well as against the attractive Mme. Liu, against whom Chiang Ching clearly holds a number of highly feminine grudges. Although this factor has not been decisive in turning Mao against Liu, it has probably had its effect.

More obvious, and probably more significant, is the role of Marshal Lin Piao. In his favor was his brilliant military record, the great although vague prestige that he consequently has in China, and his age (born in 1908; Mao Tse-tung in 1893). He also has the reputation of remaining comparatively aloof from factional disputes, although in fact he was a rival of P'eng Te-huai and other military leaders who have had ties with the opposition. Lin's overt politics have been confined mostly to praise and support for Mao, with how much sincerity it is difficult to say. Despite his perennially poor health, he began a rapid political rise after 1949, and especially after 1954. He succeeded P'eng Te-huai as Defense Minister in 1959 and soon began to politicize the armed forces along Maoist lines, in contrast to P'eng's strong professional tendencies. Mao's conviction of the armed forces' great political importance would alone have been enough to confer on Lin, as their head after 1959, a major political role. As it was, Mao came to think of him as the best candidate for an even higher position.

Another leader of great importance, whose political allegiance appears too complex to permit him to be classed simply as a supporter of Mao, is Premier Chou En-lai. He is not only a first-rate administrator but a skilled politician able to reconcile into a workable synthesis the discordant views of others. He apparently has never aspired to the highest position in the party and is therefore trusted by the others. Although lacking an obvious "power base," he has widespread connections and influence, in the army among other places. As far as one can tell, he is content with great influence behind the scenes combined with considerable public exposure and prestige in his capacity as premier (and, until 1958, as foreign minister also). Being, among other things, an administrator, he is committed to policies that by Chinese Communist standards are pragmatic and even moderate, but on the major issues he has supported Mao to such an extent that in 1957, in an unpublished portion of a major speech, Mao mentioned Chou as his probable successor. For this stand by Chou there appear to be two main reasons. First, he has had personal and jurisdictional disputes with leaders of the opposition, notably party General Secretary Teng Hsiao-p'ing. Second, he apparently reasons that the survival of his governmental bureaucracy and rational development will be better served by supporting Mao, whom he evidently regards as indispensable and unbeatable in a direct confrontation, than by opposing him. An analogous problem is that of stopping a runaway horse; the best way is to run alongside, grasp the animal's lower lip, and bring it gradually to a halt, instead of standing in front of it. In short, Chou sees that Mao can be managed but hardly overcome. It is possible that Chou hopes not only to survive Mao but to become the real power in China after his death, with Lin Piao as his own glorified front man and Mao's nominal successor.

Before 1949, Liu Shao-ch'i served in effect as the main bridge between Mao and the party apparatus, whose leading figure he thereby became. By about 1945 he was the second ranking figure in the party, after Mao. Although at first a subscriber to the Mao cult and often unfairly thought of abroad as a fanatical Stalinist, Liu appears to have intelligence, integrity, practical ability, and independence of view. He is not as strong a personality or as ruthless a political operator as Mao, however. He has apparently leaned increasingly to the moderate side since the early 1950's, and since about the time of the Great Leap Forward he can be considered the leader of the opposition.

Teng Hsiao-p'ing, a man evidently of less integrity and statesmanship than Liu, has long specialized in party organization. He is a leading member of the powerful Szechuan faction, which has been for many years in a state of restrained tension with Mao. Teng broadened this base by becoming the working head of the party apparatus about 1954, in succession to Liu Shao-ch'i. In that capacity, he built up an impressive personal following, especially after the powerful regional bureaus of the party Central Committee were revived in late 1960, in order to cope with the conditions created by the collapse of the Greap Leap Forward, opened up some important posts to which he could secure the appointment of his supporters.

THE CULTURAL REVOLUTION IS LAUNCHED

The economic recovery beginning in 1962 inescapably confronted the Chinese Communist leadership with the question of whether the pragmatic, essentially non-Maoist, policies that had evoked it should be perpetuated on the ground that they had proved their usefulness or abandoned because they were no longer needed. As might be expected, Mao Tse-tung took the second position, and in doing so he reinjected himself into domestic policy making more deeply than he had since 1958.

MAO'S COMEBACK

Mao's attitude met with great opposition, one sign of the disagreement being that the Third Five Year Plan, which ought to have commenced in 1963, did not go into effect until 1966. Liu Shao-ch'i began trying to fortify his prestige by bringing out a revised version of a work of his published in 1939, *How To Be a Good Communist,* on August 1, 1962. The disgraced P'eng Te-huai, sensing no doubt that he had been proved right and enjoyed much unofficial support, unsuccessfully demanded his rehabilitation.

Mao succeeded in gaining the support of a majority of the party Central Committee at its Tenth Plenary Session (September 1962), to which he propounded the slogan, "Never forget class struggle."

The keynote of the session's proceedings was militant and Maoist, the need for continuing struggle against "revisionism" at home and abroad.

During the two-year period following the Tenth Plenary Session, several political campaigns of Maoist origin were launched, but with little effect. Apparently reluctance was widespread among the party apparatus and the populace, after a pleasant and beneficial interval of comparative relaxation, to go back to anything resembling the traumatic days of the Great Leap Forward. Probably the most important of these campaigns was the Socialist Education Campaign, which began in 1963 and whose object was to regenerate party discipline and revolutionary enthusiasm among the lower cadres and through them among the peasantry. Another was a campaign, beginning in the spring of 1963, to persuade the country to imitate the simpleminded Mao-worship of a young soldier named Lei Feng, who was said to have died shortly before but who may in fact have been invented. Another, beginning at the end of 1963, exhorted the people to "learn from the People's Liberation Army," which Lin Piao's leadership was believed to have transformed by that time into an assemblage of Lei Fengs. Early in 1964 came a campaign to transform the youth into "revolutionary successors" to the aging party leadership.

In the spring of 1964 Mao began to apply increased pressure not only to the intellectuals but also to that portion of the party's propaganda apparatus, headed by Chou Yang, which was supposed to control them. The main target was a "revisionist" philosopher, Yang Hsien-chen, who was an alternate member of the party Central Committee. At about the same time, political officers and political departments, organized in military fashion and often staffed by political personnel from the armed forces, began to be set up in party bodies, especially propaganda organs, and in economic agencies and enterprises.

Later developments have made some personalities in these campaigns seem interesting and significant. The wives of the two top party leaders, who like their husbands appeared increasingly as mutual rivals, became active and prominent in public life during this period. Chiang Ching (Mme. Mao Tse-tung) undertook in 1963–64 to "revolutionize" Peking opera, possibly because the party leadership still had reservations about her involvement in politics but considered this a fairly safe activity and appropriate to her record of interest in the arts; in fact, however, Chiang Ching's work brought her close to the propaganda apparatus of the armed forces, which was to play an important part in the Cultural Revolution. Evidently not to be outdone, Wang Kuang-mei (Mme. Liu Shao-ch'i) was active during 1964 in the Socialist Education Campaign in the countryside.

More significant than the activities undertaken by these ladies, however, was the position assumed by P'eng Chen, the able, energetic, and outspoken mayor of Peking and chairman of its municipal Party Committee. Although not a member of the elite seven-man Standing Committee of the party Politburo, P'eng was a regular Politburo member. Signs multiplied during 1964 that he stood very high in Mao's favor, and that Mao had put him in overall charge of the campaigns just described and may have intended that, if P'eng accomplished his task to Mao's satisfaction, he should replace the increasingly distrusted Liu Shao-ch'i as Mao's successor. One of the reasons why Mao approved P'eng probably was that, of all the top Chinese leaders, P'eng was the most outspokenly anti-Soviet in his personal pronouncements. Later developments were to suggest, however, that P'eng may have adopted this militantly anti-Soviet stance partly to gain Mao's favor and to help divert him from domestic affairs to the relatively harmless task of chastising the erring Russians.

MAO'S INTERESTS

From 1962 until 1967, the initiative in formulating policy and making decisions within the CPC rested almost entirely with Mao Tse-tung. Since it was during this period that the Cultural Revolution was conceived and launched, the nature and purposes of the latter cannot be understood without comprehending Mao's attitudes, and in particular his view of his own problems.

Although his propagandists' writings would occasionally lead one to doubt it, Mao was presumably aware that he was mortal. And not only mortal, but old; he turned seventy on December 26, 1963. And not only old, but none too well; he is widely believed to suffer from Parkinson's disease. He could hardly help fearing that time was working not only against him but against his "thought," and that his opponents both in China and abroad were counting on time to relieve them of this affliction. He was probably none too pleased to learn that, in a speech delivered ten days before Mao's seventieth birthday, United States Assistant Secretary of State Roger Hilsman had cautiously predicted that in time a more rational and pragmatic generation of Chinese leaders would appear, and he implied it would be easier for the United States to deal with than the present one.

It did not require a speech, however, to convince Mao that many of his colleagues and subordinates in the party were infected with "bureaucratism" and "revisionism," that unlike him they had become "divorced from the masses." He knew that the party apparatus was becoming a New Class, and that it was involved to varying degrees in self-enrichment, nepotism, and the like. As he indicated in a document, usually known as "the Twenty Three Articles," which he wrote in January 1965, the dry rot extended as high as the departments of the party Central Committee. His accusation reflected clearly if indirectly on General Secretary Teng Hsiao-p'ing, who presided over those departments, and through him on Liu Shao-ch'i. Mao certainly feared that the party apparatus would soon slip out from under his control unless he took drastic measures to bring it back into line.

Clearly Mao was also worried about the youth of China. He believed that many, probably the majority, were soft, nonrevolutionary, and dedicated to personal advancement. For those who were not, the potential channels of upward mobility were clogged with self-serving careerists. A large part of the problem, as Mao saw it, was the fact that the country had not recently experienced any great crises, such as those he and his colleagues had undergone before 1949, which could temper them into true revolutionaries. Mao came to the conclusion that he must create such a crisis, and that in so doing he could use his main allies, the army and the segment of the youth that responded positively to his revolutionary appeal, to confound and defeat his opponents.

For several years, and especially since 1961, Mao had been increasingly incensed at what he called "Khrushchev revisionism," or in other words the politico-economic order that was emerging in the Soviet Union. He feared that it might strongly appeal to the "revisionist" and "bureaucratic" elements within the Chinese party apparatus, and indeed it seems to have done so with Khrushchev's concepts of the "party of the whole people" and the "state of the whole people." At all costs, Mao reasoned, "Khrushchev revisionism" must be prevented from taking hold in China, and, together with the other trends just mentioned, deprive the country of the revolutionary momentum that Mao had worked so hard to impart to it.

Finally, Mao was unquestionably eager, for personal as well as political reasons, to vindicate his own reputation for revolutionary and creative statesmanship, notably about the Great Leap Forward, and to refute and silence his various critics, both inside and outside the party.

There is much to be said, for the sake of vividness and authenticity, for seeing Mao's interests expressed in his own words, or something very close to them. The language is sufficiently esoteric that we have first presented an analysis in less specialized language; we can now go to the original.

In mid-1964, in the last of nine major editorial blasts against Khrushchev and all his works, it was stated rather startlingly that[1]

> . . . there is grave danger of a restoration of capitalism in the Soviet Union. . . . And this sounds the alarm for all socialist countries, including China, and for all the Communist and Workers' Parties, including the Communist Party of China. . . . Is our society today thoroughly clean? No, it is not. Classes and class struggle still remain, the activities of the overthrown reactionary classes plotting a comeback still continue, and we still have speculative activities by old and new bourgeois elements and desperate forays by embezzlers, grafters, and degenerates. There are also cases of degeneration in a few primary organizations; what is more, *these degenerates do their utmost to find protectors and agents in the higher leading bodies.* We should not in the least slacken our vigilance against such phenomena but must keep fully alert.

The editorial went on to map out a fifteen-point program for combating "revisionism" within the CPC, with special attention to training "revolutionary successors." The language was rather vague, perhaps because Mao did not wish to show his hand but more probably because he had not yet decided precisely what to do.

In January 1965, Mao told the American journalist Edgar Snow about China's future, that (as paraphrased by Snow):[2]

[1] "On Khrushchev's Phoney Communism and Its Historical Lessons for the World: Ninth Comment on the Open Letter of the Central Committee of the CPSU," *People's Daily* and *Red Flag,* July 14, 1964. Emphasis added.

[2] Edgar Snow, "Interview with Mao," *The New Republic* (February 27, 1965), p. 23.

> There were two possibilities. There could be continued development of the revolution toward Communism, the other possibility was that youth could negate the revolution, and give a poor performance: make peace with imperialism, bring the remnants of the Chiang Kai-shek clique back to the mainland, and take a stand beside the small percentage of counter-revolutionaries still in the country. Of course he did not hope for counter-revolution. But future events would be decided by future generations, and in accordance with conditions we could not foresee.

In an interview with a French visitor held during the following summer, Mao put the point more forcefully: "Youth must be put to the test."[3]

PRECIPITANTS OF THE CULTURAL REVOLUTION

Chinese Communist sources officially date the inauguration of the Cultural Revolution, or the "Great Proletarian Cultural Revolution," as it is formally known, from September 1965, for reasons that will become apparent shortly. It seems likely that something had happened during the preceding months to convince Mao that launching such a movement was both more urgent and more opportune, and perhaps to give him a clearer idea of how it should be done.

The search for the immediate, as distinct from the original, causes of the Cultural Revolution may reasonably begin with the fall of Khrushchev in mid-October 1964. Three months later Mao told Edgar Snow that "China would miss him as a negative example."[4] In plainer language, Mao, who had built his pre-Cultural Revolution policies primarily around attacks on Khrushchev, was determined to show that the Soviet "revisionist's" fall had not exhausted Mao's creativity or eliminated the need for his leadership. To prove the point, Mao had to hurry; in time Khrushchev's memory would fade, and Mao would need it as a means of discrediting both his domestic opponents and the new Soviet leadership, with whom Mao early decided to maintain a state of political confrontation as he had with Khrushchev himself; in fact, when Mao began to denounce Liu Shao-ch'i publicly,

[3] André Malraux, "I Am Alone with the Masses — Waiting," *The Atlantic*, Vol. 222, No. 4 (October 1968), p. 113.

[4] Snow, *loc. cit.*, p. 21.

the epithet usually employed was "China's Khrushchev." Mao may also have feared, and with some reason, that with the fall of Khrushchev, who by his high-handed, anti-Chinese policies had antagonized virtually all the top Chinese leaders, his policies, the essentials of which were being continued by his successors, would become more attractive to "revisionist" elements within the CPC.

In Mao's eyes, the need to discredit the new Soviet leadership in China and if possible everywhere was rendered urgent by that leadership's decision, made shortly after Khrushchev's removal, to inaugurate a more active Asian policy, notably in Vietnam, in obvious competition with the Chinese. This decision would have been a fact, and a problem for Mao, even if there had been no American escalation in Vietnam. Beyond Asia, Khrushchev's successors manifested a determination to become more active in the Third World as a whole, again in obvious competition with the Chinese, for example by pressing for Soviet representation at the conference of Afro-Asian states scheduled to open at Algiers in late June 1965. From Mao's point of view, these policies of the Soviet leadership, and their potential effect on China, seem to have been a kind of continuum with the policies of his domestic opponents; a blow against any segment of this continuum would be a blow against the whole.

The American escalation in Vietnam, beginning in February 1965, which a month earlier Mao had predicted to Edgar Snow would not occur, obviously created some danger, how great it could not be said with certainty, of Chinese military involvement. It brought on a major strategic debate (which will be examined in the next case study), and it also seems to have provided Mao's opponents with a plausible basis for maintaining that this was not a time for dramatic initiatives at home. On the whole, public debate on domestic policy yielded to the strategic debate for several months. As usual, Mao drew the conclusion opposite to that chosen by his opponents; he insisted that the American escalation in Vietnam, whether or not the United States went so far as to attack China also, created a major crisis with which China could cope only if it adopted the more revolutionary domestic policy that he was demanding. His argument carried the greatest weight in the area where, in the Chinese Communist political system at any rate, domestic and foreign policy overlapped most: the armed forces. In late May 1965, with the Vietnamese crisis creating an appropriate atmosphere, all titles and insignia of rank were abolished in the armed forces, whose "guerrillaization," nominally for external military purposes but actually more for domestic political purposes, was thereby accelerated.

Mao's belief in the political vulnerability of his opposition was probably increased by some serious setbacks suffered in 1965 by the policy, evidently somewhat favored by Liu Shao-ch'i in competition with the program championed by Mao of promoting revolution "from below," of improving China's relations with friendly states "from above." The Algiers conference collapsed during the summer and was never held, mainly because of the objections by other states to the extreme demands made by the CPR. In September, President Ayub Khan of Pakistan, who had visited Peking the previous March and whose relations with the CPR, on a common anti-Indian basis, were considered close, refused, to Peking's annoyance, to continue a losing war with India over Kashmir and instead accepted a cease-fire ordered by the United Nations and based on mediation by the Soviet Union. Mao could and probably did say that these developments indicated that Liu's policies were bankrupt, as the fall of Khrushchev indicated that his own were viable and correct.

Apparently Mao believed that his domestic program could be promoted most effectively by linking it with the external crisis, whose nature could be suitably distorted, for example by alleging that the American threat to China took the form of a possible invasion. In this way, for one thing, he could enhance the political prestige of Lin Piao's armed forces and proclaim the necessity and appropriateness of their guerrillaization. By late 1965, Mao was probably coming to think of Lin Piao, rather than Liu Shao-ch'i or P'eng Chen, who had already begun to demonstrate something less than enthusiasm for Mao's program, as his successor. Mao's estimate that the armed forces were crucial to the forthcoming Cultural Revolution would have made Lin an obvious choice, and Lin may even have taken advantage of his own indispensability to bargain for the honor of being heir apparent. It is also possible that Chou En-lai may have been supporting Lin for this role.

Mao probably saw an ideological appropriateness in the shift of heirs. He intended to bring China back to the spirit of the "socialist revolution" before 1949, when the army's political as well as military influence in the rise of the Chinese Communist movement to power was critical. These were probably among the reasons why Lin Piao's name was chosen to appear on a major programmatic article, "Long Live the Victory of People's War." It appeared on September 3, was clearly intended to have domestic as well as external significance, and was probably designed among other things to help create a suitable psychological climate for launching the Cultural Revolution. The main theme is the historical experience of the CPC, which is portrayed as one of "self-reliant" struggle ("people's war") against "imperialism," as a model both for the China of today and for the Third World (the "world countryside").

THE STRUGGLE AGAINST P'ENG CHEN

Later in September 1965, Mao took his case for the Cultural Revolution to a meeting of the Standing Committee of the Politburo and the leaders of the party regional bureaus; it lasted into October. According to the subsequent sketchy official accounts of this meeting, Mao's main point was a summons to "criticize bourgeois thinking," presumably among the intellectuals and within the academic community at first. It can be safely assumed that the argument went beyond that. By this time it was reasonably clear to his colleagues that Mao was impatient to get on with a radical domestic program, although as yet they appear to have had no idea of the lengths to which he was prepared to go, or that some of them were to be his principal targets. During the debate in which both sides probably cited the Vietnamese crisis as a major argument, Mao failed to evoke a clear-cut majority in favor of his position. The outcome therefore was an inconclusive compromise. A "Group of Five," apparently consisting of P'eng Chen, Lu Ting-yi (the head of the party's Propaganda Department), K'ang Sheng (a Maoist member of the party Secretariat), Wu Leng-hsi (the editor of the *People's Daily*), and Chou Yang, under P'eng Chen's chairmanship, was created to supervise a program of pressures on the intellectual and cultural life of the country that could be expected to be of rather limited intensity. Already P'eng Chen seems to have been reluctant to move to a mass campaign, as Mao desired, and instead was determined to confine the program's application to specific groups, preferably without involving friends and associates of his in Peking who were guilty of having criticized Mao in their writings. Perhaps in part because of fear for the survival of the capital city, P'eng also seems to have favored a less abrasively anti-American line than Mao's, and in spite of his earlier record as an articulate critic of the Soviet Union he may even have become attracted by the "united action" on Vietnam that Moscow was then preaching. He was probably shocked by the disastrous failure, at the beginning of October 1965, of the mostly "self-reliant" coup launched by the Indonesian Communist Party, with whose fortunes he himself had had a close, recent association. He may have concluded that leftist revolutions in Asia could be expected to succeed only if they were less "self-reliant" than Mao and Lin Piao insisted they should be, or in other words if they received substantial aid not only from China but from the Soviet Union.

In late October or early November Mao withdrew from Peking to the vicinity of Shanghai, where he stayed until the following spring. He was not seeking merely rest and a milder climate, although his health does appear to have been poor during this period. According to later Red Guard accounts, he found the political atmosphere of Peking so adverse as to be stifling. A hypothesis made more plausible by the subsequent unfolding not only of his campaign against P'eng Chen but of his later campaign against Liu Shao-ch'i and Teng Hsiao-p'ing, would be that Mao was planning and preparing for a time when P'eng might make a false move serious enough to make his overthrow possible. Mao was accompanied by some of his key political advisers and propagandists, and perhaps by Lin Piao; Chou En-lai, who seems to have thrown in his lot with Mao by this time, stayed in Peking and may in effect have functioned as one of Mao's agents there, in addition to keeping his bureaucracy going.

Thus the dual leadership present within the party since 1959 was now paralleled by a geographic separation. Ominous rumblings emanated from the Maoist headquarters in the Shanghai area from time to time; the region was reasonably controllable, since its First Secretary, K'o Ch'ing-shih, had died in the spring of 1965 and had not been replaced. On November 10, the Shanghai newspaper *Wen Hui Pao* printed an attack on Wu Han, an associate of P'eng Chen's who had criticized Mao allegorically in a play entitled "The Dismissal of Hai Jui," for having purged P'eng Te-huai. This move, which was of course indirectly aimed at P'eng Chen, acquired additional force when it was picked up by the *Liberation Army Daily.* The close relationship in Mao's mind between the domestic and the external aspects of his struggle against "revisionism" was dramatized by the appearance on November 11 of an editorial proclaiming the impossibility of "united action" with the Soviet Union, over Vietnam or anything else. In November Lin Piao became increasingly prominent, not in person but in the form of directives on political and cultural matters to the armed forces. Mao, on the other hand, disappeared from public view late in November, but as though by way of compensation more publicity than ever began to be given to his "thought." Another prominent figure who disappeared from public view at the end of November was Chief of Staff Lo Jui-ch'ing, who had objected to the guerrillaization of the armed forces, had disagreed with Mao and Lin on strategic issues, and may have appeared to be something of a political threat to Lin's position.

The disappearance of the relatively professional-minded Lo Jui-ch'ing was not the only sign that, since P'eng Chen and the civilian party apparatus were most unlikely to serve as the prime mover of the Cultural Revolution, it was to be the armed forces. In December 1965–January 1966, during an important conference of military political personnel, it was officially stated that the armed forces were the "main instrument of the dictatorship of the proletariat." It is very probable that at the same conference those present were informed that Mao intended the armed forces to act as the organizer and energizer of the vast youth movement that he visualized as the heart of the Cultural Revolution. Indeed, personnel of the armed forces' political apparatus had appeared on some academic campuses as early as the previous September.

During February 1966 some obscure developments appear to have made a crisis of sorts, subdued but potentially important. There was great tension over seeming external threats. At the end of January, the United States had resumed bombing North Vietnam after a "pause" of thirty-seven days. The Soviet Union, greatly disturbed by the radical and unpredictable trend in China, had apparently decided to exert any pressures of a sobering kind it could, short of actual involvement, presumably hoping to lend encouragement to Mao's opponents. The political difficulties in the way of Soviet effectiveness were enormous. Moscow had few friends within the Chinese leadership and could only harm them by endorsing or supporting them. It distrusted P'eng Chen for his record of anti-Soviet pronouncements and his apparent tendency to advocate a softer line toward the United States. As later in Czechoslovakia, the means available to the Kremlin for influencing a political situation in a neighboring "socialist" country were mainly military. In January 1966, Moscow very ostentatiously renewed its defensive alliance with Outer Mongolia, whose target could hardly be any country other than China, and under cover of this arrangement began to move troops into the eastern part of the country, where they would be as close as possible to Peking and thus appear to pose a threat to it.

It was in the menacing climate created by these external developments, and perhaps somewhat connected with them, that one important event occurred, and another appears to have occurred, in February. The more readily documentable of them, as revealed by later official (Maoist) sources, was the issuing by P'eng Chen on February 12, without the knowledge of the other members of the Group of Five, of an "Outline Report" seeking to steer the current stage of the Cultural Revolution, which centered around the charges against Wu Han, away from controversial political questions and into the comparatively harmless realm of literary criticism and academic discussion. The other event, much more obscure if it occurred at all, was an alleged plot by P'eng Chen, Lo Jui-ch'ing, Lu Ting-yi, and Yang Shang-k'un (who held a highly confidential post within the party Secretariat) to stage an armed coup, allegedly with the aim of seizing power. It seems possible that something of the sort occurred, and that it was precipitated by a belief that Mao was dead or dying. A competent and reliable eyewitness has informed the writer that pictures of Mao were taken down in Peking at about this time, and the rumor spread that he was dead. Not only was this rumor, like the one relating to Mark Twain, greatly exaggerated, but it may have been started by the Maoists as a provocation, to test and if possible trap the anti-Maoists. If the affair did occur but had such a disreputable origin, the later occasional denials by prominent Maoists, notably Chou En-lai and K'ang Sheng, that it had occurred would be understandable, as would their disavowal of Red Guard charges that other prominent figures, including Liu Shao-ch'i and Teng Hsiao-p'ing, had been implicated in the plot.

If, on the other hand, there was a plot, it was evidently nipped in the bud. P'eng continued active for the time being, but Lo Jui-ch'ing seems to have been purged and arrested at about this time, and the Public Security Forces under his control, which could not necessarily be expected to cooperate with the regular army in launching a highly disorderly youth movement, were all but dismantled. This indeed may have been the intended result of whatever fabrication or provocation the Maoists may have engaged in for the plot.

Not long afterward the anti-Maoist side was weakened by a prolonged absence from the country (March 26–April 19) of Liu Shao-ch'i. He left two weeks after the overthrow of President Sukarno by the Indonesian army, in all but name. This event, an obvious and menacing forerunner of his own possible fate, may well have startled him into trying to improve his political position by a visit to friendly Asian states, notably Pakistan and Burma, with whose chiefs of state he evidently considered himself to be on good terms. It is uncertain whether the Maoists encouraged his trip, and his illusion, with the aim of getting him out of the country so as to facilitate their own operations, or whether they merely took advantage of his absence to move ahead. It is certain that when Liu returned he was greeted with none of the formalities considered appropriate to a chief of state.

Early in February a high ranking Japanese Communist delegation began a trip lasting several weeks to North Vietnam, the CPR, and North Korea. Its main purpose seems to have been to persuade the Chinese to stop denouncing and obstructing the Soviet call to "united action" on Vietnam and to cooperate instead, and secondarily to persuade the CPC to send a delegation to represent it at the forthcoming Twenty Third Congress of the Soviet party, a cordial invitation to which was sent to Peking on February 24. On February 4, at about the time the Japanese mission set out, its newspaper *Akahata* published a long and important editorial. Going through the motions of denouncing the Soviet party for its various "revisionist" sins, the editors proposed a compromise formula probably intended to be acceptable to the CPC by demanding that the Soviet leaders "extend more influential and effective assistance to the Vietnamese people, and put a stop to any actions which are obstructing the strengthening of international united action and a united front against imperialism and the aggressive war of U.S. imperialism in Vietnam."[5]

The Japanese mission failed in China, and no joint communique was issued, mainly because Mao insisted, and his guests would not agree, that Soviet "revisionism" and "united action" must be publicly repudiated. In addition, Mao urged the Japanese, who had been

[5] "For the Strengthening of International United Action and United Front in Opposition to American Imperialism," *Akahata*, February 4, 1966.

greatly shocked by the bloody failure of the Communist coup in Indonesia, to take up arms in Japan. On March 22, furthermore, while the Japanese delegation was still in China, the CPC rejected with abuse the Soviet invitation to send a delegation to the Twenty Third Congress. P'eng Chen accompanied the Japanese delegation during much of its stay and clearly had extensive talks with its leaders. There is some basis for believing that his thinking, which as we have seen may already have been turning in a less anti-Soviet direction, was somewhat influenced by these talks. For one thing, although the Chinese press, including the *People's Daily,* carried occasional editorial blasts against "united action" during this period, the *People's Daily,* over which P'eng as boss of Peking exerted some influence, reprinted the *Akahata* editorial of February 4 on February 25, a few days after its editor, Wu Leng-hsi, had also talked with the Japanese delegation. P'eng's last public appearance was at the end of March. When an Albanian delegation, representing a country of whose leadership and policies Mao had long been expressing total approval, appeared on March 26, P'eng did not turn out to join the distinguished gathering that received it. He undoubtedly objected to what the Albanians stood for, and in any case the political pressures on him may have been too great by that time to allow him the opportunity to take part in public meetings.

For in April 1966, the *Liberation Army Daily,* with the belated and probably reluctant support of the *People's Daily,* intensified its editorial offensive against P'eng Chen by propaganda attacks on persons close to him, notably Wu Han and another prominent official and writer who was considered to have criticized Mao, Teng T'o. In addition to being held liable for his efforts to protect these men, P'eng may also have seemed dangerous for his softness toward the United States, which seemed to be finding an echo in Washington in the hearings on China conducted in March by the Senate Foreign Relations Committee.

By early May, Mao had decided that his politico-military preparations were sufficiently advanced to enable him to move against P'eng Chen. Whatever Liu Shao-ch'i's attitude may have been at that time, Teng Hsiao-p'ing was evidently willing to let himself be won over by the Maoist camp, perhaps because P'eng, as the ranking member of the Secretariat next to himself, was a formidable potential rival. Teng made a militant speech in Shanghai early in May, and when on May 10 Mao's long disappearance from public view was ended by an announcement that he had recently talked with the Albanian delegation, a photograph was published showing the latter on Mao's left and Teng immediately on his right, in the place of honor, flanked by Chou En-lai and Lin Piao in that order. To emphasize that great events were impending, the *Liberation Army Daily* published an especially militant and significant blast against Teng T'o, and on May 9 a nuclear test (China's third) was conducted.

With his political resurrection thus duly dramatized, Mao returned to Peking shortly afterward. What happened next is decidedly obscure, but it seems very probable that he and Lin effectively used a threat of military force, probably accompanied by some actual movements of troops loyal to them, to neutralize P'eng Chen's power base in Peking and overawe a majority of the party leadership into siding with Mao and against P'eng. On May 16, in the name of the Central Committee, an important directive was issued — although it was not published until a year later — in which P'eng's Outline Report of February 12 was repudiated, and the Great Proletarian Cultural Revolution was officially and publicly proclaimed for the first time, with a clear indication that anyone who opposed it, no matter how highly placed, would be made into a political unperson.

Within a few days, the overthrow of P'eng Chen had been accomplished. The effective means were probably an adverse vote by the Standing Committee of the Politburo, some form of military pressure, and vociferous agitation by units of Red Guards. For it was at this time, in late May 1966, that the first Red Guard units began to appear, under army auspices, on the campuses of universities and middle (high) schools in Peking. Similar units of Red Guards were soon formed in other places as well. On June 1 the Maoists took control of the *People's Daily*, which on the following day assumed a more Maoist coloration, and on June 3 announced a new municipal party leadership for Peking, minus P'eng Chen, of course.

UNFINISHED BUSINESS

By this time the Cultural Revolution had been launched in earnest, and its basic techniques — constant invocation of the authority of Mao Tse-tung and his "thought," massive and forceful propaganda, military pressures, mobilization of the more radical among the youth, and ruthless reshuffling of the party leadership by means known hardly if at all to the party constitution — were already in evidence. The inauguration of the Cultural Revolution was announced to the world, or at any rate to that part of it of which Mao approved the most highly after China, namely Albania, by Chou En-lai in a speech delivered at Tirana on June 27, 1966. Chou explained the rationale of the Cultural Revolution:[6]

> Owing to the corroding effect of the influence of the bourgeoisie and the spontaneous forces of the petty bourgeoisie, and owing to the presence and influence of the forces of habit from the old society, some persons within the Party and government organs and cultural and educational institutions may degenerate and become new bourgeois elements. At the same time, imperialism, modern revisionism and the reactionaries of all countries try every means to carry out encirclement and penetration against us, as well as subversive activities. All this creates in our country the danger of the emergence of revisionism and the restoration of capitalism.

Since we are examining the launching of the Cultural Revolution, there is no need to review the ensuing phases in detail. The next case study will be more interesting and easier to understand, however, if we briefly consider the main trends.

At the beginning of June, Mao again withdrew to the Yangtze Valley; in this way he left the party apparatus to cope with the serious problem presented by the emerging Red Guards, and in all probability he was consciously laying a trap for Liu Shao-ch'i and Teng Hsiao-p'ing as he had earlier for P'eng Chen. While waiting, he purged the party's propaganda apparatus and put T'ao Chu, the able and rising First Secretary of the Central-South region, stretching roughly from Wuhan to Canton, in charge of it. Liu and Teng, who clearly felt little enthusiasm for the disorderly Red Guards, responded predictably and bureaucratically to the challenge that they presented by adopting the tested Chinese Communist procedure of sending "work teams" of cadres to deal with them and bring them under some control. Even more predictably, the Red Guards resented and rejected these efforts, and the serious issue that developed enabled Mao to make support of the Red Guards a test of loyalty to him and the Cultural Revolution. Again after appropriate politico-military preparations, he returned to

[6] Text released by New China News Agency, June 27, 1966.

Peking late in July and, using methods similar to those he had employed against P'eng Chen, succeeded in extracting a decision in favor of the Red Guards and the Cultural Revolution from the Eleventh Plenary Session of the party Central Committee, which met from August 1 to 12, 1966.

From August 18 until late November, Mao appeared before eleven million Red Guards, brought by military transportation from all over China, at eight gigantic rallies. At these rallies he made it clear that Lin Piao was his new heir and displayed the new party ranking order that he had decided on with the consent of the Eleventh Plenary Session; one of the main features of this new order was a sharp drop by Liu Shao-ch'i. During this period the crushing Maoist coalition and the Red Guards almost annihilated the central Secretariat of the party, which Mao had come to regard as the opposition's stronghold, or at least prevented it from functioning; it has never recovered.

Having fulfilled this mission and having seen Mao plain, the Red Guards were shooed out of Peking, which they were congesting badly, and were told to go and "make revolution" in the regions and provinces, where the powerful and entrenched local party bureaucracies remained to be dealt with. Whatever Mao may have thought, Chou En-lai was anxious that the Red Guards in dealing with the local party apparatuses should not disrupt the urban or the rural economies. But a movement so titanic could not be so precisely controlled and aimed. In a number of provinces a complex and chaotic struggle involving not only Red Guards and supporters of the local party leaders, but in many cases workers and peasants as well, followed. The danger to the nation if this sort of thing should continue was obvious, and in January 1967, Mao, Lin Piao, and Chou En-lai agreed that the only instrumentality capable of restoring order, the army, must be called in. Mao's objectives being what they were, he insisted on saddling the army with an impossible dual objective, whose mutual incompatibility he was to prove slow to realize. One was to restore or maintain order; the other was to support the local Maoists and drive the Cultural Revolution ahead. Left without clear guidance, the army emphasized first the one and then the other of these tasks, until growing disorder and an act of defiance by a major regional commander in midsummer showed how serious the situation was becoming. Mao and even his militant wife, then reluctantly gave the army a reasonably clear mandate to restore order even at the expense of the Red Guards

During the autumn of 1967, accordingly, public order improved considerably. A similar cycle occurred in 1968, beginning with a leftist offensive by the Red Guards, spurred on by Chiang Ching from Peking and directed primarily against Chou En-lai, in the late spring, followed by a counteroffensive led by Chou En-lai, probably with Mao's reluctant acquiescence, which curbed Chiang Ching and produced firmer repression of Red Guards by the army than ever before. By the late summer "Revolutionary Committees," seemingly Maoist in inspiration and loyalty but in reality controlled most often by the local military authorities, had come into existence in all the provinces and major municipalities of the country. It appeared improbable, although possible, that the extreme Maoists could overcome this adverse trend and regenerate the Cultural Revolution in more than name.

SELECTED BIBLIOGRAPHY

Since the study of Chinese politics is a complicated business, and since the views expressed in the foregoing study are not unanimously held by other specialists, it seems desirable to recommend a few other basic studies covering similar ground. One such work, difficult but standard and important, is Franz Schurmann, *Ideology and Organization in Communist China,* 2nd ed., enlarged (Berkeley, Calif.: University of California Press, 1968). Another valuable work, somewhat more specialized and based mainly on interviews with selected refugees in Hong Kong, is A. Doak Barnett, *Cadres, Bureaucracy, and Political Power in Communist China* (New York: Columbia University Press, 1967). Professor Barnett has examined the formative period of the Communist regime in *Communist China: The Early Years, 1949–55* (New York: Praeger, 1964). A very valuable study of the ensuing years is to be found in *Communist China, 1955–1959: Policy Documents with Analysis* (Cambridge, Mass.: East Asian Research Center, Harvard University, 1962). Important secret Chinese military documents dating from 1961 have been translated in J. Chester Cheng, ed., *The Politics of the Chinese Red Army* (Stanford, Calif.: Hoover Institution, Stanford University, 1966). A series of useful case studies by various scholars is available in A. Doak Barnett, ed., *Chinese Communist Politics in Action* (Seattle, Wash.: University of Washington Press, 1969).

On the specific subject treated in this study, the origins and launching of the Cultural Revolution, a number of valuable periodical articles are available. The Chinese political scene in the years immediately preceding the Cultural Revolution is analyzed in A. A. Cohen and C. F. Steffens, "Disillusionment within the Ranks," *Problems of Communism,* Vol. XII, No. 3 (May-June 1963), pp. 10–17; Chalmers Johnson, "Lin Piao's Army and Its Role in Chinese Society," *Current Scene* (Hong Kong), Vol. IV, Nos. 13–14 (July 1, 15, 1966);

Charles Neuhauser, "The Chinese Communist Party in the 1960s: Prelude to the Cultural Revolution," *The China Quarterly,* No. 32 (October-December 1967), pp. 3–36; Edgar Snow, "Interview with Mao," *The New Republic,* February 27, 1965, pp. 17–23.

The history of the Cultural Revolution has been interpreted, from various points of view but in all cases with valuable results, in Philip Bridgham, "Mao's 'Cultural Revolution': Origin and Development," *The China Quarterly,* No. 29 (January-March 1967), pp. 1–35; The Editor, "Mao and the Crumbling Monolith," *Current Scene,* Vol. V, No. 12 (July 31, 1967); Harry Gelman, "Mao and the Permanent Purge," *Problems of Communism,* Vol. XV, No. 6 (November-December 1966), pp. 2–14; John Israel, "The Red Guards in Historical Perspective: Continuity and Change in the Chinese Youth Movement," *The China Quarterly,* No. 30 (April-June 1967), pp. 1–32; Franz Michael, "The Struggle for Power," *Problems of Communism,* Vol. XVI, No. 3 (May-June 1967), pp. 12–21; Michel Oksenberg, "China: Forcing the Revolution to a New Stage," *Asian Survey,* Vol. VII, No. 1 (January 1967), pp. 1–15; "The Power Struggle in China," *China Topics* (London), YB412 (February 2, 1967); Henry G. Schwarz, "The Great Proletarian Cultural Revolution," *Orbis,* Vol. X, No. 3 (Fall 1966), pp. 803–822; "Thoughts on the Present Situation in China," *China Topics,* YB387 (July 21, 1966).

HAROLD HINTON

4 Vietnam Policy, Domestic Factionalism, Regionalism, and Plotting a Coup

On October 16, 1964, as though to salute the fall of Khrushchev announced the day before, Communist China conducted its first nuclear test. The triumphant statement issued by Peking immediately afterward insisted, among other things, that the test would act as a "great encouragement to the revolutionary people of the world." In all probability this typically Maoist phrase was intended to suggest little more than a psychological influence, but it is vague enough to permit more drastic inferences about Chinese involvement in revolutionary struggles in various parts of the world.

About a month later, shortly after the American presidential election, it became clear that highly placed persons in the United States were advocating air attacks on North Vietnam as a means of counteracting the rapidly deteriorating situation in South Vietnam. In Korea fourteen years earlier, a comparable beginning had led in a few months to an American invasion of North Korea that had to be repelled by sizable Chinese forces. Foreign Minister Chen Yi had warned in July 1964 that any similar American invasion of North

Vietnam or northern Laos, areas adjacent to China, would also be met with a Chinese military response on the ground. The prospect of American invasion of North Vietnam seemed all the greater because Hanoi was known to be planning to send regular North Vietnamese army units into South Vietnam for the first time, not only to accelerate a Communist victory but to ensure Hanoi's control over the presumably triumphant Viet Cong.

The new leadership in Moscow evidently took the situation in Southeast Asia very seriously. It probably reasoned that Khrushchev had mistakenly allowed the conflict to develop to its current stage by a policy of essential noninvolvement, and that Stalin had contributed to the Sino-American confrontation in Korea by his caution following the American decision to defend South Korea against the North Korean invasion. This time it would be better to involve the Soviet Union from the beginning, by providing sophisticated defensive military equipment to Hanoi, in the hope of deterring the United States, preempting China and if possible keeping it out altogether, and keeping North Vietnam manageable.

It was probably with some such purposes as these in mind that Premier Kosygin went to Hanoi in early February 1965. As might be expected, he was given routine and even chilly treatment when he passed through Peking on his way south. While he was in Hanoi, American air attacks on North Vietnam began and soon developed to a scale that had not been anticipated in any Communist capital. With the crisis raised to a new level, it is understandable that on his way back Kosygin was received in Peking by the top Chinese leadership, including Mao Tse-tung, on February 11. But events were soon to show that the Chinese leadership was divided as to how to deal with the war in Vietnam, and that domestic Chinese developments were further to complicate the problem of working out an effective policy toward it.

INTRAPARTY DIFFERENCES ON FOREIGN POLICY

The differences over domestic policy between the Maoists and the leaders of the party apparatus appear to be closely paralleled in foreign policy, and again Chou En-lai and the administrators have tended to support the Maoists. Both, to be sure, would undoubtedly agree in principle that both the security and the influence of China ought to be enhanced as much as possible. Both would agree that China's relationship with the United States was and ought to be fundamentally an adversary relationship, for reasons of ideology and history and to promote control and mobilization in China. Both would agree that features of Khrushchev's policy, notably his tendency toward détente with the United States culminating in the test ban treaty, his eagerness to compete with China in the Third World, and his withdrawal of aid to China in 1959–60, were unacceptable and justified a Chinese political counterattack.

But beyond these general points of agreement lie some serious items of disagreement.

With respect to the United States, Mao appears to be fixated on the idea that his party's revolutionary experience, as interpreted retrospectively by himself, forms a universally valid model for the developing countries, and that the workability of that model hinges on a Communist-led confrontation, rising when possible or necessary to highly politicized revolutionary warfare, with "imperialism," Japanese or American, under cover of which domestic opponents can also be disposed of. Although such an attitude permits occasional tactical avoidance of direct confrontation with "imperialism," such as China has indeed practiced since 1958, it clearly rules out political concessions that threaten to turn into agreements in principle. It also implies an unwillingness to gamble on the distant future, except in the sense that any revolution may require two or more decades for its successful completion, as that in China did. Pressure on "imperialism," whether it takes the form of warfare at any time or not, must be as continuous as possible.

Liu Shao-ch'i and other opponents such as P'eng Te-huai, on the other hand, preferred a strategy requiring less provocation of and less active struggle against "imperialism" in the short run, the better to build up, eventually, the economic and military power of the Chinese state so as ultimately to give more effective support to struggles against "imperialism" in other parts of the world. This school seems to regard "people's war" as being of doubtful effectiveness under present circumstances and no doubt recalls that for China a full-scale Japanese invasion was required to make it effective. The oppositionist attitude seems to permit maneuver against and even compromise with "imperialism," as well as confrontation with it, and appears similar to the views that have generally prevailed in Moscow since the death of Stalin.

As for policy toward the Third World, Mao has always stressed the revolutionary component, or a strategy "from below" (a phrase favored by analysts of Communism). In principle, this approach envisages overthrowing all governments that are not anti-"imperialist," and transforming those which are as soon as possible into Communist regimes. The basic strategy to be employed is that of "people's war," or revolutionary warfare, Chinese style. Although Mao favors Chinese guidance, incitement, training, arms, and funds for such movements, he also holds that they must remain "self-reliant," or in other words that the recipient movement's political control over its revolution must not be jeopardized as long as it is vigorous and that China must not expose itself to undue risks of "imperialist" retaliation by excessively overt involvement. The opposition, on the other hand, is less interested in propagating armed revolution and the Chinese model, in the short run at any rate, than in promoting that which it regards as the national interest of the Chinese state. This attitude gives rise to what may be called a strategy "from above." It involves extensive diplomatic dealings, including on occasion treaties of friendship and aid programs, with governments which, whether Communist or not, are considered anti-"imperialist," or which it is hoped can be wooed over to an anti-"imperialist" stance by such means. Those who have received benefits from China under this approach have included leftist, but non-Communist, Afro-Asian leaders and the apparatuses of various Communist Parties, both in and out of power. Again the long-run promotion of the power and influence of the Communist Chinese state, rather than fostering general revolution in the short run, is the primary consideration.

Beyond the general points of agreement already mentioned, attitudes toward the Soviet Union appear to diverge quite sharply. It is clear that Mao strongly disliked both Khrushchev's attack on Stalin and Khrushchev's domestic program (notably his "party of the whole people" and his "state of the whole people"), which seemed to threaten Mao's personal position and his own domestic program of austerity and intensive mobilization through political appeals. But in addition to Khrushchev he disliked, and still dislikes, his bureaucratic colleagues and successors, whom he regards as the counterparts of the opposition that he has come increasingly to detest in China. Finally, since the death of Stalin at any rate Mao has displayed no tolerance for any significant Soviet role in the Third World and indeed no interest in any sort of major accommodation with the Soviet Union.

The opposition, on the other hand, though it clearly objects to Khrushchev's impulsive and anti-Chinese policies, appears to have hoped and believed that his replacement by more stable and bureaucratically minded colleagues would make possible an improvement in Sino-Soviet relations, including a resumption of Soviet aid to China. The opposition does not seem to have objected to Khrushchev's attack on Stalin or to his domestic policy nearly as strongly as Mao did. It also has appeared willing to accept an active Soviet role in the Third World, it is to be hoped in cooperation rather than in competition with China, and to have favored and perhaps insisted on active Soviet opposition to American "imperialism" in the crisis in Vietnam.

Although unjust from any other perspective, it was therefore not unreasonable from the Maoist standpoint for Red Guards to charge Liu Shao-ch'i, during the Cultural Revolution, with having espoused the "three unities and the one diminution" (*san-ho-i-shao*), or in other words with having favored unity with "imperialism, reaction, and modern revisionism" and the diminution of aid and support for "national liberation movements."

These differences over foreign policy, like the corresponding differences over domestic policy, became somewhat institutionalized and intensified with a dual leadership that appeared in the spring of 1959 with the election of Liu Shao-ch'i as Chairman of the Chinese People's Republic, whereas Mao retained the chairmanship of the party Central Committee. For the time being, however, foreign policy differences were transcended by or submerged in common resentment of Khrushchev's China policy, notably his abrupt withdrawal of economic aid in 1960. Thus the Tenth Plenary Session of the party Central Committee (September 1962), which signaled Mao Tse-tung's comeback in domestic policymaking, also proclaimed support for the essentials of his foreign policy. The communique dealt with foreign affairs before domestic affairs, a rather unusual procedure, and strongly denounced those Maoist demons, "the imperialists, the reactionaries of various countries, and the modern revisionists,"[1] in other words respectively the United States, all but the most strongly leftist non-

[1] Text released by New China News Agency, September 28, 1962.

Communist leaders of other countries outside the "socialist camp," and the Soviet Union. There was apparent agreement between the two schools that Khrushchev's setback in Cuba must be exploited, and his effort to maneuver an international Communist conference to condemn the Chinese must be countered, by an intensive effort to swing over the leaderships of other Communist Parties, notably those of Asia, to the Chinese side of the Sino-Soviet dispute, or to split them and set up rival "Marxist-Leninist" parties if this could not be done.

It also appears likely that both sides agreed, perhaps after much debate, however, on attacking the Indian Army along the Himalayan frontier in the autumn of 1962, the opposition probably for what it regarded as national security and the Maoists no doubt also in the hope of promoting the cause of revolution in India and elsewhere. The border war produced a major crisis in China's relations with the Third World, to an extent that had probably not been anticipated by the opposition and was therefore not welcome to it. In the late spring of 1963, accordingly, Liu Shao-ch'i paid a state visit to Burma, Indonesia, Cambodia, and North Vietnam, apparently with the purpose, among others, of repairing the Chinese image. He was to be strongly criticized for this trip during the Cultural Revolution. Mao, for his part, showed the direction in which his thoughts about the Third World ran by publishing, at almost exactly the same time, a volume entitled *Selected Military Writings of Mao Tse-tung,* the theme of which was the familiar one of politicized revolutionary warfare against "imperialism" and domestic "reaction."

Once again, however, Khrushchev seems to have helped to prevent differences within the Chinese leadership over foreign policy from becoming serious. The test ban treaty that he signed in late July 1963 was evidently unacceptable to both schools, although not necessarily for exactly the same reasons, as witnessed by the fact that the Chinese government as well as the Chinese Communist Party protested formally against it. Presumably the Maoists objected primarily because the treaty represented the ultimate to date in détente between the Soviet Union and the West, the opposition because it tended to embarrass and complicate the Chinese nuclear weapons program.

The fall of Khrushchev in mid-October removed this convenient bit of cement. His successors projected an image and inaugurated a policy just similar enough to his to enrage Mao Tse-tung, and yet just different enough to interest the opposition. The crucial issue created in Peking by his fall, and by the mounting crisis over Vietnam, seems to have been whether the United States or the Soviet Union was really China's primary enemy. Mao had contrived to confuse the issue at the theoretical level, while creating the impression that in practice he regarded the Soviet Union as the more objectionable of the two. Certainly by thus opening a kind of second front he had diminished the chances that China could oppose the United States effectively in Asia. The issue after Khrushchev's fall was whether this line should continue in effect, or whether China should take steps to put itself into a position to oppose the United States effectively even if this meant a limited, pragmatic reconciliation with the Soviet Union. The Maoist refutation of this possible course of action, as might be expected, was the sweeping charge that the United States and the Soviet Union were "colluding" with one another.

VIETNAM AND SZECHUAN

The Maoists showed their objections to Soviet efforts to organize an international Communist conference and to Soviet policy toward Vietnam, which apparently envisaged an attempt to bring about negotiations, by staging a riot by Chinese and North Vietnamese students outside the American Embassy in Moscow on March 4, 1965. Presumably because of the opposition's efforts, a Sino-Soviet agreement was nevertheless reached, on March 30, for the passage of Soviet military equipment across China to North Vietnam. To have done otherwise would have seriously alienated Hanoi, and the Maoists were probably consoled by the thought that the main rail line to North Vietnam ran through the Central-South region, then under the leadership of T'ao Chu, who stood high in Mao's favor to all appearances, or at any rate higher than the other regional first secretaries.

A much more serious policy problem was presented by a Soviet request, made on April 3 and again on April 17, 1965, for air base rights in Southwest China. The rights requested apparently included constructing facilities, manning them with Soviet personnel, and staging other Soviet personnel through them to North Vietnam. The request does not appear to have included a demand for bases from which to provide Soviet air cover for North Vietnamese targets threatened by American air attacks. Thus the military risk that acceptance would have entailed, although not negligible, was not likely to have been the main reason why this proposal was far more controversial in Peking than the request for rail transit facilities. The main difficulty, at least in the eyes of the Maoists, was probably that accepting such an arrangement would have tended to strengthen the Southwest regional party machine and Soviet influence in that region and perhaps elsewhere in China; that indeed may have been one Soviet objective.

The crisis in Vietnam threw into sharper relief than ever, in Peking's eyes, the precariousness of its hold over South and Southwest China, especially the latter. A backward and in many places sparsely populated region, with a substantial proportion of non-Chinese minorities, and poorly connected with the rest of China by modern means of transportation, it could hardly avoid seeming to confront Peking with a serious problem of security and control at a time of a major crisis almost next door. The problem must have seemed especially acute to the Maoists, who are essentially centralizers and regard centrifugal tendencies with horror, whereas the opposition has displayed greater flexibility and a willingness to make concessions to regionalism as a means of staving off possible complete disintegration.

The key province in the Southwest, by any standards, is Szechuan. This province is larger than France and contains more than seventy million people. It possesses substantial natural resources, as well as important defense industries. It is strategic in that it borders on eight provinces (more than any other province of China) and is clearly essential to secure control from the center over Tibet, whose eastern marches it in fact includes. From the standpoint of any central government, it is a traditionally insecure province, given to rebellion and separatism, and difficult to control because of its comparative geographic isolation from much of China Proper. Szechuan possesses most if not all the basic prerequisites for nationhood; if independent, it would be one of the most populous states in the world, and by no means one of the smallest. It served, after a fashion, as the Chinese Nationalists' base area during seven years (1938–45) of their struggle against Japan. Szechuan has naturally contributed substantially to the ranks of the Chinese Communist movement, as to those of others in modern times. Indeed, the influential Szechuanese faction in the party tried in 1935, during the celebrated Long March, to have the party make its main base in Szechuan. They were outmaneuvered by Mao

Tse-tung, however, and ever since tension seems to have remained between Mao and some at least of his Szechuanese colleagues, as well as with some non-Szechuanese who made their careers in the Southwest for a time after 1949 and seem to have espoused the outlook and interests of the region. The substantial number of Szechuanese, by birth or adoption, who were to suffer politically during the Cultural Revolution includes General Secretary Teng Hsiao-p'ing, Marshal Ho Lung, and Chief of Staff Lo Jui-ch'ing. Finally, even if one discounts the later Red Guard charges against him, it does appear that Li Ching-ch'üan, the first secretary of the Southwest Regional Bureau of the party Central Committee, was guilty of "revisionism" in some of his policies, notably his agrarian policies, and of making his region into something of an "independent kingdom."

On April 9, 1965, K'o Ch'ing-shih, the first secretary of the East China Bureau of the party Central Committee, died in Chengtu, the capital of Szechuan, according to the official announcement "after a serious illness that did not respond to medical treatment."[2] It is not clear why he died there, or for that matter whether his death was really due to natural causes. It is possible that he had been squeezed out of East China by outside pressures, presumably Maoist since he went to Szechuan rather than Peking. It is certain that no one was appointed to succeed him in East China, and with that piece of conscious omission the dismantling of the Regional Bureaus can be considered to have begun. His funeral was attended by, among others, Marshal Chu Teh, Ho Lung, and Marshal Nieh Jung-chen, all Szechuanese by birth or adoption. It is of course possible that they knew of, discussed, and approved of the Soviet request of April 3 for air base rights in the Southwest; it is even more likely that they were suspected by the Maoists of doing so. For their part, the Maoists found the proposal totally unacceptable and succeeded in blocking it.

THE STRATEGIC DEBATE

The two schools of thought in Peking approached Vietnam, and the rest of their major problems at that time, in quite different spirits. Mao seems to have regarded Vietnam as secondary, apart from its potential value in vindicating the principle of "people's war" and

[2] New China News Agency despatch, April 9, 1965.

generating "people's wars" elsewhere. He had predicted to Edgar Snow, on January 9, 1965, that the United States would neither escalate the struggle in Vietnam by attacking the North nor attack China itself, and even though he had been proved wrong in the first respect he seems, in spite of occasional propaganda statements to the contrary, to have continued to believe himself right in the second. His main problem was the domestic situation, which he considered bad for reasons already indicated, and the possible aggravating effects on it of "Khrushchev revisionism." The opposition, on the other hand, tended to be satisfied with the domestic situation as it was and to be slow to realize how intense was Mao's dissatisfaction with it and the lengths to which he was willing to go to change it. The opposition, or at least some segments of it, was deeply worried over Vietnam and the resulting risk to China but was also impressed – it appears – with the potential benefits to China that might accrue from a use of the crisis to improve relations with the Soviet Union, at least in the economic and military fields.

The main public participants in the strategic debate, which continued intermittently until the Eleventh Plenary Session of the Central Committee in August 1966, were, on the Maoist side, Defense Minister Lin Piao and (until he was purged in May 1966) Peking municipal boss P'eng Chen; on the opposition side, Chief of Staff Lo Jui-ch'ing (until he was purged in early 1966) and to a lesser extent Liu Shao-ch'i. The debate was an extremely complex and subtle give-and-take, a complete account of which is available to anyone interested.[3]

The main issues argued in the debate were five: the proper strategy for the Vietnamese Communists to pursue (or be encouraged to pursue), the proper strategy for China in the struggle in Vietnam, the implications of the latter for the political situation in China, the appropriate state of Sino-Soviet relations in the Vietnam crisis, and the threat to China from the United States.

As for strategy in Vietnam, in early 1965 Hanoi was beginning to send its regular army units into South Vietnam, apparently for com-

[3] Uri Ra' anan, "Peking's Foreign Policy 'Debate,' 1965–1966," in Tang Tsou, ed., *China in Crisis*, Vol. 2, *China's Policies in Asia and America's Alternatives* (Chicago: University of Chicago Press, 1968), pp. 23–71.

bined military and political reasons. The Maoist spokesmen[4] evidently opposed this move, believing that the struggle in South Vietnam should be as "self-reliant" as possible, and favored a protracted guerrilla warfare that in time would lead to a Communist victory with minimum escalation on either side. The opposition, or at least the exceptionally hawkish Lo Jui-ch'ing, seems to have supported sending regular North Vietnamese units to the south, calling this move "active defense."[5]

As for Chinese policy toward Vietnam, the Maoists[6] again emphasized "self-reliance," or in other words the idea of minimum Chinese involvement; they stressed the prosecution of the struggle in the south, as against the security or other interests of North Vietnam, and seemingly tried to split Hanoi and the Viet Cong by making a thoroughly hypothetical Chinese intervention in the struggle conditional on a request from the latter alone. The opposition[7] advocated somewhat more active support, mainly logistical, on the principle that China should be the "reliable rear area" in the conflict. It felt strong interest in the security of North Vietnam, as well as in the struggle in the south. Although in practice probably somewhat more willing than the Maoists to commit Chinese forces if necessary, it defined the conditions for such a commitment rather more realistically as a request from both the Viet Cong and Hanoi (the latter being even more unlikely than the former to make such a request), as evaluated in Peking on the basis of the objective necessity for Chinese intervention.

As for the implications of the Vietnamese crisis for China, the Maoists used the argument that the crisis required the "guerrillaiza-

[4] Li Tso-p'eng, "Strategically 'Pit One Against Ten,' Tactically 'Pit Ten Against Ten,'" *Red Flag,* December 22, 1964 (in American Consulate General, Hong Kong, *Selections from China Mainland Magazines,* No. 453, January 25, 1965) (reprinted in 1966 in an edited version that stressed even more heavily the strategy of guerrilla as against conventional warfare); Lin Piao, "Long Live the Victory of People's War," New China News Agency release, September 3, 1965 (published as a booklet by the Foreign Languages Press).

[5] Lo Jui-ch'ing, "Commemorate the Victory over German Fascism! Carry the Struggle Against U.S. Imperialism through to the End!" *Red Flag,* May 10, 1965 (published as a booklet by the Foreign Languages Press).

[6] Lin, *loc. cit.*

[7] Lo, *loc. cit.;* Liu Shao-ch'i, statement of July 22, 1966 (*Peking Review,* July 29, 1966, p. 9).

tion" of politics and life in general, the better to be able to cope with anything that might arise out of the crisis. They really meant, of course, that the crisis could and should be exploited so as to create a suitable atmosphere (a "siege mentality") for the "guerrillaization" that Mao desired, for the deprecation of the "expert" in favor of the "red."[8] The opposition held that the Vietnamese crisis could be used to promote, and they may have genuinely believed that it required, a high level of professionalism in economic and military life and, against the possibility of an American attack, extensive preparations and pre-attack mobilization; as Lo Jui-ch'ing put in on one occasion, "A thousand and one things need to be done in preparation."[9]

As for Sino-Soviet relations, the Maoists insisted strongly that no "united action" with Moscow on Vietnam, such as the Soviet Union was demanding, was desirable or possible.[10] The main stated ground was that the Soviet Union was a "revisionist" power that was "colluding" with the United States and would betray China and North Vietnam under the guise of "united action." Foreign Minister Chen Yi even went so far, in a celebrated interview given on September 29, 1965, as to insist that the Soviet Union was contemplating joining with the United States, Britain, Japan, and India in an invasion of China.[11] The real ground was probably that to have collaborated with the Soviet Union even to this limited extent would have seemingly made nonsense of the Maoist domestic and foreign policy and would have strengthened the hand of the opposition. The latter, Lo Jui-ch'ing in particular[12] and Liu Shao-ch'i[13] and Teng Hsiao-p'ing[14] less outspokenly, seem to have favored at least some "united action" both in the hope of improving their domestic position and re-establishing Soviet aid to and protection of China, as well as winning victory in Vietnam.

As for the danger to China from the United States as a result of

[8] Notice the abolition of military ranks and titles in May 1965.

[9] Speech of September 3, 1965 (New China News Agency despatch, September 4, 1965).

[10] "Refutation of the New Leaders of the CPSU on 'United Action,' " *People's Daily* and *Red Flag*, November 11, 1965.

[11] See *Vice-Premier Chen Yi Answers Questions Put by Correspondents* (Peking: Foreign Languages Press, 1966).

[12] See note 5.

[13] In the speech cited in note 7, Liu refrained from denouncing the Soviet Union (the only speaker on this occasion to do so).

[14] Teng Hsiao-p'ing, speech of July 20, 1965, before the Ninth Congress of the Rumanian Communist Party (*Peking Review*, July 30, 1965).

the crisis in Vietnam, the Maoists held that although the United States possessed strong ground forces it was unlikely to attack China, especially if it were distracted by "people's wars" fought at the guerrilla level in Vietnam and elsewhere. If an American attack on China did occur, it would take the form of an invasion that could be crushed by a guerrillaized army and a popular militia led by the Communist Party inspired by Mao Tse-tung's "thought," as had allegedly occurred when Japan invaded China in 1937–45.[15] The opposition, on the other hand, and again Lo Jui-ch'ing in particular, held that the United States was in a highly bellicose mood and alleged that its weakness in ground forces would probably lead it to attack China by air, with thermonuclear weapons. Clearly a fully professional defense establishment would be required to deal with such a threat.[16]

The actual policy pursued during 1965–66 was something of a compromise between the views of the two schools, although the compromise assumed an increasingly Maoist flavor as the Maoists increasingly acquired the ascendancy over the opposition in domestic politics. There was a buildup of Chinese forces opposite Vietnam, but it was not large. Some air raid precautions were taken, but not very extensive ones, mainly around Canton. Rice and weapons, mainly light infantry weapons, were shipped to North Vietnam. Between 50,000 and 100,000 engineer troops were sent to North Vietnam, equipped, it would appear, with nothing heavier than side arms and antiaircraft guns, to help keep open the rail lines between North Vietnam and China, which form an important part of the South China rail net. Soviet military equipment was shipped by rail across China to North Vietnam, but it was occasionally delayed or diverted until an agreement not to do so was reached in March 1967, perhaps under the pressure of the recent stationing of B-52's in Thailand by the United States; at about that time, the disorder caused by the Cultural Revolution began to disrupt the shipments. Occasional threatening statements about Chinese intervention in the war were presumably designed to deter American escalation against North Vietnam or possible American military pressures on China, but these grew increasingly vague. China's second nuclear test occurred on May 14, 1965, possibly by way of response to a statement by President Johnson the previous day that

[15] Lin Piao (see note 4); P'eng Chen, *Speech at the Aliarcham Academy of Social Sciences in Indonesia* (May 25, 1965) (Peking: Foreign Languages Press, 1965).

[16] See note 5.

China would never be allowed to dominate Southeast Asia, but it took place during a brief pause in the American bombing of North Vietnam and the accompanying statement from Peking omitted the usual assertion that the test would be a "great encouragement to the revolutionary people of the world."

The balance in policy toward Vietnam seems to have been tipped decisively in favor of the Maoists mainly by the progress of the domestic power struggle, but perhaps also by an exchange at Warsaw between the American and Chinese ambassadors that was interpreted in Peking as an indirect American pledge that, even though the United States had resumed bombing North Vietnam at the end of January 1966, it would not attack China unless the latter intervened directly in Vietnam. It is conceivable that without this assurance of sorts, which was given in the spring of 1966, Mao would not have dared launch his final political offensive against P'eng Chen in May.

The Twelfth Plenary Session of the party Central Committee (August 1–12, 1966) handed a blank check for future policy toward Vietnam to the Central Committee and the government, meaning in effect to the Big Three on the Maoist side: Central Committee Chairman Mao Tse-tung, sole Vice Chairman Lin Piao, and Premier Chou En-lai. Here, as in domestic politics, Mao had triumphed in policymaking. The Maoists appear to have had less difficulty in implementing their Vietnam policy than in implementing their domestic policy. The former has restricted actual Chinese involvement in the Vietnamese crisis almost to the minimum, continued to repudiate "united action" with the Soviet Union, continued to advocate a protracted "people's war" in South Vietnam under the greatest possible conditions of "self-reliance," and opposed any form of negotiations. Hanoi's decision in the spring of 1968 to begin some kind of talks with the United States, even without a complete bombing halt, reduced relations between Peking and Hanoi to a very low point.

THE "FEBRUARY COUP"

We commented briefly in the preceding case study on an alleged plot or coup said by the Maoists to have occurred in February 1966, and we attempted a tentative and inconclusive interpretation. It is now possible, and will help the reader to understand the subject of this case study, to present a fuller treatment of this obscure episode, since it falls within the area of overlap between domestic and foreign policy.

About the beginning of 1967, newspapers and wall posters of Red Guard origin began to refer to a plot or coup said to have occurred in February 1966. Chou En-lai was reported to have told a group of Red Guards on September 9, 1966, that P'eng Chen had planned a military coup; assuming that Chou made such a statement, and ignoring for the time being the truth or falsity of the charge, we may reasonably conclude that Chou's purpose in making it at that time was to establish a rapport with his audience, prove his own Maoist militancy, and improve the prospects for the acceptance by the Red Guards of his demand that they not disrupt the economy. In January and February of 1967, Lin Piao began to enlarge greatly the charges regarding the "February coup" by naming not only P'eng Chen but Lo Jui-ch'ing, Lu Ting-yi, and Yang Shang-k'un as the main conspirators, and accusing Liu Shao-ch'i, Teng Hsiao-p'ing, and T'ao Chu of having supported them. A Red Guard poster added the charge that Ho Lung had tried to prepare a base in Southwest China as a fall-back position in case the coup should fail. Regardless of the truth of Lin's charges, their motivation is easily understood because of the Maoist assault on the party Secretariat (with which all the accused except Ho Lung were connected in one way or another), the fact that some of them were or had recently been so high in the party as to inconvenience Lin Piao in his new role as Mao Tse-tung's heir apparent, the commitment of the army at that time to a key role in the Cultural Revolution, the assault on the provincial and regional party apparatuses, and the accompanying effort to set up Revolutionary Committees. Many of the specific charges were clearly implausible, inaccurate, or downright false. Ho Lung, for example, was seemingly in high favor with the Maoists, including the Red Guards, for a time after August 1966, which he would probably not have been if he had been involved in a plot several months earlier. At a meeting held on April 28, 1967, Chou En-lai and K'ang Sheng expressed doubt that there had been a "February coup" at all. Neither their expressed doubts nor the flaws in the earlier charges, however, completely dispose of the problem. Chou and K'ang, for their part, were probably saying on behalf of two of the top leaders (Chou for himself and K'ang for Mao) that the third, Lin Piao, had gone too far, and since a Revolutionary Committee had been proclaimed in Peking on April 20 they were probably also trying to cool off the overheated political atmosphere of the city.

Insofar as the charges relating to a "February coup" appear to have any historical validity, as contrasted with a retroactive political purpose, they appear to apply to P'eng, Lo, Lu, and Yang. Beginning early in 1965, it has been alleged, they, and P'eng and Lo in particular, launched war preparations, including the accumulation of stockpiles in the vicinity of Peking. Since Lo, as Chief of Staff, seems to have feared an American air attack growing out of the escalation in Vietnam, and since P'eng as boss of Peking would naturally have been worried by such a possibility, this charge appears neither implausible nor sinister. In May, it is also alleged, they began to try to create a war scare; the reference is probably to the publication on May 10 of Lo's statement of his strategic views, which has already been discussed.

By the beginning of 1966, the divergence between these men and their more Maoist colleagues had become much more acute. P'eng Chen of course was deeply involved in trying to manage the first stage of the Cultural Revolution in such a way as to contain and neutralize Mao Tse-tung's pressures for a more radical program. Lo was trying to counter the insistence of Mao and Lin Piao on even more intensive propagation of the "thought of Mao Tse-tung" in the armed forces; this issue became especially serious after an important conference of political personnel in the armed forces in January 1966. Lu Ting-yi was evidently unenthusiastic about, and may have been actively opposing, Mao's insistence on printing enormous numbers of his *Selected Works* and other, simpler volumes (such as the famous Little Red Book) for mass consumption. Yang Shang-k'un, who held an important and confidential administrative position in the Secretariat, may well have served as a point of contact and coordination among the three others.

There was an important political weakness in the position of these four men. The Secretariat is not, strictly speaking, a body in which decisions are made on major policy questions. The body in which this is done at the highest level is (or was then; the situation has become obscure since 1967) the Standing Committee of the Politburo (its full title is the Political Bureau of the Central Committee). None of the four "plotters" was a member of this exalted body. Of the seven men who were, both earlier evidence and later developments strongly suggest that Chou En-lai and Lin Piao were then supporting at least the essentials of Mao's domestic and foreign programs, and that Liu Shao-ch'i, Chu Teh, and Chen Yun were opposed to or at least unenthusiastic about them to varying degrees and probably not with any great amount of coordination. This otherwise even split conferred great importance on the seventh member, General Secretary Teng Hsiao-p'ing. As the senior, although not necessarily dominant, figure in the party Secretariat, Teng obviously had close working relationships with the four "plotters," was presumably accessible to them, and might be thought likely to have sympathized with them. It would have been logical for the "plotters" to try to convert him to their views and persuade him to lead, or at least create, an effective anti-Maoist majority in the Politburo Standing Committee. At least one consideration was favorable: Teng had tried on a number of occasions to enhance his own influence in the State Council (cabinet), Chou En-lai's bailiwick, and in so doing had clearly aroused a good deal of resentment on Chou's part. On the other hand, in spite of his current differences with Mao, P'eng Chen had been so much more in the public eye (as a result of his extroverted personality and his prominent position in Peking) than Teng that he had probably aroused jealousy and insecurity on Teng's part. It would have been logical for the "plotters" to advance a particular interpretation of the external situation as a means of influencing Teng, and especially, in view of his occupational tendency toward a bureaucratic and therefore pragmatic view of Sino-Soviet relations, an argument on desirable Chinese policy toward the Soviet Union that would have been likely to appeal to him. Even if this did not happen, the external situation at that time can hardly have failed to influence, in one way or another, the thinking and behavior of China's principal policymakers.

Hoping to induce some reciprocity and improve the chances for a peaceful settlement, the United States had suspended the bombing of North Vietnam just before Christmas, 1965, and had launched an energetic "peace offensive." In January, with the bombing "pause" still in effect, Moscow, which seemed to prefer some political settlement provided one could be achieved without alienating the North Vietnamese leadership, sent the first of a series of delegations to Hanoi to press its views. At the same time, it made an extraordinarily ostentatious display of renewing its thirty-year-old defensive alliance with Outer Mongolia and seems to have moved military striking forces, including perhaps surface-to-surface missiles, into the eastern part of Outer Mongolia, where they would be as close as possible to Peking. The immediate aim was probably to deter the Chinese from making any serious trouble either in Outer Mongolia or in Southeast Asia in the event a Vietnamese settlement began to materialize (which of course it did not); a more extended aim was probably to induce greater soberness and moderation in Chinese domestic policies and thus reduce Mao's influence, if possible. Also in January and February of 1966, the Soviet party circulated, first within its own ranks and then among selected foreign Communist parties, a secret letter charging the Maoist leadership with extreme nationalism as manifested in such behavior as rejecting "united action" and obstructing Soviet military equipment bound for North Vietnam. On February 24, having made acceptance difficult or at least highly controversial, the Russians invited the Chinese party to send a delegation to represent it at the forthcoming Twenty Third Congress of the Soviet party, which was due to convene at the end of March. Roughly at the mid-point in this complex and important chain of events, on January 31, the United States resumed the bombing of North Vietnam.

There can be little doubt that the Maoists were distressed by the increase, however slight, in the chances, however negligible, of a Vietnamese settlement, and that they welcomed the resumption of bombing for this reason. Their view, although not fully valid or even rational, appears to have been simple. External tension short of actual Chinese involvement in a war, whether in Vietnam or along the Sino-Soviet border, was domestically beneficial, because it facilitated pressures on the non-Maoists or anti-Maoists within the top party leadership and helped to create an atmosphere conducive to political mobilization of the populace along Maoist lines. In all probability, war could be avoided by good management and by somewhat unorthodox methods of deterrence such as vague threats of a "war without boundaries" in Southeast Asia in the event of an attack on China. Even if war should break out and take the form (predicted with questionable seriousness by the Maoists) of an invasion of China, the Chinese army and people under their Maoist leadership could cope with the threat by "luring the enemy in deep" and crushing him in a "people's war."

The non-Maoist segment of the party leadership, including the four "plotters," viewed this entire argument with the deepest reservations from beginning to end. Lo Jui-ch'ing's hawkish statements of 1965 on Vietnam suggest that they were divided as to the desirability of a Vietnamese settlement at that time, but they were probably alarmed at the resumption of American bombing, with its accompanying danger of escalation against China itself, occurring as it did amid very bad Sino-Soviet relations. Even if this situation did not actually bring war to China, it would tend to promote Mao Tse-tung's distasteful domestic program in the way already indicated. A possible, partial way out seemed to be offered by the Japanese Communist Party's position, as expressed in the *Akahata* editorial of February cited earlier. This editorial was accordingly resurrected and reprinted in the *People's Daily* on February 25, the day after the Soviet invitation to send a delegation to the Twenty Third Congress. The Japanese position can reasonably be interpreted as being that "united action" on Vietnam under some Soviet leadership would be acceptable, and even desirable, provided the Soviet Union displayed a genuinely anti-"imperialist" stance by dropping its pressure, however gentle, on Hanoi for a political settlement and by leaving the unfettered power of decision on this critical question to Hanoi itself. If that was the actual Japanese view, it must have been acceptable not only in Hanoi but in Moscow, for it corresponds with the line that the Soviet Union has followed since early 1966, as far as can be judged. The Maoist objection to this seemingly reasonable position was the argument that, in principle, since the Soviet Union was a hopelessly "revisionist" power in "collusion" with the United States, "united action" with it could not be considered under any circumstances whatever.

In this situation, later Red Guard charges that the "plotters" made contact with the Soviet Union through Yang Shang-k'un and Soviet Ambassador Lapin appear plausible. They may well have indicated that they would be interested in sending a delegation to the Twenty Third Congress provided the Soviet Union accepted the Japanese position on "united action," as it was probably in a mood to do. On the Chinese side, the implementation of any such plan would of course require a favorable majority in the Politburo Standing Committee; the situation was such that four men on this body could claim with authority to speak and act in the name of the entire Central Committee. As already suggested, Teng Hsiao-p'ing's attitude would be crucial; later developments indicate that he was never dependably won over to the side of the "plotters."

The Soviet leadership was evidently puzzled, and possibly divided, as to what to do. It was well aware of P'eng Chen's record of strongly anti-Soviet statements and probably found it difficult to believe that any combination in which he was a moving spirit could be trusted even if its line appeared reasonable. Moscow may have hoped that if it kept the pressure at the current level and waited, without exerting further pressure, a favorable majority might materialize in the Politburo Standing Committee on the questions of "united action" and the Twenty Third Congress. Premature action of any kind on behalf of P'eng Chen, who was considered to favor some relaxation of tension with the United States, would have tended to prejudice the situation in the Politburo Standing Committee and in any case would have seemed inappropriate when the Soviet leadership was becoming genuinely disturbed over the prospect, however remote, of an easing of Sino-American tension seemingly raised by developments in the United States, such as the opening of a major series of public hearings on Vietnam and China by the Senate Foreign Relations Committee. Soviet policy accordingly fell between two stools, neither of which, to be sure, was very sturdy. On the one hand, it refrained from giving convincing assurances that it would ease its border pressures on China. On the other hand, it seems not to have tried seriously to arrange to support an effectively planned coup in China, for example with air drops of arms and possibly personnel. Either course of action, if it had been seriously tried and had proven feasible, might conceivably have affected the internal situation in China in a way favorable to Soviet interests. As it was, Soviet indecision may well have contributed to the nonemergence of an anti-Maoist majority in the Politburo Standing Committee, or in other words to a failure to win Teng Hsiao-p'ing to the position favored by the "plotters."

The next stage of the controversy is even more open to differences of interpretation, but considerations of plausibility and some evidence both indicate that at some time during this period, probably in the last few days of February or the first few days of March, Mao Tse-tung experienced a medical crisis and was thought to be in danger of dying. There was certainly a fairly widespread impression to that effect, and the superstitious found confirmation of it in such portents as the appearance of a particularly murky dust storm over Peking (a "black sky"), which traditionally had been one of the signs accompanying the death of an emperor. In fact, it seems possible that

Mao was suffering from throat cancer or some other affliction of the vocal cords, serious enough to require an operation that impaired his powers of speech. If true, this would explain why he appears to have made no public speeches since that time, even when it was he who appeared rather than the double employed on some occasions to spare him fatigue, and even when he appeared in the late summer and autumn of 1966 before huge crowds of Red Guards longing to hear him speak to them. In the tense atmosphere of that period, such a serious event was bound to have significant political consequences, especially since all the Chinese leaders must have remembered the disastrous Communist coup and the massacre that had followed President Sukarno's illness a year earlier.

It is possible that the "plotters" tried to extemporize a coup with the resources, mainly military, which were available to them at that time. If so, they obviously failed to bring it off. It is equally possible, or perhaps more likely, that the Maoists decided to move against them preemptively. Either hypothesis gains credibility from the later Red Guard charge that at some time in early 1966 P'eng Te-huai held talks with Southwest regional First Secretary Li Ching-ch'üan at Ipin, in Szechuan. P'eng still had some influence in Northwest China as well as good connections with Ho Lung, who was influential in the Southwest. The insistence of Mao and Lin, whose political strength lay mainly in the eastern regions of the country, on launching the Cultural Revolution and putting pressure on the party apparatus was already raising the obvious possibility of an east-west split, and accordingly P'eng Te-huai's materialization in the Southwest may have aroused even more alarm among the Maoists than it warranted. Still more serious was the obvious possibility that Mao's incapacitation might paralyze Maoist operations within the Politburo Standing Committee, to the advantage of the non-Maoists, including the "plotters."

These circumstances meant that an answer to the Soviet invitation to the Twenty Third Congress had to be put off. More important, Lin Piao, who was in a pivotal position in the armed forces by virtue of his roles as Chairman of the Military Committee of the party Central Committee and as Defense Minister, evidently organized and executed a military blow against Lo Jui-ch'ing, his most conspicuous rival within the army and the most dangerous of the "plotters," and Lo's military supporters. The stockpiles accumulated by Lo and P'eng Chen were taken over, Lo was seized, and his followers in the army were dismissed and probably disciplined in sterner ways as well. Lo was interrogated, made some sort of confession on March 12 that was rejected as inadequate, and allegedly attempted suicide on March 18. By the latter act he tended to discredit himself politically, since it seems to be a Chinese Communist rule that suicide is the worst of all crimes since it puts the offender beyond the possibility of further communication and ultimate "remoulding."

At about this time Mao must have recovered sufficiently to take part in Politburo Standing Committee discussions, still from the Shanghai area rather than Peking. Teng evidently remained, or was somehow kept, on the Maoist side; in an important photograph published early in May, Mao was shown in the center of an obviously posed group, with an Albanian delegation to his left, Teng in the place of honor on his right, then Chou En-lai, and Lin Piao on the extreme right (from the standpoint of the men involved, not of the viewer). With the back of the "February coup" broken and a workable Maoist majority in the Politburo Standing Committee, a strongly worded rejection of the invitation to the Twenty Third Congress was sent to Moscow on March 22, nearly a month after its receipt. Four days later, Liu Shao-ch'i left on a foreign tour lasting more than three weeks. During his travels he stopped more than once in Urumchi (in Sinkiang, a part of Northwest China) and in Kunming (in Southwest China) and had talks with local leaders. If, as seems possible, he was sounding them out on the possibility of support for some move against the Maoists, he probably had little success, for the Maoists were being careful at that time not to alarm the regional leaders any more than necessary, and he may well have weakened his position in Peking further by being absent at an important time.

In any event, the Maoists continued to employ their technique of dealing with the February "plotters" one at a time, and in descending order of urgency. Lo having been disposed of in March, P'eng Chen was overthrown late in May, and Lu Ting-yi and Yang Shang-k'un evidently some weeks later. Roughly in mid-1966, at about the time that Yang was taken care of, an unpublicized withdrawal of the Soviet ambassador from Peking and of the Chinese ambassador from Moscow occurred. Down to the spring of 1969, they had not been replaced. During this same period, Yang Ch'eng-wu, a general closely associated with Lin Piao, succeeded Lo Jui-ch'ing, but probably in deference to or at the insistence of the regional military commanders who did not want to see too great an increase in Lin's already impressive influence at the military center of the country, Yang was given only the title of acting chief of staff and was in this way presumably kept more vulnerable to removal. Similarly, Lu Ting-yi was succeeded at the head of the party's huge propaganda apparatus by T'ao Chu, the first secretary of the Central-South region but also the most acceptable (at that time) of the regional leaders to the Maoists in Peking.

During the months preceding the critical Twelfth Plenary Session of the party Central Committee, the Mao-Lin-Chou coalition had outmaneuvered the minority faction in the Politburo Standing Committee and deprived it of two possible sources of support. The February "plotters" had been crushed. The Soviet Union, which in any case appears to have been understandably irresolute and to have had few effective means of leverage on the situation, had been offered no usable opportunities for significant intervention, and its presence in China had been further reduced by the withdrawal or expulsion of its ambassador.

SZECHUAN AND KWANGSI AND THE CULTURAL REVOLUTION

After the Soviet request for air facilities in Southwest China was rejected in the early spring of 1965, the pressure of external events on domestic politics tended to shift to Kwangsi, the province through which runs the major rail link between South China and North Vietnam. The subsequent influence of the Cultural Revolution on Szechuan is an important and interesting topic in its own right, however, because of the province's size and its great significance for control over the entire western region of China, notably of course the Southwest.

The first secretary of the Southwest Bureau of the party Central Committee, with headquarters in Chengtu, was Li Ching-ch'üan, a man with old and close personal ties with Ho Lung and political ties with Teng Hsiao-p'ing. Li had served in the Southwest almost continuously since 1949 and had benefited politically from both the absence and the favor of Ho and Teng when they moved their base of operations to Peking in 1952. He had become First Secretary of the Szechuan Provincial Party Committee in 1955 and had been elected to the Politburo in 1958.

During the retreat from the Great Leap Forward that followed the economic disaster of 1960, Li energetically promoted the cause of good public administration and pragmatic economic development, by Chinese Communist standards, in the Southwest. These policies were intrinsically distasteful to the Maoists, and Li encountered particularly loud objections from two cadres in the Ipin Special District, a husband and wife team named Liu Chieh-t'ing and Chang Hsi-t'ing. According to later Red Guard accounts, Li Ching-ch'üan kept them under detention from 1962 to 1965; after their release they stayed in Peking, where it is very likely that they intrigued against Li.

Again according to Red Guard accounts, Li, in cooperation with Ho Lung, began in late 1965 to create a military base, including some "black troops" (a small private army), in Szechuan, allegedly in conjunction with the forthcoming "February coup." The frustration of the latter, plus of course Li's record as one of the most "revisionist" of the regional party leaders, rendered him a prime target of the Maoists when the Cultural Revolution began to spread from Peking to the provinces in the late summer of 1966. At that time Red Guard units invaded Szechuan and began to demonstrate against him. These activities were sufficiently widespread, and sufficient disorder resulted, so that Li apparently thought it best to make a show of conciliating the Red Guards, if only to get on the right side of Mao if possible against a later day when he might have to take forceful action against the Red Guards. He went to Peking in October 1966, told Mao that he had not been suppressing the Red Guards, and on his return to Szechuan in November made a "confession" of his past errors, hoping to appease his critics. This he evidently failed to do, and disorder continued in the huge province. By December there was fighting in Chungking and Chengtu, the two principal cities of Szechuan, between pro-Mao students and pro-Li workers.

The disorder in Szechuan was no doubt one of the most critical of the provincial problems that brought Mao Tse-tung and Lin Piao to agree, in January 1967, that the army must enter the political arena. In February, Huang Hsin-t'ing, a man associated with Ho Lung, was replaced as commander of the Chengtu Military District by Liang Hsing-ch'u, a former deputy commander of the Canton Military Region and an associate of Lin Piao. Although this action reduced the disorder by curbing activities by Red Guards, its main purpose was to weaken, not strengthen, regional party bureaucrats like Li Ching-ch'üan. It would not have been surprising if Ho Lung was among those objecting to the commitment of the Army to the Cultural Revolution; at any rate, posters denouncing him began to appear about the middle of January.

Disturbed by anti-Red Guard measures taken by local commanders, the Military Commission of the party Central Committee, headed by Lin Piao, issued a directive on April 6 to the effect that the army should not repress "revolutionary" organizations. The confused and uncomfortable commanders thereupon eased their pressures on the Red Guards, and a major upsurge of disorder was the result. In Szechuan, there was more fighting in Chungking and Chengtu in early May, and it provided an incentive, or at least a pretext, for a step evidently contemplated for some time in Peking, the formal unhorsing of Li Ching-ch'üan, who had apparently taken advantage of military intervention in Szechuan to strengthen his position.

Liang Hsing-ch'u having proved inadequate to cope with Li Ching-ch'üan's regional machine, it was decided to reinforce him with another powerful military man from outside the province. He was Chang Kuo-hua, commander of the Tibet Military Region. Although not even an alternate member of the party Central Committee (alternates are entitled to attend meetings of the Central Committee and to speak, but not to vote; they also provide a panel from which vacancies among the regulars are normally filled), he had earned great prestige in Peking by his successful management—not necessarily the tactical command—of the brilliant operations against the Indian Army in the autumn of 1962. In August 1965 he had become first secretary of the Tibet Party Committee, whereas the previous incumbent, Chang Ching-wu, moved up to become a secretary of the Southwest Bureau directly under Li Ching-ch'üan. In September, Chang Kuo-hua presided almost simultaneously over the proclamation, after a decade of preparation, of an "autonomous" regional government for Tibet and over a degree of Chinese intervention, largely verbal to be sure, and aimed at keeping Pakistan in the war by putting India under pressure, in the Indo-Pakistani hostilities over Kashmir.

Chang Kuo-hua was in Peking for May Day, 1967, and by that time the central Maoist leadership had evidently selected him as its man for Szechuan. His military background and connections would obviously be useful amid such turbulence, especially if it should prove advisable or necessary to bring troops in from Tibet. Chang had treated the Red Guards in Tibet rather roughly, and he could hardly be expected to lose all his influence there simply by being moved to the next province under such honorable circumstances, but at least his interest would be engaged in the situation in China Proper and he might be discouraged from trying to set up some sort of "independent kingdom" in Tibet if he were tempted to do so. From Chang's point of view, the promise of greater power and prestige was apparently sufficient to induce him to accept a large and troublesome responsibility. In addition, he may have been tempted by the opportunity to end the political career of Chang Ching-wu, who while in Tibet had been senior to him and perhaps something of a nuisance, along with that of Li Ching-ch'üan. On May 7, the dismissal of Li Ching-ch'üan and the creation of a Preparatory Group (for a subsequent Revolutionary Committee) were proclaimed in Peking. Chang Kuo-hua was chairman of the Group, and Liang Hsing-ch'u one of the vice chairmen; they were balanced by the two Maoists, Liu Chieh-t'ing (the other vice chairman) and Chang Hsi-t'ing (a principal "organizer"). In reality, of course, there would be a strong tendency for the two military men, even though they came from outside the province, to outweigh the two Maoists.

It was one thing to proclaim the ousting of Li Ching-ch'üan in Peking, and another to deal with him on the spot, as suggested by the fact that when a public propaganda campaign was opened against him in June it was launched from the neighboring province of Kweichow, where the Maoists had been in control since the beginning of the year. It may have been as late as August before Li was actually disposed of and the new quadrumvirate effectively installed in Chengtu. Even then, the division between Maoist and non-Maoist elements within the Preparatory Group, as well as within the leadership of the Military Region, combined with the strength and turbulence of the "revolutionary" organizations including Red Guards, made it impossible to restore more than limited order. These difficulties frustrated the central Maoist leadership's desire to see a Revolutionary Committee formed in Szechuan.

On March 15, 1968, before a meeting in Peking attended by a large number of representatives of various Szechuanese factions, Chang Kuo-hua and Liang Hsing-ch'u were accused by several prominent members of the central Maoist leadership, notably Chou En-lai and Chiang Ch'ing, of having approached Szechuan's political problems in an insufficiently revolutionary spirit. On the other hand, they were no removed or punished; they were apparently irreplaceable for all practical purposes. The central Maoist leadership wanted Revolutionary Committees established in all provinces where they did not yet exist, almost regardless of their individual political complexions, and this desire made it necessary to accept in most cases the current leadership of the province as the leading element in the Revolutionary Committee.

In early May, accordingly, Revolutionary Committees began to be formed in Szechuan at the local level, and a provincial Revolutionary Committee was proclaimed on May 31. Its chairman was Chang Kuo-hua; among its fifteen vice chairmen were Liang Hsing-ch'u, Liu Chieh-t'ing, and Chang Hsi-t'ing. The other vice chairmen were divided about equally between military men and former members of the party apparatus on the one hand, and members of "revolutionary" organizations on the other. In reality, it appeared that the creation of the Revolutionary Committee would do little to change the political situation in the province, beyond perhaps promoting a limited reduction in disorder. The strongest element was clearly the army, although it appeared to be neither totally united nor in complete control of the province. But barring unforeseen circumstances the central Maoist leadership was now bound to recognize the legitimacy of this power balance and to take the views of its holders into account when trying to work out arrangements, including a Ninth Party Congress, for a more stable political order to succeed the turbulence of the Cultural Revolution.

The situation in Kwangsi got out of hand just as Szechuan was beginning to take on at least the semblance of stability. Kwangsi is formally known as the Kwangsi Chuang Autonomous Region because the mountains in the western part of Kwangsi are inhabited by about 8 million Chuangs, out of a total population of some 23 million. The Chuangs are of Thai stock, relatively backward, and are the largest minority "nationality" in mainland China. To lend credibility to the official myth that the Chuangs enjoy autonomy, the most important or at least the most conspicuous personage in Kwangsi during the pre-Cultural Revolution period was a sinicized Chuang, Wei Kuo-ching. An alternate member of the party Central Committee, he also served as governor of Kwangsi, first secretary of the Kwangsi Party Committee, and political officer ("commissar") of the Kwangsi Military District.

As might be expected, Wei's relations with Red Guards and other "revolutionaries" in Kwangsi during the Cultural Revolution were bad. As might also be expected, the "revolutionaries" were drawn overwhelmingly from among the Han (ethnic Chinese) population of Kwangsi, rather than from among the Chuangs, who resented the turmoil engendered by the Cultural Revolution. There were two main "revolutionary" organizations, the Revolutionary Rebel Grand Army and the Kwangsi Alliance Command, each claiming to be far better Maoists than the other. Regardless of what may have been the real as distinct from the nominal issues between them, large-scale fighting began in the spring of 1968. Some military units were attacked and weapons seized from them. The fighting was especially serious at Wuchow, on the eastern edge of the province near the border with Kwangtung, in April and May. By the second half of June, dozens of corpses, mainly those of young people of both sexes who had been tied up before being killed, were floating down the West River past Canton to Hong Kong and Macao. From the standpoint of the central Maoist leadership in Peking, it was perhaps even more serious that there was widespread disorder elsewhere in Kwangsi as well, including interruption of train service along the main rail line leading to North Vietnam and some actual seizures of equipment—whether of Chinese or Soviet origin, or both, is not clear—bound for Hanoi.[17]

On June 13, accordingly, an urgent telegram dealing with this situation was despatched to the political and military authorities in Kwangsi by the four agencies that in a formal sense compose what is called here the "central Maoist leadership": the party Central Committee (of which Mao Tse-tung is the chairman and Lin Piao the sole vice chairman), the State Council (or cabinet, headed by Premier Chou En-lai), the Military Affairs Commission of the party Central Committee (chaired by Lin Piao), and the Central Committee's Cultural Revolution Group (chaired by Mao's favorite propagandist Chen Po-ta but with K'ang Sheng and Chiang Ching as its most active and important members). The telegram insisted that the existence of a war in Vietnam made it imperative to restore order in Kwangsi. The measures demanded were obvious and included the cessation of fighting, the return of all seized military equipment and of all supplies destined for Vietnam, and the resumption of normal employment and assign-

[17] Based mainly on *The New York Times,* July 14, 1968; *The Washington Post,* August 7, 1968.

ments. On June 19 Chou En-lai followed this telegram with a telephone call demanding the full restoration of service on the main rail line by June 22.[18] These directives were evidently not very fully observed by the "rebels," and on July 3 the central Maoist leadership despatched another directive, this one personally endorsed by Mao Tse-tung, to the same effect.[19] It seems likely that one, although by no means the only, reason for the difficulty in restoring order was that Kwangsi as yet had no Revolutionary Committee and this deficiency was in turn due in part to the fact that Peking had not yet decided whether it could accept Wei Kuo-ching, whose relations with both the "rebels" and some sections of the local military establishment were bad, as the head of a Revolutionary Committee for Kwangsi.

The disorder and the delay in forming a Revolutionary Committee were bad enough for domestic politics, or in other words for the desire of the central Maoist leadership to see Revolutionary Committees, wearing resoundingly Maoist labels even though the reality in most cases was very different, in all provinces as soon as possible, so that the convening of a Ninth Party Congress and the stabilization of a new political order, whose exact shape to be sure had apparently not been agreed on, could take place. In addition, considerations relating to foreign policy seem to have lent great urgency in the eyes of the central Maoist leadership to restoring political stability, essentially because the lack of it had greatly diminished China's effectiveness on the international scene when such effectiveness seemed to be growing more and more desirable. The relationship between the war in Vietnam and events in Kwangsi has already been mentioned; other aspects of this problem are discussed below. On August 13, a Revolutionary Committee was proclaimed in Yunnan (the other province through which runs a railway leading to North Vietnam, although this line is less useful and important than the one through Kwangsi). On August 19, it was Fukien's turn. Kwangsi proclaimed its Revolutionary Committee on August 26, with the controversial Wei Kuo-ching as chairman.[20] The other two holdouts, Tibet and Sinkiang, followed on September 5. On September 7, Chou En-lai declared the entire country (barring Taiwan, which "remained to be liberated") "red."[21]

[18] Texts in American Consulate General, Hong Kong, *Survey of the China Mainland Press*, No. 4226 (July 26, 1968), pp. 1–3.

[19] Text in *Survey of the China Mainland Press*, No. 4232 (August 6, 1968), pp. 1–3.

[20] New China News Agency despatch, August 27, 1968.

[21] New China News Agency despatch, September 9, 1968.

CONCLUSIONS

Since 1965, more than at any time since 1949, domestic politics appear to have had priority in Peking over foreign policy, with damaging effects on the latter. Because of the greater urgency of domestic politics for all, it has proven more difficult for Mao Tse-tung to get his way in this field than in foreign policymaking. Indeed, even from his point of view the harm wrought by the Cultural Revolution has so far exceeded the gains that this colossal enterprise must be considered a failure.

One of the reasons for this conclusion has been the growing unhappiness of the powerful regional military commanders, even those close to Lin Piao in the past, not only over the turmoil created by the Cultural Revolution but over the growing influence of Lin himself in military affairs, notably after Lo Jui-ch'ing was replaced by Yang Ch'eng-wu as acting chief of staff in early 1966. For Lin was then in a position to dominate the entire central military apparatus of the regime as never before, to the possible detriment of the regional commanders, some of whom had been entrenched in their satrapies for years. It was apparently pressures from this direction that brought about the removal of Yang in March 1968 and his replacement by a regional military figure, Huang Yung-sheng. Yang seems to have antagonized Chiang Ching and her fellow militants at an earlier date, but he could survive their enmity, whereas he could not survive that of the regional military.

An important, related trend working in the same direction has been the ability of Chou En-lai to remain indispensable to nearly all, as he has for more than forty years, and to resist the considerable pressures brought to bear against him from time to time by Chiang Ching and her supporters. Presumably he has done this by maintaining somehow at least workable relations with Mao, Lin Piao, and the regional military.

By about the middle of 1968, it appears, Mao had become reluctantly convinced by events (mainly continuing disorder) and by various pressures on him that it was important to bring the Cultural Revolution to an end, in theory of course in an atmosphere of brilliant victory. This step would require proclaiming Revolutionary Committees in all the remaining provinces, as a prelude to such further measures of consolidation as calling a Ninth Party Congress. Estab lishing Revolutionary Committees in those provinces where they had not yet been set up would require in practice the acceptance by Mao of the predominantly military control in those provinces, combined with a minimal role for representatives of "revolutionary" organizations in the Revolutionary Committees. Parallel with Mao's growing acceptance of this proposition was a new, somewhat informal, top leadership body consisting of 14 (sometimes 15) persons and including not only the top party figures, Chiang Ching among them, but a generous sprinkling of men connected with the armed forces and the public security apparatus, or what remained of it. Even while Lin Piao's influence over the armed forces was being challenged, the role of the army in policymaking, including foreign policy, seemed to be on the increase. By July it appeared that Chiang Ching was being shunted into a mainly cultural role, from which she could do little to protect the interests of her Red Guards. In July and August, under the cover of exhortations from Mao and other high leaders to accept the leadership of the working class, Red Guard units began to be severely repressed and disbanded by local military units. It was in this atmosphere that the last of the Revolutionary Committees were formed, culminating with Tibet and Sinkiang on September 5.

There can be no doubt that the Cultural Revolution, and in particular such developments as domestic disorder (notably the disruption of service on the railway leading through Kwangsi to North Vietnam), the heavy involvement of the army in political activity, and the slowing of the nuclear weapons program, harmed both China's image and its actual influence in foreign affairs. The year 1968 saw a number of important foreign developments of great interest to the Chinese leadership, which it was in a very poor position to influence. The main examples are the seizure of the U.S.S. *Pueblo* and the ensuing ension in Korea, the beginning of talks on Vietnam in Paris in April, and the Soviet invasion of Czechoslovakia and the resulting crisis in Eastern Europe. About the last of these developments, the Chinese eadership may well have reflected bitterly on the superior ability of he Soviet Union, as compared with China, to maintain political conrol at home and assert itself abroad under the cover of an effective uclear deterrent. It seems likely that in Peking a sense of virtual elplessness abroad contributed to the decision to reassert order and ontrol at home, as an essential step toward a more effective role on ie international stage.

It is too early to say whether a stabilization of the political situation in China, assuming that it in fact occurs, will bring the Chinese leadership anything like the increase of influence abroad that it would almost certainly like. It does seem possible, however, to sketch the outlines of Peking's main recent and current interests abroad.

The apparent trend toward a thinning out of the American military presence in Asia, notably in Vietnam, seems to arouse mixed feelings in Peking. On the one hand, the trend superficially enhances the security, and potentially the influence, of China itself and of other anti-American regimes in Asia. On the other hand, the trend is also associated with negotiations of some kind on Vietnam, which to the Maoists at least are intrinsically unacceptable. Furthermore, it would be logical for a reduction of the local American military presence to be accompanied by increased strategic watchfulness for real or apparent Chinese efforts to take advantage of the reduction. Peking can hardly have forgotten the events of 1950, when the United States first proclaimed its intention not to defend any area on the Asian mainland against hostile attack, only to change its stand abruptly a few months later when South Korea was invaded. The Chinese leadership is probably concerned over the American decision, announced in September 1967, to build a "thin," or at least nominally anti-Chinese, anti-ballistic missile defense (ABM). Peking may be afraid that the United States is putting itself in a better position to launch a nuclear first strike, either aggressively or by way of retaliation for some real or fancied offense on China's part. Certainly the Chinese have talked far less than before about their own nuclear weapons program since the summer of 1967, and the cause may well be a fear of further stirring up the United States as well as the evident slowing of the program by the effects of the Cultural Revolution. From a political point of view, the only politico-military initiative on China's part that would make much sense would be a probe in the Taiwan Strait, which if successful might create a favorable backdrop for domestic political developments and bring the "liberation" of Taiwan closer; from the military point of view, however, such a move would be risky in the extreme.

As for Vietnam, it appears that Peking has been apprehensive of some breakthrough toward a political settlement as a result of the American presidential campaign and the Soviet invasion of Czechoslovakia. Since their first major public statement on the latter sub ject from Peking, a speech by Chou En-lai on August 23, 1968, the Chinese have been alleging that the Soviet Union has recognized an American sphere of influence in the Middle East and Southeast Asia in exchange for American recognition of a Soviet sphere in Eastern Europe. Although these charges are obviously aimed at currying favor with the Arab states and North Vietnam, in whose eyes China's standing has declined, there is no doubt that China feels profoundly distrustful of the ambivalent Soviet role in the Vietnamese crisis. Current trends in North Vietnamese politico-military strategy, combined with the apparent ascendancy of the supposedly pro-Chinese Truong Chinh, suggest that the Maoist idea of "protracted war" on an essentially guerrilla and "self-reliant" basis, rather than the quasi-conventional warfare with sizable Soviet aid that has been tried since 1965, is exerting increasing influence in Hanoi, even as it shows increasing interest in negotiations. On the other hand, acceptance by Hanoi of an essentially Chinese strategy, at least in military matters, does not mean acceptance of Chinese influence, let alone control. Chinese options in the Vietnamese crisis are obvious, but limited in number, attractiveness, and probable effectiveness: more arms for Hanoi, intrigue with the National Liberation Front to split it from Hanoi and encourage it to carry on the struggle, disengagement, or direct intervention.

The Soviet invasion of Czechoslovakia (August 20, 1968) aroused fears in Peking of similar action against Rumania, Yugoslavia, and Albania, with all of whom China was on more or less good terms. Worse still, a series of Soviet statements appearing to justify military intervention in another "socialist" country whenever "socialism" was judged in Moscow to be in danger may well have created an apprehension that, once it had tidied up its affairs in Eastern Europe, the Soviet Union might turn toward China, before the latter's nuclear stockpile became threateningly large, and put military pressure on it, whether amounting to actual invasion or not, so as to influence its domestic and foreign policies and if possible the composition of its political leadership.

The most immediate problem was Rumania; Chou En-lai publicly promised it "support" in case of a Soviet invasion, on August 23. By this time Albania had already denounced the Soviet invasion of Czechoslovakia in the strongest language and set in motion steps for its withdrawal from the Warsaw Pact, which was formally announced on September 12. The timing of this step suggested that the Albanians regarded the nominal stabilization of the Chinese political scene, in the form of the proclamation of the last of the Revolutionary Committees, as an important step in their favor. On September 16, China sent a diplomatic note to the Soviet Union accusing the latter of having conducted flights over China's border regions between August 9 and 29. Assuming this charge to have had some validity, it is possible that these flights, which began about the time that the Soviet Union initiated the final "maneuvers" that escalated into the invasion of Czechoslovakia, may have been aimed at seeing whether the Chinese seemed to be contemplating any military pressures on the Soviet frontier or Outer Mongolia at that time. For steps of that kind, perhaps more than sending aid to Eastern European countries, would be the most obvious way in which China could help to take Soviet pressure off other areas.

In late September, for the first time since January-February 1967, an Albanian military delegation paid an official visit to China. It was given a thunderous reception, and Chou En-lai on September 30 pledged full support for Albania and again accused the Soviet Union of pressures on the Sino-Soviet border. On its way home in early October, the Albanian delegation spent several days in Sinkiang, rather than taking the more common route via Kunming and Rangoon. It seems likely that it was given a tour of, and briefings on, both the border region and the Chinese nuclear installations, the most sensitive of which are in Sinkiang. Presumably the delegation was informed rather precisely of what it could and could not expect of China, so as to avoid costly miscalculations. For example, in spite of the superficial attractiveness from the Chinese and Albanian viewpoints of the idea of Chinese nuclear missiles in Albania covering the Ukraine, the fact is that the Chinese MRBM program does not appear to be very advanced, the Suez Canal is closed, and all remember what happened when Khrushchev tried to find forward sites for some of his abundant MRBM's and IRBM's in Cuba, so as to acquire strategic leverage with which to press for a favorable German settlement. What China is able and willing to do for Albania, or for that matter any East European country threatened by the Soviet Union remains to be seen.

Much as the Vietnamese crisis of 1965 had contributed to Mao Tse-tung's decision to launch the Cultural Revolution, so the Czechoslovak crisis and its aftermath probably had a great deal to do with a strong leftist trend in domestic policy that set in during the autumn of 1968 and was sanctioned by the Twelfth Plenary Session of the party Central Committee in October. Partly at least with the aim of preparing the country to fight a Maoist "people's war" if necessary, millions of people were moved from the cities to the countryside, and policies resembling those of the Great Leap Forward, such as a trend toward artificial equalization of peasant incomes, were introduced in the rural areas.

With the virtual suppression of the Red Guards by the army in the late summer of 1968, the balance of power within the central Maoist leadership appears to have shifted against the extremists like Chiang Ching and in favor of the moderates, notably Chou En-lai. During the last few weeks of 1968 and the first few weeks of 1969, when Mao was evidently on winter vacation and perhaps ill as well, policy tended to swing in a moderate direction, notably in the foreign field. When Mao resumed active charge of affairs in late January, however, there was another shift to the left, and an invitation to the United States to resume ambassadorial talks at Warsaw, which had been extended on November 25, was abruptly withdrawn on February 19.

Having used the army to dispose of the Red Guards and curb the influence of Chiang Ching, however, Chou En-lai seemed to be trying to manage Mao in such a way as to reduce the domestic political power of the army, which no longer appeared necessary or desirable now that the Red Guards were no longer a serious problem. A number of indications suggested such a maneuver on Chou's part, and perhaps the most plausible hypothesis that can be advanced to explain the Sino-Soviet border clashes along the Ussuri River in March 1969 is an effort to remind the army and the public that the army has other, more urgent tasks than running the country, at any rate above the provincial level.

The provincial military authorities were in a strong position, however, when the much postponed Ninth Party Congress met at last on April 1, 1969. Chou En-lai and his administrative group suffered an erosion of influence in the new Politburo and Central Committee that emerged from the Congress. From their point of view, however, some hope remains for a return to centralized administration and stable development in the form of a high proportion in the new leading party bodies of nationally and professionally oriented military men, who appear to have reservations about the deep involvement of their provincial colleagues in local administration. In fact, since neither Maoism nor a restored orthodox Leninist party apparatus appears likely or viable as organizing principles, China's future may lie along one of two lines: a modern version of warlordism, if provincial militarism prevails; or, if it does not, the centralized military-bureaucratic domination recently predicted by Milovan Djilas.

APPENDIX

Dramatis Personae

Chang Huo-hua. Formerly commander, Tibet Military Region. Chairman, Szechuan Revolutionary Committee since 1968.

Ch'en Po-ta. Party propagandist and close associate of Mao Tse-tung. Leading member of the Cultural Revolution Group.

Chen Yi. Foreign Minister since 1958. Close associate of Chou En-lai.

Chiang Ching. Mme. Mao Tse-tung.

Chou En-lai. Premier. Foreign Minister until 1958.

Chou Yang. Leading party specialist in relations with intellectuals until purged in 1966.

Chu Teh. An aged soldier. Member of the Standing Committee of the Politburo. Unpopular with Red Guards but not purged.

Ho Lung. A senior soldier purged about the end of 1966.

Huang Yung-sheng. Commander, Canton Military Region and chairman, Kwangtung Revolutionary Committee. Also Chief of Staff (since March 1969).

Li Ching-ch'üan. Formerly first secretary, Southwest Bureau of the party Central Committee. Purged in 1967.

Liang Hsing-ch'u. Commander, Chengtu Military Region since 1967.

Lin Piao. Defense Minister since 1959. Mao's chosen successor since 1965 or 1966.

Liu Shao-ch'i. Second ranking figure in the party and Mao's apparent successor until 1966, then purged.

Lo Jui-ch'ing. Minister of Public Security, 1949–59. Chief of Staff, 1959–66, then purged.

Lu Ting-yi. Party's leading propagandist until purged in 1966.

Mao Tse-tung. Chairman of the party Central Committee. Chairman of the Chinese People's Republic, 1949–59.

P'eng Chen. Politburo member and municipal boss of Peking until purged in 1966.

P'eng Te-huai. Defense Minister, 1954–59, then purged.
Teng Hsiao-p'ing. General Secretary of the party Central Committee, 1956–66, then purged.
Wei Kuo-ching. Party and government chief of Kwangsi Chuang Autonomous Region (formerly Kwangsi Province) and chairman of its Revolutionary Committee since 1968.
Wu Leng-hsi. Chief editor of the *People's Daily* until purged in 1966.
Yang Ch'eng-wu. Acting Chief of Staff, early 1966–March 1968, then purged.
Yang Shang-k'un. Director of the General Office of the party Central Committee until purged in 1966.

SELECTED BIBLIOGRAPHY

Since the emphasis in this study falls on Chinese foreign policy and its relationship to domestic policy, it may be helpful to mention a few general works on Chinese foreign policy. An excellent introduction, although it tends to overstress Chinese reactions to real or imagined American threats as a leitmotif, is David Mozingo, "The Maoist Imprint on China's Foreign Policy," in *China Briefing* (Chicago: Center for Policy Study, University of Chicago, 1968), pp. 23–51. A standard study, valuable although somewhat dated, is A. Doak Barnett, *Communist China and Asia; Challenge to American Policy* (New York: Harper, 1960). A detailed, more recent analysis is Harold C. Hinton, *Communist China in World Politics* (Boston: Houghton Mifflin, 1966). Probably the best study of the Sino-Soviet confrontation is Donald S. Zagoria's excellent *The Sino-Soviet Conflict, 1956–1961* (Princeton: Princeton University Press, 1962).

The main available original documents relating to the debate on policy and strategy in 1965 are: Lo Jui-ch'ing, "Commemorate the Victory over German Fascism! Carry the Struggle Against U.S. Imperialism through to the End! *Red Flag,* May 10, 1965 (also published as a booklet by the Foreign Languages Press, Peking); P'eng Chen, *Speech at the Aliarcham Academy of Social Sciences in Indonesia* (Foreign Languages Press, 1965); Lin Piao, *Long Live the Victory of People's War* (Foreign Languages Press, 1965); *Vice-Premier Chen Yi Answers Questions Put by Correspondents* (Foreign Language Press, 1965). Additional relevant documents and analysis may be found in William E. Griffith, *Sino-Soviet Relations, 1964–1965* (Cambridge, Mass.: Massachusetts Institute of Technology Press, 1967). Two valuable analyses of the debate are Uri Ra'anan, "Peking's Foreign Policy 'Debate,' 1965–1966," in Tang Tsou, ed., *China in Crisis,* Vol. 2, *China's Policies in Asia and America's Alternatives* (Chicago: University of Chicago Press, 1968), pp. 23–71; Ishwer C. Ojha, "China's Cautious American Policy," *Current History,* Vol. 53, No. 313 (September 1967), pp. 135–140, 175–176.

The domestic aspects of the material presented in this study are analyzed in American Consulate General, Hong Kong, "Collection of Materials Against

Ho Lung," *Current Background,* No. 859 (August 8, 1968); The Editor, "Stalemate in Szechuan," *Current Scene* (Hong Kong), Vol. VI, No. 11 (July 1, 1968); "Li Ching-ch'üan and His 'Independent Kingdom' in the South-West," *China Topics* (London), YB437, August 18, 1967; "Tibet and the Cultural Revolution," *China Topics,* YB502, August 30, 1968; "The February Coup," *China Topics,* YB426, May 11, 1967.

A good analysis of domestic political events in 1968 is presented in Richard Baum, "China: Year of the Mangoes," *Asian Survey,* Vol. IX, No. 1 (January 1969), pp. 1–17.

PART IV INDIA

The third great political system of Asia is the complex, federated Union of India, which has a rich history blending modern and traditional, British and Hindu institutions and is an amalgam of all the heterogeneous strains of an ancient and inventive people. On the surface and at the highest pinnacles of power the system seems to be easily recognizable as a close descendant of British traditions. Yet closer examination soon reveals that influences stemming from traditional Indian ways are felt at these top levels and even more at the lower level in state and district politics.

The building of India as a nation state was associated with the dual processes of modernization and evolution toward self-government. Thus when India achieved independence it was natural for her leaders to conceive of her goals in political development to be the continuing effort to establish a secular state and to diffuse more modern ways of life throughout the society. Yet it has become increasingly clear that old practices and beliefs are not entirely irrelevant to a new India and that traditional considerations can reinforce and give dynamic life to newer institutions.

Consequently, much of contemporary Indian public affairs no longer involves denying traditional ways and respecting only modern practices; rather there is now a conscious seeking of ways to link old and new, to make traditional forms functional for modern developments and to bring together on a common footing village life and national politics.

The first of our Indian case studies illustrates this basic problem, dealing with the attempt to codify and formalize for the whole nation some elementary principles of traditional Hindu culture. The very idea of codifying, and in this sense secularizing, elements of Hindu social life that had always been supported by religious sanctions violated the deepest feelings of traditionalist Indians who saw secular law as a product of foreign influences and social customs as the very core of Indian identity. On the other hand, those who champion a modernized India feel it essential to bring together customary practices and modern forms. The story of the Hindu Code Bill in fact describes this effort to put old practices into the framework supplied by modern legal institutions. More important, it is the story of modern social change in Asia, in which the initial effort to achieve modern forms inevitably brought radical changes in old ways. Once the Indian leaders sought to codify the rules of marriage, divorce, and inheritance they found that they could not resist the temptation to reform these ancient social norms according to modern standards.

In the second case study we see how an Indian village, still deeply identified with traditional India, was brought into the national system of politics. Introducing elections and revitalizing basic village institutions caused profound changes in an otherwise isolated rural community. The result was a new system of local government that made village leaders a part of a national system of politics. Thus, ending the parochialism of rural communities and building a broadly structured national system is the very essence of modernization and political development in India as well as in much of the rest of contemporary Asia.

GENE D. OVERSTREET

5 The Hindu Code Bill

The transfer of power from British to Indian authority may of course be understood as a specific act: the formal establishment of Indian independence in August, 1947. It may also be understood as a process: the gradual evolution of effective self-government. This process neither began nor ended with the formal transfer of sovereignty; it encompassed the preparatory phase of step-by-step admission of Indians to governing institutions under British authority, the constituent phase of the drafting of new institutions by Indian authority, and the implementation phase wherein the Indian leadership initially employed the new forms and, in so doing, defined and revealed the locus of power and the operative conventions for its use.

As a case study for the analysis of this process the Hindu Code Bill seems eminently useful. The successive phases of formulation and consideration of the Code cover a large part of the transition period – a span of almost 20 years from the late 1930's to the mid-1950's. During this time the Code evoked intense interest and feeling, for it was surely one of the most important measures undertaken by the Indian national leadership. The process by which it became law should illuminate the nature of both the old and the new political systems in India, and in significant degree contribute to the definition of the new system.

ORIGIN OF THE CODE

In tracing the origins of the Hindu Code Bill it is necessary, first, to indicate and explain the fact that India did not have on the achievement of independence a civil code—a set of rules uniformly governing private relations among its citizens or within the Hindu community. Why had custom and usage not been codified earlier, or not, at any rate, since the great ancient codes?

It is a commonplace that Indian culture is, and for centuries has been, extremely heterogeneous. The more highly developed subcultures of India—the Bengali, Tamil, Punjabi, Maharashtrian, and so on—are as unalike as some of the cultures of Europe. Such a diversity of ethnic-linguistic groups has given rise to, and in turn been reinforced by, a diversity of subcastes (since subcaste boundaries are in general contiguous with ethnic boundaries). Furthermore, ethnic and caste differences are overlaid by religious differences, not only those among Hindus, Muslims, Zoroastrians, and Christians, but more to the point here, among sects within or closely related to the Hindu community—Sikhs, Jains, Buddhists, and reform groups such as the Brahmo Samaj and the Arya Samaj.

This quality of heterogeneity characterizes, specifically, Hindu customary law on private relations. Great differences prevail among the various ethnic groups, castes, and sects in the rules of marriage and divorce, succession and inheritance, adoption and guardianship. The best known example, perhaps, is the difference between a matriarchal basis of family organization, prevailing among the Nayars of the Malabar Coast, the Gonds in Assam, and certain hill tribes, and a patriarchal basis. Another very important difference is that between the Dayabhaga school of Hindu law, prevailing mainly in Bengal, and the Mitakshara school. On the devolution of jointly owned property, for example, the former school provides for inheritance of a deceased owner's share by his heirs, while the latter accords possession of that share to the surviving owner. Furthermore, within the major Mitakshara school there are a number of subschools, centering in Madras, Bombay, and certain other major cities. On the matter of the right of a woman to dispose of property, for example, there are significant differences between the Bombay and the Madras subschools.

Such has been the diversity of Hindu private law that the British long proclaimed the impossibility of effective codification. In an often quoted statement of about 1870 on the subject, Sir Henry Maine declared:

> The age of miracle is past, and I hardly expect to see a code of Hindu law which shall satisfy the trader and the agriculturist, the Punjabi and the Bengali, the Pandits of Benares and Rameswaram, of Amritsar and of Poona. But I can easily imagine a very beautiful and specious code, which should produce much more dissatisfaction and expense than the law as at present administered.[1]

Apart from the vast diversity in Hindu private law, a serious obstacle to its codification lay in the fact that the law was traditionally legitimized by religious values. The ancient laws of the Hindus had indeed been codified from time to time, as in the classic Code of Manu, but this was accomplished not by kings but by pundits, not by political authority but by religious authority. In the traditional system, the Brahman pundit was superior to the Kshatriya king; the religious leadership defined the law, which was regarded as divinely sanctioned and was executed by its divinely sanctioned agent in the palace. To put it another way, in the classical system there was a concept of natural law (*dharma*) eternally prescribing the order of man's relation to other men and to his environment; this law was revealed by the pundits and enforced by the king.

For the orthodox Hindu, then, it was unnatural for a government to define law, and it was unthinkable for an alien (that is, a non-Hindu) government to do so.

Confronting this situation, the British chose neither to import an alien law nor to codify Hindu law. As early as 1780, in the Declaratory Act, they pronounced a fundamental and fixed policy of applying the customary law prevailing among the various ethnic, caste, and religious groups of the subcontinent. They did, of course, undertake to abolish a few customary practices deemed inhumane; in connection with the status of women, for example, they sought to prohibit *suttee* (self-immolation of widows on the funeral pyres of their husbands) and to inhibit child marriage. But by and large they took the law as it was. British courts, employing Hindu pundits, gradually created a vast and complex accumulation of common law based upon the classical codes

[1] Quoted in *Report of the Hindu Law Committee, 1941* (Simla: Government of India Press, 1941), p. 12. On the background of the code see J. D. M. Derrett, *Hindu Law Past and Present* (Calcutta: A. Mukherjee and Co., 1957).

and observed custom. British judges seemed at times to delight in scholastic feats of application of the most obscure manuals of Hindu law.

By the 1930's it was generally acknowledged that Hindu private law had become, like a luxuriant jungle, virtually impenetrable. Moreover, there was complaint that it had become quite inflexible; custom was frozen and reform inhibited by the policy of an alien authority. In these years, and especially after the Government of India Act of 1935 which created a Central Legislature composed primarily of elected Indian representatives, the demand rose for the codification and reform of this dense and rigid system of private law. Indian legislators, products of modern British legal training, naturally were repelled by the backwardness of the law and as naturally sought a legal solution.

THE RAU COMMITTEE

The first result of this demand was a series of piecemeal bills aimed at simplifying and reforming private law in certain spheres, such as that of a Hindu woman's right to property (the Deshmukh Act of 1937). But the problem of coordination became increasingly acute. Accordingly, the Government of India by resolution of January 25, 1941, appointed a special committee to enquire into the problems arising in application of the Deshmukh Act and its relation to other pending bills; implicit was a charge to enquire into the question of codification.

The Hindu Law Committee (better known as the Rau Committee, after its chairman, Sir Benegal N. Rau) spent some five months ascertaining informed opinion and preparing its report. It sent a questionnaire to judges, lawyers, members of the legislatures, pundits, and to reform and women's organizations. It was especially scrupulous in welcoming the views of religious leaders; it expressed gratification that "two learned pundits have paid us the compliment of sending their answers in Sanskrit."

In a cautious and moderate report, the Committee concluded that "the time has now arrived to attempt a code of Hindu law" but that this should be accomplished not in one stroke but rather by a planned series of acts.[2] This would, it said, be "a reasonable compromise be-

[2] *Ibid., passim.*

tween piecemeal legislation and wholesale codification." It proposed step-by-step codification beginning with "the most urgent part" of private law, that dealing with succession, then the part on marriage, and so on.

The Committee affirmed the need for reform as well as codification of the law, pointing in particular to injustices in the status of Indian women. For illustration it described certain kinds of inequities occurring in some or all of the schools of Hindu law: a girl married in adolescence without her consent to a feeble-minded boy may be unable later to escape from such an arranged marriage, in the absence of provision for divorce; a widow thrown out of her home by her father-in-law may be unable to claim an inheritance or even maintenance, in the absence of property rights; a village girl married in the traditional arranged manner may later be rejected by her husband on his acquiring a more modern outlook and a second, more educated wife, in the absence of a prohibition against bigamy.[3]

Yet the Committee disclaimed any revolutionary intent to depart from the ancient Hindu tradition. The principle of equality could be implemented simply by a "judicious selection and combination of the best elements" of the classical system of law, it said; that system was a "spacious structure" and contained the basis for a progressive code.

On the approval of its report, the Committee furnished to the government two draft bills: the Intestate Succession Bill and the Marriage Bill. These were considered in the houses of the Central Legislature in 1942 and 1943, but at length both houses recommended that their passage be postponed until the entire code could be formulated. For this task, the government in 1944 revived the Rau Committee with virtually the same membership.

THE CODE AND THE RESPONSE

The Committee within a year published a draft Code, incorporating the earlier bills, including some provisions of the Deshmukh Act, and adding sections on divorce, maintenance, guardianship, and

[3] Anyone who has been in India will know how often it happens that a young couple, after moving to a city, grow estranged. The husband, through his work and the resulting associations, becomes dissatisfied with his more traditionally oriented wife. She frequently does not know English, as does the husband, and so is isolated from his professional life and, more and more, from his social life.

adoption. Considered as a whole, it constituted a long step toward equality for the sexes and castes in India and, more generally, toward a contractual basis for social relations in place of inherited status. Considered in detail, it proposed many specific changes in personal relations in the Hindu community.

Following an introductory section on scope and definitions, the Code dealt first with succession and inheritance. It adopted the Dayabhaga system providing that on the death of a joint owner of property, whether inherited or self-acquired, his share should pass to the heir rather than the surviving joint owner. It abolished most aspects of discrimination against women: it provided that a widow should receive an equal share with sons and grandsons of a deceased husband's property, and that a daughter should receive half a son's share (while a son would receive half a daughter's share of a deceased mother's property). It further provided that women should have an absolute right in the use and disposal of property, both inherited and self-acquired, rather than a limited estate.

The other controversial section of the Code was that on marriage and divorce. Its main features were the prohibition of polygamy, the legalization of intercaste marriages, and provision for nullification and dissolution of marriage. For sacramental marriages, the Code provided a minimum age of 16 for the bride and prohibited union of persons having common ancestors seven generations or less removed in the male line or five in the female line. In the case of civil marriages, the Code declared that they could be contracted without the loss of membership in the Hindu community or a Hindu family, which had formerly been the penalty for such marriages. Annulment of marriages was permitted for specified causes—an illegal marriage (within prohibited degrees of relationship), polygamy, impotency, or the use of fraud or force. Divorce was permitted in case of insanity, leprosy, venereal disease, desertion, conversion to another religion, and having or being a concubine.

The draft Code was widely disseminated in the 12 major Indian languages, and then for several years the Rau Committee sought by various means to ascertain the public response to it. Not content as before with soliciting written comment from specific individuals and organizations, the Committee undertook a very extensive and strenuous tour to hear oral testimony of interested persons. In the course of almost two months, it visited nine cities and held hearings at which a total of 378 persons testified. The majority of the witnesses were spokesmen for associations, and more than 100 groups were thus represented. Except in Madras and Calcutta, where the response was especially intense, all persons requesting an opportunity to testify were accommodated. A large number of witnesses were specially invited, and the Committee went to the lengths of convening in the homes of witnesses who were ill, visiting institutions for ill and destitute women, and attending pundits' *parishads* (meetings). It even visited Natore Palace in Calcutta to hear the views of the Maharani and women in *purdah* (seclusion) there.

In its report the Committee acknowledged that there were public demonstrations against the Code in five of the cities visited, and friendly demonstrations in only two; anti-Code demonstrators on occasion besieged the automobiles of members of the Committee or entered their train compartments.[4]

In the testimony before the Committee, similarly, organized opposition to the Code exceeded organized support. Expressions of support came from a number of prominent liberal individuals and a few organizations representing women and social workers; the main group represented was the All-India Women's Conference, which sponsored a program of meetings and publications in favor of the Code. But a wider array of interests demonstrated opposition to the Code. There was clearly strong opposition from propertied interests; organizations such as the Bombay Provincial Landowners Association, the Ghee Merchants Association of Calcutta, and the Marwari Chamber of Commerce attacked the Code in general and its provisions on inheritance in particular. Orthodox organizations were also strongly represented; religious groups such as the Hindu Panchayat and the Hindu Women's Association joined orthodox political parties such as the Hindu Mahasabha against the Code. Minority religious groups representing Buddhists and Sikhs also expressed opposition. The orthodox interest in the matter led to the formation of ad hoc groups, most notably the Hindu Code Deliberation Committee and the All-India Anti-Hindu Code Committee. The latter, in particular, conducted an extensive program of public agitation against the Code; through an apparatus of local chapters it organized a considerable number of public meetings.

In addition to the testimony of representatives of organized groups,

[4] *Report of the Hindu Law Committee, 1947* (Delhi: Manager of Publications, 1947), *passim*. The draft Code is on pp. 51–82.

there was opposition to the Code from prominent and influential persons—pundits, professors, judges, editors, and members of the princely aristocracy. It should be noted, finally that while the record of testimony does not permit a precise measure, a large part of the legal profession was against the Code; many lawyers and also state and local bar associations expressed opposition.

From an account of the organized activity prompted by the Code it is evident that it was an urban phenomenon, confined largely to the literate, activist elite of the country. There is, in the entire history of the Code, no evidence that information or concern about it penetrated into the villages of India to a significant extent.

Without attempting to tabulate the number of persons represented, for and against the Code, in testimony and demonstrations, the majority in the Committee came to the conclusion that "taking quality into account, the opinion which favours codification decidedly outweighs that which is opposed to it." It asserted that the bulk of educated Indian women approve of the Code; women expressing opposition "seemed to us to be merely reflecting the views of their menfolk." Further, the vast majority of Indian youth favor the Code, it said, and "this is a circumstance from which we have derived the utmost encouragement."

In the final analysis, the Committee said, the real question is not how many are for or against the Code, but "whether the proposals themselves are on the right lines and worthy of acceptance." It declared its confidence that the Code "will earn public approval."

One member of the Committee came to the contrary conclusion. Only a "microscopic minority" of those whose views were accessible to the Committee were in favor of codification, he said. As evidence, he presented in his minority report a lengthy summary of statements, written or oral, received by the Committee; it showed, for example, that on the question of legalizing divorce, 78 persons and groups were in favor and 103 against, and on the question of prohibiting bigamy, 75 were for and 99 against. It is clear, he said, that the "majority of Hindus" oppose codification in general and many provisions of the Code in particular. Accordingly, he himself believed that it was neither possible nor desirable to formulate a Code.

If to some the Code seemed a revolutionary measure, the Committee majority nevertheless portrayed it as a renaissance of the best in traditional Hindu society. The Code was formulated, it said, not by intruding alien or novel concepts, but simply by choosing and refurbishing the most progressive features from the various classic texts and schools of Hindu law. Yet it is clear that the Committee majority regarded its role, and the role of the Code it proposed, to be fundamentally an educative one.

Less than two months after the Committee Report, in the spring of 1947, the Hindu Code Bill was introduced in the Central Legislature. But here for the time being it languished, for the rush of events during this year profoundly altered the political environment and the institutional framework in India.

THE CODE IN THE CONSTITUENT ASSEMBLY

The transition to independence in India was accelerated sharply with the election of a Labour government in Britain in 1945; negotiations begun soon thereafter resulted in the formation of a Provisional government to preside over the transfer of sovereignty. A Constituent Assembly was created in July 1946, through elections by the provincial legislatures, and it convened in December to begin the work of constitution-making. In the meantime an Interim government, or executive, was also created; in the absence of cooperation between the Indian National Congress and the Muslim League, the cabinet was composed only of Congress representatives, headed by Nehru. With partition of the subcontinent into its Hindu and Muslim components, these bodies became the government of independent India; the Constituent Assembly assumed the additional function of interim Parliament, and the Interim government became the cabinet.

As the pending status of the Hindu Code Bill indicates, the Indian government did not begin with a clean slate; already on the agenda were measures of reform originating much earlier. It is evident, then, that the new government, acting in an institutional framework that required little modification, proceeded with a legislative program that was in large part already defined.

Other issues were of course of greater immediate concern to the new government, and the Code did not come up for legislative consideration until the spring of 1948. On April 9 it was referred to a Select Committee. In British parliamentary procedure, referral to a standing committee constitutes approval of the general principle of the bill, and some Indian legislators attributed this meaning to the action on the Code. But in the Constituent Assembly procedural conventions were still uncertain, and there was not unanimous agreement on the matter.

The Select Committee reported the bill, with some changes, four months later. The motion to consider the Committee's report, which would provide opportunity for discussion of the broad features of the bill, was presented on August 31.

By this stage in the consideration of the Code a crucial position had been assumed by the Chairman of the Select Committee and Law Minister, B. A. Ambedkar. His attitudes and style came to have great influence in the treatment of the bill. Well known earlier as the principal leader of the untouchable community in India, through his Scheduled Castes Federation, Ambedkar had waged a militant and dedicated campaign for profound social reform. Brought into the government by Nehru, he fell to the task of piloting the Hindu Code Bill through the legislature with a naturally intense commitment. He was uniquely fitted to represent in his person the powerful will for change among the underprivileged elements of Indian society. His subsequent behavior was likely to reflect the release and upsurge of this will after independence, and to express the expectation and demand that the freedom of India should be used to secure equality for the underprivileged groups.

But Ambedkar was also uniquely fitted to offend orthodox Hindus. Their opposition to the Hindu Code Bill was likely to be aggravated by the spectacle of an untouchable quarreling with the pundits and proposing to tamper with Hindu customary law. In any event, there was with independence a release and upsurge also of conservative sentiment, and an expectation and demand that the freedom of India should be used for the revival and affirmation of cherished traditional ideals.

The subsequent course of debate on the Code showed increasingly intense and bitter rivalry between what may roughly be called the modernists and the traditionalists. The bill became a major focus in the general and pervasive conflict between these two elemental forces in Indian politics. A notable feature in legislative debate on the bill from the outset was the fact that many of those members who spoke against it were members of the Congress party. While representatives of orthodox opposition parties also participated, the most telling opposition came from within the ruling party. The widening cleavage between modernists and traditionalists within the Congress became the primary fact of Indian politics.

THE CONGRESS DIVIDED

The contrasting persons of Nehru and Gandhi are a dramatic and revealing—though to some extent misleading—representation of the duality of Indian nationalist leadership. Nehru was avowedly secularist and rationalist, his ideology almost exclusively a product of the modern British milieu; Gandhi was profoundly though eclectically religious, and his ideology was a kind of Hindu populism. Yet Gandhi's ideas and behavior defy strict labels, and the traditionalist faction of the nationalist movement had other, more consistent, leaders and spokesmen in the persons of Vallabhbhai Patel, Pattabhi Sitaramayya, and Purushottamdas Tandon. Patel, in particular, was exceedingly powerful both in the party and in the government, in which he assumed the position of Home Minister. Indeed, he might well have assumed the position of Prime Minister but for the decisive influence of Gandhi in support of Nehru—and this is an example of the bafflingly complex behavior of the Mahatma.

To outsiders, Nehru's ascendancy in the government seemed to signal the ascendancy of the modernist wing in the Congress party, and particularly so after the assassination of Gandhi early in 1948. But in fact the traditionalist wing was stronger than before. If Nehru was to dominate the government, Patel evidently determined to dominate the party. This was reflected in the election as President of the Congress of Sitaramayya in 1948 and of Tandon in 1950. In the latter event, particularly, the factional lines were clear-cut, for Patel supported Tandon and Nehru favored Acharya Kripalani. Nehru's position seemed further weakened thereafter with the defection from the party of Kripalani and a group of his followers, who formed the Kisan Mazdur Praja (KMP) party in opposition to the Congress. On the other hand, the right-wing position was somewhat weakened in 1950 by the death of Patel. The right wing nevertheless intensified its attempt to control government and party policy; in the words of Michael Brecher, it was "in revolt" against Nehru.[5]

It is against this background that the legislative process on the

[5] Michael Brecher, *Nehru: A Political Biography* (London: Oxford University Press, 1959), p. 432.

Hindu Code Bill must be considered in the years 1949 to 1951. But one other factor influencing the process must be mentioned. This is the inexperience of the legislators and the heavy workload of a legislative body which undertook both to make a constitution and to make law. Apart from the fact that the government could not count on effective party discipline to assure the automatic passage of this official bill, it did not have clear priorities and timetables for its legislative program; nor did the legislature have a clearly defined set of procedures for its enactment. All of these factors contributed to the difficulties and delays encountered with the bill, although they do not fully explain them.

Second reading of the Hindu Code Bill was formally initiated, as has been noted, with Ambedkar's motion to consider the report of the Select Committee. Debate on the motion began in February, 1949, but it could proceed only sporadically; time was assigned for debate during four days in February, one in March, and two in April; the total was about 20 hours, during which 14 members spoke. The government finally moved to a conclusion of the debate in December, during which it used more than 30 hours with 33 members taking part. Passage of the motion was achieved on December 19. Closer examination of this phase of the legislative process on the bill may reveal some of the problems and procedures involved in its passage.

On the evening before resumption of debate on December 12, the Congress Parliamentary party held a closed meeting to discuss the disposition of the bill. Although it was well known to members that Nehru had declared at the beginning of this session that the government would "stand or fall" on the bill, some expressed continued opposition to it and urged postponement. To meet overt or covert opposition Nehru proposed, according to press accounts, that an informal representative committee be formed to iron out differences on the bill, after passage of the motion to consider but before the clause-by-clause consideration of the bill—the final stage of the crucial second reading.[6] Implicit in this was a willingness to contemplate further delay in an effort to accommodate all possible attitudes on the bill.

As debate opened, the presiding officer, the Deputy Speaker, ruled that there should be no time limit on speeches but urged a self-imposed limit of one-half hour. The public galleries overlooking the

[6] The following account is drawn from the *Hindustan Times* (New Delhi) and the *Hindu Weekly Review* (Madras), supplemented by Parliamentary debates.

floor of the House were packed with spectators, and according to the press an "excited atmosphere" prevailed. Outside the House a demonstration had just been broken up by police; some 500 persons, including many women, had massed in opposition to the bill, and for some time an atmosphere of violence prevailed. The demonstrators interfered with traffic in the vicinity, molested MP's arriving for the sitting, damaged the car of Sheikh Abdullah as it arrived, and fought with police. The police made a charge on the crowd, wielding *lathis* (long heavy sticks tipped with metal). They detained about 40 of the demonstrators and arrested 12. Some of the demonstrators were injured, as were six policemen.

The first speaker to take the floor of the Assembly, Mukut Behari Lal Bhargava, declared in opposition to the bill that it was profoundly anti-Hindu and antidemocratic. The bill was pervaded with Muslim and Christian principles, he said, and would destroy such Hindu institutions as the joint family. It violated the right of the masses of the people, through customary law, to determine the rules of personal relations. Moreover, he said, the bill would have serious economic effects in promoting fragmentation of property, and it would also promote excessive litigation over property rights. In any event, he said, the House was incompetent to pass the bill, since it lacked a mandate or power to undertake such fundamental social reform; the bill should await consideration by the Parliament to be elected under the new constitution.

As debate wore on through the week, the majority of speakers supported the bill. A Harijan MP spoke in favor, observing proudly that the bill was another feather in Ambedkar's cap. Several women Members declared their support, as did several members of the Select Committee.

Other speeches opposing the bill included one by the Maharaja of Dharbanga. But the most important speech in opposition, and indeed in the week's debate, was that by the Congress President himself. Sitaramayya expressed very plainly his opposition to passage of the bill in its present form and by the present legislature. Urging postponement, he declared that the bill had been improperly formulated; the subject had not been adequately studied and the persons involved, such as Rau and Ambedkar, were incompetent for the task because they were steeped in alien Western values and out of tune with their society. The people themselves had not been consulted, since the bill was not an element of the Congress electoral program; they must be educated further for fuller understanding and consent on the matter. Demonstrations against the bill in New Delhi and elsewhere showed, he said, that the people were sullen and bitter toward the Congress, and passage of the bill would have serious repercussions in the future election for the new Parliament.

Sitaramayya concluded with a veiled threat of withdrawal of support to Nehru. He recounted a story about the German General Staff in World War I which in November, 1918, was called upon by the Kaiser to fight on but answered that he must immediately flee the country since the army refused to fight. Obviously addressing Nehru, Sitaramayya said, "Please reconsider your position."

As if to underline the refusal of the Congress conservatives to support Nehru on the bill, newspapers reported during the debates the public statements of a number of party leaders opposing immediate passage. One interesting report concerned the Delhi Provincial Congress Committee; it decided to educate the public on the bill, but in the meantime party members were instructed to go about the city and "educate the public about the need for employing non-violent methods to fight against the proposed measure, if they so desired."

CONCESSIONS AND DELAYS

Demonstrations, for the most part nonviolent, continued daily outside the House through the week of debate, and various other manifestations of feeling on the bill appeared. The president-elect of the conservative Hindu Mahasabha, N. B. Khare, declared the opposition of his organization to the bill; Hindu law is a sacred matter, he said, and no secular government can interfere in it. A deputation of leading citizens of Delhi, led by Pandit Sharma, called upon the Prime Minister to urge postponement of the bill. A letter from the head of the Anti-Hindu Code Bill Committee, Swami Karpatri, stated that since the present legislature was a caretaker agency it could not act on such vital matters; its doing so would undermine confidence in constitutional means of redress, he said, and would prompt the public to take nonviolent direct action. A demonstration against the bill was reported in Amritsar, sponsored by Hindu and Sikh organizations and various orthodox women's groups.

If there was public support of the bill, it was at this time largely inarticulate. One manifestation of qualified support appeared, however, in a statement by the general secretary of the All-India Hindu Code Review Committee, Lakshmi Datta Dikshit. Opposition to the bill, he said, was confined to a small but well-organized sector of the public; in evidence he offered the results of a questionnaire he had sent to about 55 prominent persons in the fields of social work, religion, education, and politics. The majority, he reported, believed that the bill should be passed if appropriately amended; only ten were totally opposed, while only three supported the bill without qualification.[7] Among the majority Dikshit listed Sitaramayya, who of course demanded severe qualifications; thus the meaning of the poll struck many as rather ambiguous.

At the end of the week of debate on the bill, the Congress Parliamentary party held another meeting to consider disposition of the bill. According to press reports, it decided by a vote of 55 to 15 to pass the motion to consider the Select Committee's report on the following Monday. At the same time Nehru made a major concession to opposition within the party by assuring members that they would have full freedom to vote as they chose in the subsequent clause-by-clause examination of the bill. By thus relaxing party discipline he openly acknowledged that the bill was no longer literally a test of confidence in the government. He also reiterated, according to the press, that there would be an informal committee set up in the meantime to scrutinize the bill further and suggest improvements.

On Monday the public galleries were again packed and hundreds waited outside; it was estimated to be the largest group of spectators in the history of the legislature. Nehru arose in the House immediately after question time to speak on the motion. He now proposed not an informal committee but rather a process of consultation to accommodate opposition. Probably because of an objection, from the Law Minister among others, that another committee would simply repeat the work of the Select Committee, he now promised that the Law Minister would invite conferences with individuals known to desire modification of the bill. Nehru said he attached the greatest importance to passage of the bill and hoped that it could be accomplished during the next session. But he stressed his desire to proceed in a spirit of conciliation. While the government must offer leadership, he said, it should gain the approval of the great majority of the people on major legislation such as the bill.

[7] *Hindustan Times Weekly*, December 11, 1949.

Following Nehru's remarks, the Minister of Parliamentary Affairs and Chief Whip, Satyanarayan Sinha, moved closure. It was passed by voice vote with a few dissenting voices. Then the Law Minister rose to answer debate. He spoke surprisingly briefly and in an unusually pacific tone, emphasizing the degree of agreement achieved on the bill. He was frequently interrupted and heckled, but in general he maintained a remarkably conciliatory manner.

The opposition was not altogether pacified, however; a few MP's now made one more attempt to halt consideration of the bill. Two amendments were moved to the motion under debate: one to circulate the bill (delay debate and invite the expression of public opinion) and another to recommit the bill to the Select Committee. Both amendments were defeated by voice vote, and when division was demanded on the second amendment, it was shown to have only five supporters.

In the vote on the motion to consider the Committee report, a division was again demanded; voting against the motion were only 11 members. There was a considerable number of abstentions, but the motion carried. Among those voting for the motion was Sitaramayya. The accommodation made or promised by Nehru had succeeded in accomplishing one more step in the passage of the Hindu Code Bill. But the decisive step remained.

It may be speculated that Nehru had privately conceded to the opposition a further delay in passage of the bill. At any rate, he was soon forced to do so. The Hindu Code Bill was not included in the legislative agenda at the next session, nor in fact until September 1951 – more than 20 months after completion of the first phase of the second reading.

The delay had, evidently, at least one positive result – it persuaded some adherents of the bill of the need to organize more effectively. Acknowledging that they had heretofore been lethargic and had assumed that the bill would be passed without supporting pressure from organized opinion, some of them now set out to mobilize such pressure. All the evidence suggests that supporters continued to be on the whole less articulate than opponents of the bill, but there were a few manifestations of increased public activity in favor of the bill after 1950.

An interesting illustration is the activity of the Dharma Nirnaya Mandal, an organization in Poona which described itself as a group of "great savants" engaged in "social and religious reforms."[8] Led by T. K. Tope, Professor of Hindu Law of Bombay University, and by Pandit Raghunathsastri Kokaje, the Mandal undertook a program of systematic public agitation for the bill, utilizing to a rare degree in India methods customary in Western countries. It organized a speaking tour in the states of Bombay and Madhya Pradesh, in which 28 cities and towns were visited and up to seven public meetings held in each. In general it designed these meetings to reach particular elements of the population – women, lawyers, students, and local dignitaries. Pamphlets and brochures were widely distributed, and special attention was given to dissemination of sample resolutions to be adopted in support of the bill and forwarded to the government. In addition to these activities the Mandal sought interviews with newspaper editors not only to secure publicity but to inspire editorial support for the bill, and it also approached scholars and local notables to carry on its work in various centers.

In its report on its work the Mandal said that in all but the largest cities in the region it was the first and only organization working for the bill. Anti-Code Bill Conferences had been held often, and agitation against the bill had been conducted in such places as Hindu temples, with the result that the "meek masses have been fooled." Political party and social-work organizations even when sympathetic to the bill uniformly refused to endorse it officially; since the uneducated public was in general apathetic or resistant, local organizations were reluctant to commit themselves for fear of "loss of popularity." What was needed above all, said the Mandal – and what was most striking in its absence – was more active propagation of the bill by the Congress party.

Organized support for the bill came also from at least one other source – The All-India Women's Conference.[9] This organization seems, however, to have operated sporadically and without a real mass base. It later formed a special agency for work in favor of the bill, called the Fundamental Rights Organization, but its effects seem to have been restricted mainly to women MP's.

The pressure politics of these groups seem not to have influenced

[8] Trimbak Krishna Tope and Harihar Sitaram Ursekar, *Why Hindu Code?* (Lonavla, District Poona: Dharma Nirnaya Mandal, n.d.).

[9] Renuka Ray, "The Background of the Hindu Code Bill," *Pacific Affairs* (September 1952), pp. 268–278.

party or Parliament substantially, for when the bill once again came on the agenda opinion among MP's was "hardening against" it, according to press reports. This feeling could be attributed in large part to an unpropitious situation in the latter part of 1951.

CRISIS IN THE CONGRESS

Following the promulgation in 1950 of the new federal constitution defining a bicameral central legislature, it was determined that the first general election for the lower house, the Lok Sabha, would be held in the winter of 1951–1952. As that time approached, members of the Constituent Assembly became increasingly aware of their lame-duck status. Moreover, many of them wanted to take up electioneering work. Yet the pressure of legislative work, if anything, increased, with a backlog of measures such as the Hindu Code Bill on which action had been frequently postponed because of an overly full legislative calendar. While Members grew increasingly restive, the government was increasingly uncertain as to priorities in its legislative program in these waning days of the interim Parliament.

An even more serious obstacle to legislative action lay in the aggravation of the cleavage within the Congress party. By the fall of 1951 the division between modernists and traditionalists had taken more acute forms. The main factor contributing to the exacerbation of difficulties in the party was, probably, the rivalry between the two factions over the nomination of candidates in the forthcoming elections, which would determine the complexion of the party in Parliament thereafter. Certain pressing substantive issues were also involved. Apart from domestic reform measures in dispute there was, in particular, the Kashmir problem. The Hindu wing of the Congress tended to demand more militant action against Pakistan, whereas the modernist wing believed that the party and the government must be unchallengeably secular in order to claim the loyalties of the predominantly Muslim population of Kashmir. Between a theocratic and a secular orientation toward this crucial problem compromise was, if at all possible, at least exceedingly difficult. Whatever the reasons, by mid-August, 1951, there was reportedly an irreconcilable split between Nehru and the new conservative president for the Congress, Tandon.

Nehru then resorted to the ultimate sanction for the assertion of his personal power in the organization – the threat to retire. Because his popularity was considered indispensable to the party in the forthcoming elections, the threat was indeed a decisive weapon. As a token he did in fact resign from two of the central bodies of the party, the Working Committee and the Election Board. He thereby paralyzed the party and created a crisis of leadership.

During this crisis, the Congress Parliamentary party met with Nehru to plan the disposition of the Hindu Code Bill and other bills pending in the current session of the legislature. According to press reports Nehru resisted proposals for the postponement of the bill, and the party decided that clause-by-clause debate should begin on the following Monday and continue daily until passage of the bill was achieved.

On the same day Tandon resigned as president of the Congress party, stating that he could not honorably accede to Nehru's views and must therefore give way to another president. On the next day Nehru was elected to the post by the All-India Congress Committee. From a statement he made at the time, it appears that he accepted the position only when it became obvious that the traditionalist wing could not be made to accept any other candidate of his choosing.

Nehru had now established clear preeminence in both government and party. The question now arose, of course, whether he could and would use that power to push ahead on the Hindu Code Bill. His subsequent behavior would do much to illuminate the style and goals of his leadership.

THE ORTHODOX OPPOSITION PERSISTS

Early in the following week it was announced that, while the Code had to follow the Press Laws Bill in the Parliamentary agenda, it would be taken up immediately thereafter. Further, the Congress Parliamentary party would meet in daily session for clause-by-clause agreement on the bill. At the same time it was announced that the Law Minister had prepared 83 amendments to the bill, generally designed to moderate its effects and meet objections of opponents. Nehru thereby indicated a renewed willingness to accommodate opposition.

But again the opposition was not pacified; indeed, it seems to have been emboldened. The press reported rumors of an impending filibuster in the legislature. Members were said to feel that if the Code bill were given precedence over other pending bills the legislature would have little or no time for other business before adjourning for the elections. More important, the press reported rumors of opposition to the bill from another quarter which had hitherto not played a crucial part — the President of India, Rajendra Prasad. A member of the traditionalist wing, Prasad had before his election to the presidency made known his feeling against the bill; now he reportedly chose to bring it directly to bear. He wrote to Nehru, it was said, advising him to drop the bill and reminding him that the President possessed certain constitutional powers in the legislative process; he could advise Parliament on the consideration of a bill and by withholding his assent to an act could require that it be reconsidered and, to become law, repassed.

A vital constitutional point was of course involved — the relation between the President and the prime minister. The provisions of the new constitution were somewhat ambiguous on the matter, but in sum the President was in a subordinate position and could act only on the advice of the prime minister. Yet the nature of this relationship would be spelled out crucially in operation only through development of convention, to which Prasad's behavior at this point could contribute substantially.

When subsequently a Member raised in Parliament a question about the veracity of the rumor concerning the President's advice to Nehru, the question was disallowed on the ground that reference in Parliament to the President was prohibited. The matter was officially not acknowledged. Prasad himself at this very time left New Delhi for a two-week visit to Simla, as though conspicuously to remove himself from the scene.

Whether through pressure from the President or from other sources, Nehru evidently at this point conceded the inadvisability of pushing the bill through, even in modified form. Rumors now began to circulate that the government had made the further concession of altering the order of sections of the Code, so as to take up in Parliament the less controversial provisions on marriage and divorce, with the understanding that there would not be time for the prickly issues of inheritance and succession.

It is interesting to note that at almost the same time, Nehru said in a public speech in Lucknow that he was "fed up with the Prime Ministership" and was considering resigning from that position in order to work "outside and without responsibility." This may probably be taken as a poignant expression of weary disillusionment, rather than as a weapon to force further compliance from the legislature.

As Parliament again took up the Code on Monday, September 17, Nehru announced that it should complete the first two sections within a week, but he did not reveal his intentions for the rest of the bill. The opposition immediately attacked the bill with obvious intent to forestall consideration of even this much. In connection with the introductory clauses, dealing with such matters as scope and definitions, Members introduced crippling amendments such as a provision that the Code would apply only to those persons who subject themselves to it in writing within a specified time, or that it would apply only on the passage of a referendum in each state.

On this and the next day, debate was occasionally characterized by outbursts of personal hostility. After N. V. Gadgil had spoken in support of the Code he was challenged by an orthodox member with the words, "Why have you not thrown away your sacred thread?" — meaning that Gadgil had betrayed the values of a Brahman and should renounce that status.

Orthodox opposition was expressed outside the halls of Parliament in daily black-flag demonstrations, and it took, finally, the dramatic form of a fast. Having already sent telegrams to the Prime Minister and the President, on Monday Swami Satyananda Saraswati sat under a neem tree near Parliament House on a fast against the Code. On the second day of his fast he was removed by police car and taken miles away to a remote part of the city, and there released. He walked back to his place to resume his protest, and on the third day he was again removed by the police. Again he walked back, and on the fourth day the police placed him in Irwin Hospital to protect his failing health. Police often dealt similarly with demonstrators outside Parliament House, removing batches of them to the suburbs or detaining briefly the more active leaders.

During the week of debate there appeared suspicion of opposition to the Code from still another official quarter, raising another serious constitutional issue. A newspaper in the capital published a cartoon referring to the Hindu Code Bill which showed opponents of the bill in Parliament holding back the hands of a clock and the Deputy Speaker, who had presided over most of the debate, holding the pendulum. The cartoon was generally interpreted as a challenge to the impartiality of the presiding officer, one of the most important of the procedural conventions of the legislature. The Deputy Speaker himself replied in Parliament that whatever his views on the bill he had tried to conduct the debate justly. On the next day he announced receipt of an apology from the editor and cartoonist, who explained that their intention was to show the presiding officer not obstructing debate, but trying to keep it on schedule. The Deputy Speaker declared that he was satisfied, and he was moved to say further that he had not enforced a time limit on speeches in Parliament because it was not a part of his prerogative to do so.

Suspicion of partiality on the part of the Deputy Speaker was perhaps encouraged only a few days before this episode when newspapers reported new evidence of his religious orthodoxy. He recounted in a public speech that he had cured a small girl of cobra bite through some mystical power, called forth by chanting sacred prayers.

AMBEDKAR AND NEHRU

In the middle of the week of debate the government finally confirmed rumors that the bill would be divided into a series of bills and that the more controversial elements of the Code would be postponed. It declared that only the first 55 clauses of the Code, to be called the Marriage and Divorce Act, should be passed in this session of Parliament. To facilitate passage the Congress Parliamentary party continued to meet regularly, and by the end of the week it was reported to have agreed on nearly all of these clauses.

But by the end of the week Parliament had passed only three clauses. Attendance at sittings of the House had declined steadily and a mood of apathy and impatience to leave for electioneering was observed in many Members. Supporters of the Code, in and out of Parliament, showed increasing bitterness. A convention of women convened in Delhi by the All-India Women's Conference, as a last-minute effort to check collapse of the Code, criticized both the opposition attempt to kill it by filibuster and the government decision to take up first the section on marriage and divorce; the convention insisted on prime consideration to the succession and inheritance clauses, affecting women's property rights. It sent a deputation to the Prime Minister to protest the "vivisection" of the bill.

At least once in the course of steering the bill through debate the Law Minister, Ambedkar, engaged in a furious exchange with orthodox MP's, abandoning altogether a conciliatory manner and offending religious sensibilities. Declaring that Hindu society had long been in a process of deterioration and had shown itself incapable of absorbing the doctrine of equality, he charged that only statutory compulsion could force it to give up the enslavement of women and untouchables. He made sarcastic remarks about the Hindu epic, the *Ramayana,* which orthodox members took as an insult to the religion, and for which he then apologized.

By the weekend, it was reported that the government was resigned to abandonment of efforts to get any part of the Code through the present session. The agenda announced for the following week partially confirmed this, by placing the bill fifth in order after other seemingly less important matters. The cabinet was reported to have met on the subject and to have decided to secure passage of clause 4 of the bill and then turn to other legislative business. On the next Tuesday this was accomplished. For the time being the government made no official announcement on the disposition of the remainder of the Code, but its opponents were said to be jubilant at its apparent abandonment. Ambedkar was reported to have submitted his resignation to the Prime Minister, effective at the end of the session, on medical advice.

Not until the following week was the announcement made. Nehru declared that, while he believed the Code to be of pressing necessity for the progress of the country and would continue to support it "until the last breath of my life," it had to be given up for the time being because of the press of other legislative business. Abandonment of the bill was not a matter of political expediency, he said; he was not worried about losing or gaining votes in the forthcoming elections. He sought to make it "categorically, unequivocally clear" that it was mainly a matter of lack of time.

A week later Ambedkar made public his resignation and a statement explaining it.[10] He recited four reasons, the first three dealing with his disagreement on other matters of domestic and foreign policy; the fourth reason, and apparently the most important, was the treatment of the Hindu Code Bill. He said in effect that since the government had majority support in the legislature on this matter it could and should have passed the bill. It failed to do so, he charged, because the Prime Minister declined to give it first priority, to use party discipline to control votes, and to use the party whip to control debate. In fact, he said, the Prime Minister had allowed other more powerful members of the cabinet to push their bills ahead of Ambedkar's Code

[10] *Hindustan Times,* October 12, 1951, p. 7.

Bill, allowed Congress party MP's the freedom of vote on the bill, and allowed the Chief Whip to refuse to enforce a time limit on speeches and to refuse to move closure.

The Chief Whip was a special object of attack. He was, Ambedkar said, "the deadliest enemy of the Code." He did not move closure or issue the whip, and was, indeed, "systematically absent" when the bill was debated. "I have never seen a case of a Chief Whip so disloyal to the Prime Minister. . . ."

Ambedkar said he was forced to conclude that Nehru, "although sincere, had not the earnestness and determination required to get the Hindu Code Bill through." He had wished to resign earlier, he said, but had remained in the cabinet solely for the purpose of carrying the bill through; failing in that, and not for medical reasons, he submitted his resignation.

It is interesting to note that, apart from the reference to the Chief Whip, Ambedkar made no mention of opposition to the bill in official quarters. Ignoring the alleged opposition of the President and the Deputy Speaker, he placed responsibility squarely on the Prime Minister. As well he might be, since he had been a primary influence in the drafting of the constitution, Ambedkar was evidently concerned even in this moment of renunciation of responsibility to protect the fragile conventions of responsible government.

But Ambedkar and Nehru plainly had rather different concepts of responsible government. Ambedkar evidently felt, as had Sir Benegal N. Rau, that the government should immediately implement the majority will and, more than that, that because public opinion was largely inchoate the government should define the majority will and educate the people to accept it. Nehru, no doubt influenced by the pragmatic problems of holding the Congress party together, evidently recognized more clearly that his support in the legislature was still fragile and his support in the country was still shallow. Although he was no less a reformer or schoolmaster to the people, he took the more gradual course of consensus-building, seeking at the very least a larger and more willing majority.

THE FIRST GENERAL ELECTION

It was obvious that in the forthcoming election the Hindu Code Bill would be an outstanding issue. Indeed, in the debate in Parliament at least one MP had challenged Nehru to an electoral contest on that issue. The Prime Minister of course ignored this challenge. But another, which he could not ignore, came from his home constituency.

Nehru was the Congress candidate in Allahabad constituency (six townships of Allahabad district and one of neighboring Jaunpur district) for a seat in the Lok Sabha. In a most dramatic confrontation of personalities and programs, a group of orthodox leaders put forward as an independent candidate a holy man, a *sanyasin,* who had six years earlier taken a purificatory vow of lifetime silence. He uttered not a sound during his campaign; at public meetings he sat quietly while his managers spoke for him, dressed also in religious robes. Opposition to the Hindu Code Bill was a central aspect of the campaign. Nehru had planned not to campaign in his own behalf, assuming that his was a safe seat and that he could concentrate on campaigning on behalf of the party throughout the country. But such was the popularity of the holy man that the Prime Minister was forced to take up the challenge; he said he was willing to fight the election on the basis of that single issue. He was, however, subsequently forced to retreat somewhat; in his closing speeches he suggested moderation of the Code's effects. He won the election with a vote of 233,571; the *sanyasin* was second in a field of five with 56,718 votes.[11]

It might be added parenthetically that Ambedkar was defeated for election to the Lok Sabha. He had denounced the Congress party, and after defeat he dramatically denounced the Hindu community by attemping to lead his untouchable following in conversion to Buddhism. He died in 1956.

If in the period 1949 through 1952 Nehru's leadership was severely tested and finally affirmed, it was also evidently altered. While he had been earlier the leader of a wing of the Congress, he had increasingly become the leader of the whole Congress. In the process he had to become less an initiator and more an arbiter. Between zealots of the modernist and traditionalist elements of party and government he had to pursue a course which, if not at dead center, was at any rate a compromise.

DÉNOUEMENT: PASSAGE OF THE CODE

When the new Parliament met, the government proceeded with its effort to secure the codification of Hindu private law. In December

[11] *The New York Times,* November 25, 1951, p. 3; January 31, 1952, p. 2; February 14, 1952, p. 6.

the new Law Minister, C. C. Biswas, introduced into the upper house, the Rajya Sabha, the Hindu Marriage and Divorce Bill. As before, the government proceeded cautiously; the bill was considerably revised to meet opposition objections, and after its introduction the Law Minister moved a proposal to circulate the bill (that is, to elicit public opinion) for a period of more than two months. It will be recalled that such a proposal had earlier been rejected by the government when made by the opposition in an effort to delay the Code.

The motion was accepted, but not without heated debate on it and on the bill itself. In this debate there were signs of a rise of modernist sentiment, or at least of the articulateness of the modernist element of the legislature. A number of Members expressed a readiness to adopt the bill without delay, and on the bill itself they expressed the view that it was too much compromised by conservative influence and too weakly supported by the new Law Minister. Further, some members raised the more radical charge that the bill should be comprehensive in its scope, binding not only Hindus but all Indians. By being applied only to Hindu sects, they said, it partook of a communal and discriminatory character, and was contrary to the constitutional guarantee (Article 44) of a uniform civil code.

Supporters of the bill or of a more progressive version were joined at this point in the Code's evolution by another force – the Indian Communist party. During the earlier phases of the Code the Communists had been indifferent or contemptuous, in keeping with their rejection of liberal and indeed all parliamentary solutions to socio-economic problems. During the period from 1948 to the eve of the general election the party was engaged in violent attempts at revolution and its members were underground. But now, in accordance with its new strategy and tactics, the CPI's representatives in Parliament gave qualified support to reform legislation such as the bill; Bhupesh Gupta, a Bengali Communist leader and member of the CPI Central Committee, said in the Rajya Sabha that the party welcomed the bill despite its "halting" character, and would set in motion a campaign to popularize it.

The next step in the progress of the Marriage Bill was referral to a Select Committee of the Parliament. Similar motions for referral were passed in the Rajya Sabha and the Lok Sabha, and a Joint Committee of the two houses was convened on the bill. In the Committee's deliberations a modernist spirit apparently prevailed, for in its report it recommended certain liberalizing changes. It proposed, for example, to restore the provision for a minimum age of 16 for brides, which had been reduced to 15 in earlier revisions of the Code. Further, in a zealous application of the principle of equality of the sexes it proposed that men as well as women enjoy the right to alimony.

In December, 1954, the Rajya Sabha debated the report of the Joint Select Committee. Opposition focused on the question of the minimum age for marriage, and in response the Congress Parliamentary party decided to revert to the standard of 15 years of age. With this concession the conservative resistance to the bill was in large part dissipated. The weakness of the orthodox position is illustrated by the fact that in debate in the upper house the spokesman of the Hindu Mahasabha, N. C. Chatterji, borrowed the argument that the bill violated the constitutional guarantee of a uniform civil code. The Law Minister (now H. V. Pataskar) replied that the bill was a step toward a civil code, and that it was no more than would have been done by the ancient law-giver Manu himself if he had been alive.

Within the month the bill was passed in the Rajya Sabha, and in May, 1955, it was passed in the Lok Sabha. Congress party members were granted freedom in voting but requested to act according to the party's view in support of the bill; discipline was by and large maintained, and in the Lok Sabha the lone voice heard voting nay was that of the Mahasabha leader, V. G. Deshpande.

The other controversial installment in the Hindu Code, the Hindu Succession Bill, passed through a similar process in the new Parliament. Introduced first in the upper house and then the lower, it was somewhat liberalized in a Joint Select Committee; for example, the Committee recommended that illegitimate children enjoy a position of equality with legitimate offspring in regard to succession in cases in which the father is known. The government responded to opposition by agreeing to the removal of this provision, and the bill was then passed with near-unanimity, first in the Rajya Sabha in November, 1955, and then in the Lok Sabha in May, 1956. In the latter year Parliament also adopted the Hindu Minority and Guardianship Act and the Hindu Adoptions and Maintenance Act. The Hindu Code was law.

The explanation for the rapid decline in effective resistance to the Code seems to lie, essentially, in the mollification and division of the opposition. Its objections were partially satisfied through Nehru's willingness to compromise in successive versions of the Code. But perhaps more important, its ranks were fragmented through the simple tactic of regrouping the Code Bill into four distinct bills. This partially disrupted a coalition of diverse economic and social forces, which had theretofore been combined, although some of them were opposed only to some aspects of the Code.

It need hardly be said that implementation of the law among the villages of India would be a difficult and prolonged process. But having provided statutory enablements toward equality of sexes and castes, the government had at least declared its principles and goals and made a start toward them. By rendering out of a vast and diverse mass of custom and judicial interpretation a simple and uniform code for personal relations, it contributed to the aim of unification or "nationalization" of Indian society, the aim of rendering out of a vast array of diverse subcultures a single nation. By providing legal recourse for underprivileged elements, it contributed to the democratization of the society. And by rendering custom into a statutory code, it contributed to the aim of secularization, that is, of supplanting religious by secular authority in the society.

But its passage showed how profound was the resistance to these aims, and how slow the progress toward them would be under the prevailing leadership.

GENE D. OVERSTREET

6 Village Politics and Development

It would be idle to search for a "typical" Indian village, given the great variability in the details of local political, social, and economic life in the country. But it is necessary to look at the village scene in India, for it is surely among the main sources and the main objects of national politics, given the fact that most Indians are born and spend their whole lives in this setting. The village of Khalapur,[1] although it is not identical to all villages in all details, can serve to illustrate at least the general outlines of conditions and forces at this level of the Indian political system.

THE VILLAGE

Khalapur is located on the dry, flat plain of the state of Uttar Pradesh in northern India, not far from the Ganges and the Jumna Rivers and between the capital at New Delhi and the Himalayas at

[1] The name is fictitious but the village is real. It was studied by a resident interdisciplinary field team of American and Indian scholars in the period 1953 through 1956, under the general guidance of Morris E. Opler, Director of the Cornell University India Program. The following account of the village is based on the individual reports of certain members of the project. Since the present author was not a member of the project he can only provide a composite of these reports and is obviously deeply indebted to their authors. At the beginning of the following account the present tense is used for the sake of simplicity although the details refer to the time of the study.

the border. The village and the surrounding farmland cover about 6,000 acres, and the population is slightly over 5,000. A dirt road leads from the village to the closest town, Deoband, about six miles away. With a population of about 26,000, Deoband is the administrative headquarters for a cluster of villages and has a small government dispensary and a post and telegraph office; it is located on a railroad line running between New Delhi, 90 miles away, and Ambala. Somewhat closer to Khalapur is a major highway with bus service to New Delhi and to the district headquarters at Saharanpur, 36 miles away. In Saharanpur District as a whole, it may be noted, the population density is 634 per square mile, and about 75 per cent of the population is classified as rural.

In Khalapur itself the mode of life is wholly rural. The scene is predominantly one of mud huts, which house the great majority of the inhabitants. Apart from these huts and some houses of crude brick, there are only a few permanent buildings, chiefly a small branch post office, a community hall, three small primary schools, and a secondary school called the "Intercollege" that serves both Khalapur and neighboring villages. There are also a few shops selling basic commodities such as spices and cloth.

Only recently has there developed in the village a significant cash economy. With the construction several decades ago of additional irrigation facilities, which now serve most of the village land, many farmers took up the production of a cash crop, sugar cane, in place of the customary grains and legumes. Several miles away there are now two small mills for processing the cane, and these employ a few villagers, mainly as clerks.

With the exception of the handful of employed or self-employed persons (teachers, clerks, and shopkeepers), the people of Khalapur are integrated into the farmer-retainer groups which are characteristic in Indian village organization. Dominating the groups in Khalapur, generally, are farmers of the Rajput subcaste, who make up about 40 per cent of the population and hold 90 per cent of the land. Belonging to an especially proud and vigorous subcaste of the Kshatriya caste, the Rajputs of Khalapur are divided into 34 lineages, all claiming descent from a common ancestor who acquired the village four centuries ago. Subordinated to them in an hierarchical status system are other subcastes performing their traditional services. At the bottom of the hierarchy is the next largest subcaste in the village, the untouchable Chamars, who serve mainly as farm labor. Other "unclean" subcastes are the Jatiyas (leather-workers) and the Bhangis (sweepers). In an intermediate position are some 15 "clean" artisan and occupational subcastes.

A farmer (*jajman*) may typically have, in addition to laborers, about seven retainers (*lagdars*) serving his and other families — a carpenter, blacksmith, barber, water-carrier, potter, washerman, and sweeper. For their services these retainers receive either cash or a share of the harvest (usually one-eightieth to one-fortieth of the crop). A farmer and his retainers are bound together according to conventions of mutual but fundamentally unequal obligation, and each of these groups shows, in microcosm, the traditional configuration of economic, social, and political power in the village.

In a somewhat ambiguous position in Khalapur is the Brahman caste, constituting about 6 per cent of the population. Conventionally of the highest social rank, the Brahmans are indispensable for certain services; officiating at weddings, feasts, and the like, they lend legitimacy to a great variety of social acts and relations by religious sanction. Only a few of them in Khalapur own land, however, and they therefore fall into de facto dependence on the Rajputs. Furthermore, not all of them are fit or willing to perform their religious roles, and some tend to drift into other roles and an indeterminate social rank.

In Khalapur live also a small number of Muslims. They make up about 7 per cent of the population, and almost 100 of them are descended from Rajputs converted centuries earlier to Islam. Headed by this Rajput element, the Muslims are divided into strata in some ways resembling castes; each group follows an hereditary occupation and observes customary rules restricting intermarriage and eating together. Between the Muslims and the Hindus in Khalapur relations have normally been peaceable; the Hindu and Muslim Rajputs seem to regard caste bonds as stronger than religious differences.

But elementary social harmony has not uniformly prevailed between the Rajputs and other subcastes of the village. Indeed, the village until recently had a reputation as a lawless one; theft and murder were not uncommon, and itinerant peddlers dared not remain in the village overnight. The Rajputs are known as heavy drinkers and ready fighters, and they frequently have their way with their dependents by violence or by threats.

Further, among the Rajputs themselves there have been more or less continuous factional rivalries, sometimes developing into legal battles or even violent feuds. To some extent, Rajput factionalism is based on the division of the villages into boroughs (residential neighborhoods). These units, defined as separate subdivisions for some administrative purposes, came into being gradually under British rule, and they have developed a certain degree of internal unity. They are all of mixed caste composition and dominated by the Rajput lineages clustered within them. They are not of equal power; because of the concentration of a greater number of wealthy Rajput lineages in the two central boroughs, these two in coalition have had a crucial role in village affairs.

Kinship ties and factional alignments frequently cut across borough lines, but the borough has been a significant source of identification and loyalty in village life.

VILLAGE POLITICAL INSTITUTIONS. To resolve conflicts among families, castes, and boroughs and to deal with offenses against the community the people of Khalapur generally have recourse to the traditional system of informal village councils, or *panchayats.* Resting entirely upon customary law and social sanction, the panchayats have as their aim the restoration of harmony through consensus. Though the term "panchayat" means literally "council of five," the size and composition of these councils are quite variable, generally including the heads of families or at least the notables of the group concerned.

Retzlaff distinguishes four main types of informal panchayats in Khalapur.[2] Most important, probably, is the caste panchayat, an assembly of the notables of a given subcaste or caste to deal with an internal dispute. (In the case of disputes between persons of the same caste but different villages, a caste panchayat encompassing both villages would be convened.) Endeavoring to maintain caste unity and enforce caste rules, the panchayat may, as a supreme penalty, out-caste an offending member, in which case all other members are obliged to break off relations with him, requiring him usually to leave the village.

The second type of panchayat is the general meeting, or village, panchayat, an assembly of the leaders of all or at least the main castes to deal with a dispute affecting the village as a whole. Third is the

[2] Ralph H. Retzlaff, *Village Government in India: A Case Study* (New York: Asia Publishing House, 1962), pp. 16–26.

farmer-retainer panchayat, which may be called to deal with a dispute between retainers of a particular landowner. The farmer presides over such a panchayat, and it is one of the forms he may use to maintain effective control over his system of dependents. Such a panchayat may also be convened to settle disputes between two farmer-retainer systems. A final type of panchayat is the improvised single-purpose assembly, called in cases not obviously fitted to another type; this might include intra- or interborough conflicts not involving particular castes or the village as a whole.

According to Hitchcock's description of the operation of panchayats in Khalapur, a small number of village elders who have gained a reputation as impartial arbiters play decisive roles.[3] Known as good men for their honesty, perceptiveness, tact, and above all their relative freedom from factional biases, these leaders are respected and followed in the informal decision-making process in the village.

The procedure in a panchayat is aimed at agreement and reconciliation rather than simple decision. The notion of voting is alien to the tradition; if an assembly cannot reach consensus, it postpones decision to a more propitious time. To reach a judgment in a dispute, it frequently uses the device of requiring an oath of honesty or innocence from each of the contesting parties. So seriously does the community regard an oath before a panchayat that a villager would rarely take one falsely, no matter how much he may have lied before the case came to the panchayat.

But disputes may not be amendable to resolution in the informal village agencies, and instead require outside intervention and judgment. Although they assumed that castes and villages would endeavor through their panchayats to keep their houses in order, the British also provided a local system of judicial as well as executive agencies. At the beginning of the nineteenth century, shortly after acquisition of the territory including Khalapur, the British appointed through the District Collector a number of local agents in the village. These officials, at first eight and later sixteen, were chosen by an informal process of nomination by the leading land-owning families and were therefore in Khalapur invariably Rajputs; the post was held for life and was considered to be hereditary. These officials were responsible

[3] John T. Hitchcock, "The Rajputs of Khalapur: A Study of Kinship, Social Stratification, and Politics" (Ithaca: Cornell University, Ph.D. Thesis, 1956), Section III.

both for tax collection and for law and order; they were the sole intermediaries between the villagers and the British. Their official status and powers reinforced their socioeconomic power, as Rajputs, in the village, and of course the competition for the posts tended to exacerbate rivalries and hostilities among the Rajputs.

Partly in response to this, the British at the beginning of the twentieth century separated the executive and adjudicative functions by the creation of the new post of village judge. Two were appointed in Khalapur, and as in the case of the local officers they were selected through an informal process of nomination by the Rajputs.

More important, in 1921 the British turned to the use of traditional village models with the creation in Khalapur of a statutory village panchayat. Composed of six appointed members, of whom one was chairman, the panchayat was empowered to act as a judicial agency in assessing fines and other penalties for petty crimes and in settling civil disputes. It was also given the more novel and potentially more significant function of organizing constructive activity in the village, and it was empowered to use revenue derived from fines and from government grants for village development.

Until British rule ended in 1947, the members of the statutory panchayat, like the other village officials, were chosen mainly from among the dominant landowners, though there was occasionally a low-caste member. The British evidently reasoned that if the panchayat was to be an effective agency, it must obviously be manned chiefly by the holders of effective power. But equally obviously, if it was to be an agency of development, it must be manned by persons with an interest in change rather than the status quo. Among the Rajput oligarchs such an interest would seem unlikely.

The first chairman of the statutory panchayat of Khalapur was, however, a man with both the capacity and the will to accomplish reform. He had served as village judge since 1915, and as this fact indicates he was the head of one of the leading Rajput families of the village. Indeed, he was descended from a long line of local officers and had himself also served in that capacity. In family reputation and wealth he was eminently qualified for an ascribed role of leadership. Further, in his personal qualities he was fitted for the actual exercise of leadership; he was literate, shrewd, patient, sympathetic, and impartial.

The essential functions of village leadership, as Hitchcock summarizes them,[4] include first the ambassadorial function of representing the village in formal contacts with higher officials; this the chairman did very well, for he possessed the means and the manner needed to play the gracious host when an official visited the village and to command attention and respect when he visited officials in town. A second function is that of protector, and in the case of Khalapur this was especially important; the village because of its lawless reputation had a memory and a fear of police intervention, which was occasionally corrupt and brutal, and also of litigation, which was expensive and alien, and so it valued a leader who could keep the peace in the village and protect it from external interference. This, too, the chairman accomplished with rare success, dealing expeditiously with local disorders and sometimes showing a politic forebearance toward trouble-makers whose crimes (even including murder) he did not report to higher authority. A third, and related, function of village leadership is that of conciliator; the chairman was able to advise and negotiate settlement of disputes because he had, above all, a reputation for impartiality.

But to lead the village in development he needed also a motive, and this he had through his affiliation with the Arya Samaj, a religious reform movement against both orthodox Hinduism and Westernism. Deeply influenced by Arya Samaj principles in his youth, he adopted a relatively ascetic and "pure" form of life for himself and began to proselytize for religious and social reforms in the village. Apart from organizing religious meetings and bringing about the construction of a Hindu temple and a religious school for village children, in his official positions he sought to reduce drunkenness, hooliganism, prostitution, and the use of opium and even of the hookah. He also endeavored to improve the economic lot of the village, and especially of those without land, by such measures as the creation of a common grazing ground and the digging of additional wells and tanks, and to improve the lot of the lower castes through education. In the latter case, however, his aims and activities were very modest; he did not in general oppose traditional rules governing the caste system nor those governing the status of women.

Within these limits he accomplished much in his period of leader-

[4] John T. Hitchcock, "Leadership in a North Indian Village: Two Case Studies," in Richard L. Park and Irene Tinker, eds., *Leadership and Political Institutions in India* (Princeton, N.J.: Princeton University Press, 1959), pp. 400–402.

ship from 1915 through 1935. His influence was greatest within his own caste, but so was the opposition to him, and it was, ironically, a conspicuous failure within his caste — indeed, within his family — that brought about his downfall. A young man in his family was found to be keeping a prostitute in the village, and since custom prescribed that a leader must at a minimum be able to control his own family, the opponents of the chairman were able to use this incident to discredit him. He quit his positions and shortly thereafter died.

Under his leadership both the statutory and the informal panchayats had functioned far more effectively than after his retirement. He used the statutory panchayat as a complement to the traditional assemblies, seeking settlements through the informal panchayats and convening the formal body only when an appellate or coercive agency was needed. But under subsequent chairmen the statutory panchayat fell into disuse. Competition among Rajput families for panchayat offices, if only for their prestige value, seems to have intensified. Several subsequent chairmen were removed or not reappointed because of factional opposition among the Rajputs. It may be noted that one of them was removed on the pretext that he was pro-Congress, whereas in fact the national policy and activities of the Indian National Congress seem to have had no effect or relevance in village politics.

In sum, British reforms in village government had in Khalapur some beneficial results when they were employed by effective village leadership, but such leadership proved to be exceptional; and the main long-term effect was to consolidate Rajput domination of the village and at the same time exacerbate factions within that caste. The idea that the village members should work together in constructive activities for the common good found little response.

INSTITUTIONAL CHANGES AFTER INDEPENDENCE

Although Khalapur's experience with the statutory panchayat was a common one, the Indian National Congress maintained its confidence in the viability of this form as an agency of local government and development. Although not many in the leadership shared Gandhi's idealized image of the village as an harmonious and self-sufficient pastoral commune, the Congress ideology rested firmly on a belief in the capacity of the panchayat to realize the supposedly corporate nature of the village and to express the supposedly progressive will of the villagers.

In the constitution of India of 1950, the government was enjoined in the Directive Principles to "organize village panchayats and endow them with such powers and authority as may be necessary to enable them to function as units of self-government." It was left to the states to implement this directive, and indeed one of the first accomplishments of the legislature of Uttar Pradesh after independence had been the passage of the U.P. Panchayat Raj (rule) Act of 1947. Under this law a village community constituted a corporate body to which was granted the power to own and dispose of property and to levy taxes. Each village was to elect a *gaon panchayat,* or administrative council, of from 30 to 52 members, and also a *pradhan,* or president, as chief administrative officer and chairman of the gaon panchayat. A village would elect, further, representatives to an *adalat panchayat,* or judicial council, serving a group of from three to five villages in the area. Elections had to be held every five years, with full adult suffrage.

The gaon panchayat was clearly conceived as an agency of development. Among its obligatory functions were the management of village property such as buildings and land, the improvement of public services such as village lighting, streets, water supply, sanitation, schools, medical service, and fire protection, and in general "assisting the development of agriculture, commerce, and industry."

The powers of the village and its new statutory panchayat were significantly expanded several years later, with the passage by the state legislature of land-reform legislation. According to the U.P. Zamindari Abolition and Land Reforms Act (1950), each village as a corporate body was empowered to take possession and dispose of all uncultivated land, forests, orchards, fisheries, and so forth, not included in private holdings in the village territory. For the administration of this property the gaon panchayat was to select a Land Management Committee, which was to include all members of the panchayat and be chaired by the pradhan.

The village panchayat acquired still another function relating to the land in 1953, with the U.P. Consolidation of Holdings Act, which provided that the Land Management Committee (in effect, the panchayat) should constitute also a Land Consolidation Committee to furnish information and counsel to government officials implementing the provisions of the act for the transfer and consolidation of farm plots in the village.

As Retzlaff points out,[5] the powers and responsibilities of the new gaon panchayat with respect to land involved it officially and directly in the most intensely controversial aspect of village affairs. That the Congress leadership expected, despite past experience with statutory panchayats, to revitalize and also democratize this institution of village government, and at the same time to require it to cope with the most serious source of village disputes, is a mark of the confidence that leadership had in the institution and in the people who manned it.

THE FIRST VILLAGE ELECTION IN KHALAPUR

Information about the new panchayats and the forthcoming election reached the village in 1949 in rudimentary form from a variety of higher officials, both administrative and legislative. Communication was a somewhat inhibiting factor, as it is in general in relations between Khalapur and higher levels of the political system. According to estimates by Gumperz,[6] about one-half of the adults over 25 years of age in the village are illiterate in Hindi, the language of the region, and most of the rest are semiliterate, able to read only simple texts and those with difficulty. Moreover, because of the differences between literary and vernacular Hindi and between these and the village dialect, villagers frequently have little comprehension of communication, either written or oral, from outside. In the Hindi region of India, village people residing only about 100 miles apart have difficulty understanding one another, especially if they are in the more isolated social groups, such as women and the lower castes, in which the local dialects are relatively unaffected by contact with standard Hindi.

There are five or six radios in Khalapur, but villagers rarely listen to the news or other programs in Hindi; they say that the language is too difficult. They would similarly find it hard to understand

[5] Ralph H. Retzlaff, *op. cit.*, pp. 51–54. In the various reports on Khalapur, including Retzlaff's, consideration of the election and operation of the *adalat* (judicial) panchayat is omitted, and so it is omitted here.

[6] John J. Gumperz, "Language Problems in the Rural Development of North India," *Journal of Asian Studies* (February, 1957), pp. 251–260.

officials from the state or district centers explaining to them the statutory panchayat and the forthcoming village election. On this subject the most effective means of communication to Khalapur probably was a speech given in the village by its representative in the state legislative assembly, who was familiar with the peculiarities of the local dialect.

It may be added parenthetically that although literacy and comprehension in English are far more restricted than in Hindi, officials at higher levels of government persist in using English in some direct communications to Khalapur. Gumperz points out that even after 1947 the courts occasionally issued judgments affecting parties in Khalapur only in English, and on at least one occasion issued an order, which naturally went disregarded, to the panchayat in English. Where the road from Khalapur to Deoband crosses the railroad tracks there are warning signs only in English.

But despite the difficulties of communication and the novelty of some aspects of the new system of village government, a variety of village leaders soon understood its implications in general terms. Confronted for the first time with a universal-suffrage election, the Rajput oligarchy came to feel acutely its minority status and its factional disunity; and the non-Rajput components of Khalapur began to sense their potential power in the new system and to draw together to assert it.

The Rajputs began in caste panchayat meetings to seek agreement on a candidate for pradhan, or mayor, for it was on this relatively simple element of the new system that attention was fixed from the beginning. They soon recognized that they should have to seek allies outside the caste, for a non-Rajput party, which was to call itself the *mazdur* (labor) party, began to form a united front against them. Joining this front were leaders not only of the lower castes, including untouchables, but also of the Brahmans and even of a few Rajput families. These leaders were considering as candidates for pradhan a Brahman and a merchant.

The Rajputs decided on the tactic of alliance with the Brahmans. Given the village social order this was a natural and (although still a minority) probably an unbeatable alliance. It would be indeed surprising if the lower castes defied a combination of religious and economic power in the village.

To enlist the support of the Brahmans the Rajputs evidently concluded that they must nominate a Brahman candidate. They considered four and eventually chose one who, according to one commentator, "had heretofore been virtually inactive in village politics, and possessed few discernible characteristics of leadership."[7] On the day before the election he agreed to run, and since the other Brahmans in the village would have to vote for him for the sake of caste unity the coalition was sealed and the lower-caste party gave up on nominating an opposition candidate.

According to another account,[8] this process of selecting a candidate for pradhan was supplemented by a series of village panchayat meetings, and it involved in essence a compromise between the Rajput oligarchy and the lower castes. Once the lines were drawn, a Brahman was the only candidate acceptable to both these elements of the village. But later events showed that the compromise was at best tenuous and temporary.

There was no significant advance planning in Khalapur for the selection of candidates for the new statutory panchayat. The process had to be improvised on election day. When agents of the Panchayat Raj Department of the state government arrived in the village to conduct the elections, they called a general village meeting. After explaining the law they allotted seats on the panchayat according to borough and caste, and they asked the leaders of the main castes of each borough to nominate on the spot an appropriate number of candidates. The agents explicitly required that the composition of the panchayat should correspond closely to the borough and caste distribution of the village. When the list was complete, a show of hands was called for and the panchayat was elected without open dissent. Then the single candidate for pradhan was announced and he, too, was elected without a nay vote.

That the impression of consensus given in this open election was quite spurious was immediately demonstrated by an announcement by leaders of the lower castes, angered at the Brahmans' last-minute change to a coalition with the Rajputs, that they were going on strike against the Brahmans. Thus began what was apparently the first political strike in Khalapur. There had already been at least one economic strike in the village: several years earlier the landless farm laborers joined to demand an increase of 5 rupees to their weekly wage of 25 rupees (a rupee is officially worth about 21 cents). They

[7] Ralph H. Retzlaff, *op. cit.*, p. 56.
[8] John T. Hitchcock, *op. cit.*, pp. 408–409.

refused their labor to the landowners, but the latter broke the strike after less than a week by the simple expedient of denying access to the land, which was needed for collecting fodder and fuel, to the laborers. Now the lower strata sought to use the stike as a political weapon, but with no greater success. Although they were said to have threatened a fine of 150 rupees against any subcaste violating the strike, one after another of the groups resumed their customary services to the Brahmans. The final collapse of the strike occurred when the leather-workers, after at first refusing to dispose of a dead cow near a Brahman's house, at length gave in to threats and hauled the carcass away. The strike had dwindled away through a period of several months. For the time being neither by strike nor by election could the lower-caste majority in Khalapur prevail over the higher-caste minority.

THE STATUTORY PANCHAYAT AT WORK

As state officials had presided over the election of the Khalapur panchayat, so they guided its operation during its tenure from July, 1949, to April, 1956. (According to the U.P. Panchayat Act, the duration of a panchayat, normally five years, could be extended at the discretion of the state government.) A Panchayat Secretary was appointed for Khalapur; he was the lowest link in an official hierarchy composed of local and district Panchayat Raj Officers and, at the top, the Panchayat Raj Department at the state capital. The Secretary had close and regular contact with the village, but as will be seen, neither external supervision nor internal need could assure the effective operation of the new panchayat for development in Khalapur.

Each panchayat was required under the U.P. Act to employ a systematic financial procedure and to submit annually to the village a budget of revenues and expenditures. It was empowered to assess local taxes. But in Khalapur the panchayat made little use of local resources. Meeting in August and September, 1949, it drew up a budget providing taxes on itinerant merchants and license fees charged against certain occupations; conspicuously absent was a tax on land. In sum, about 90 per cent of revenues were to be derived from the lower castes of the village.[9]

[9] Ralph H. Retzlaff, *op. cit.*, p. 70.

In the second year of its operation the panchayat added a house tax not to exceed 5 per cent of the rental value on all houses and buildings in the village. But according to records of receipts during this year, the tax was used primarily to reach members of the lower castes not touched by occupational taxes. Indeed, records over the six-year period of the panchayat showed that taxation was essentially a one-shot affair; taxed once, a villager was thereafter considered exempt, except for wealthier merchants.

According to the records, receipts of the panchayat from taxes totalled 585 rupees during the first eight months but thereafter declined to 311 rupees in the fiscal year 1950, 38 rupees in the fiscal year 1951, and a total of 64 rupees in the four remaining years. The taxation power of the panchayat fell into virtual disuse.

A contributory factor in the failure to exploit local sources of revenue, apart from the refusal of the Rajputs and Brahmans to tax themselves, was a growing suspicion as to the honesty of the tax collector, who was the pradhan himself. Villagers complained that on paying taxes they were given either no receipt or an inaccurate one; they openly speculated that the pradhan was pocketing a fair proportion of the collections. This only confirmed the traditional village distrust of official agencies and led to indifference or hostility toward the official panchayat, which could therefore not have gained the support of the village for a forceful development program even if it had wanted to.

That it did not want to is indicated by the nature and result of some of its earliest decisions. At the urging of the Panchayat Secretary, in 1949 it adopted a resolution requiring each householder to dig a soakage pit outside his house for the disposal of sewage, which was commonly tossed into the dirt lanes between houses, and providing a fine of 10 rupees for noncompliance. The panchayat later reiterated the resolution, but it did nothing more to achieve its implementation. Indeed, members of the panchayat and the pradhan himself did not bother to comply. But the state panchayat administration appeared to be satisfied with the passage of the resolutions; it did not seriously inquire into their enforcement.

Another case in which the panchayat adopted a righteous position which it would not and could not implement was the prohibition of liquor. During two meetings in 1949 with less than half of the members in attendance the panchayat passed resolutions prohibiting the sale or consumption of homemade liquor (fermented sugar cane) and providing severe fines for violations. A year later it appointed a committee to inquire into the situation. Recognizing finally that prohibition was unenforceable it passed another resolution merely censuring those who sold liquor and limiting drinkers to one bottle per person.

It was notable that in this issue and increasingly thereafter the Rajput caste was clearly divided. At the early panchayat meetings the Rajputs from the two dominant boroughs controlled the proceedings and those from the other boroughs were for the most part absent. As time wore on it became increasingly apparent that certain Rajput leaders were cronies of the pradhan and could count on favored treatment from him. Panchayat meetings came to be held virtually unannounced at the pradhan's house and often included only these favorites. Some of the untouchable members would later be asked to claim that they had been in attendance and supported decisions taken at the meetings.

Those in control of the panchayat found it useful for some purposes not within its legal authority. While the law granted it only administrative functions, the gaon panchayat in Khalapur assumed also a judicial function belonging properly to the adalat panchayat serving a larger area. It tried a number of cases of petty crimes, usually involving untouchables accused of robbery, assault, damage to crops, and so on. It generally reported that the cases were settled by mutual compromise. That the villagers acquiesced in this exercise of a judicial role by the panchayat is probably a sign not only of ignorance as to the law but also of the customary desire to settle disputes within the village rather than submit them to external authority.

Only in one instance did the panchayat play a significant developmental role. Apparently at the instigation of the Panchayat Secretary, it resolved to build a village community hall. This project took five years to complete, and it accounted for almost 70 per cent of total panchayat expenditures. Due to the declining tax revenues of the panchayat, it could not have been completed at all without an additional source of income – the proceeds from sale of land accruing to the panchayat as a result of the land-reform legislation of 1950. Under the terms of the U.P. Act the Khalapur panchayat, acting as the Land Management Committee, came into control of some 300 acres of uncultivated land, of which more than one-half was cultivable fallow land. Although the intent of the act was redistribution of such land to the landless, the panchayat set a price for it which virtually excluded all but Rajput buyers. Further, it did not observe the prohibition in the act against sale of the land to persons already owning 6.25 acres or more. Altogether the panchayat sold or rented almost one-half of the cultivable land, in almost all cases to Rajputs.

The panchayat (or rather, the pradhan, in its name) also violated the prohibition in the land-reform act against the cutting of fruit-bearing trees in village orchards. The pradhan in certain cases approved the sale to woodsellers of such trees, with a false certification that they were not fruit-bearing. An opposition faction of Rajputs hit upon this as a means of removing or discrediting the pradhan, and they filed a complaint against him at the local administrative headquarters with the accusation that he had solicited bribes amounting to 10 per cent of the price of the trees. The result was that the pradhan was enjoined to cease all activities on behalf of the Land Management Committee pending investigation of the matter. No further action was taken.

The pervasiveness of factional rivalries in Khalapur was demonstrated in another aspect of village life — youth activities. One especially zealous young man in the village, observing the failure of the panchayat to limit drunkenness, determined to mobilize youths against this social evil. He was able to organize demonstrations in the village and with his supporters to found the Ideal Youth Organization. In addition to agitation against liquor, the members began to take over other tasks neglected by the panchayat, such as voluntary work to improve sanitation. It gained the support of the pradhan but not that of many of the elders of the village, who eventually succeeded in disrupting the organization, in large part by means of inciting rivalry between boys of the two largest boroughs.

Factionalism was demonstrated also in 1954 in the election of a village judge. With the impending retirement of the holder of this office, who had grown senile and blind, the residents of three of the smaller boroughs began to combine forces to control the election of his successor. In the pre-election maneuvering three candidates appeared, but the village shrank from the open eruption of borough rivalries and eventually an informal panchayat meeting decided to form a selection committee to choose a compromise candidate. It may be noted that the untouchables did not attend the meeting and that the committee was composed of the higher castes with the exception of one member, an untouchable who happened to be passing by during the meeting and was drafted to serve on the committee.

Representing a divided community, the gaon panchayat declined steadily in activity and effectiveness. The state panchayat administration seemed to be satisfied with the symbolic passage of resolutions and the occasional mobilization of constructive activity, the occasions usually being visits of state officials to the village. The state government seemed to concentrate its forces, and with somewhat greater effectiveness, in another channel of development in Khalapur – the Community Development Program.

COMMUNITY DEVELOPMENT IN KHALAPUR

The Community Development Program of India, established in 1952, was expanded step by step in the following years and by the middle of 1953 included the village of Khalapur. It was one of 153 villages in a region of Western U.P. comprising a Community Development Block. Residing in Khalapur was a multipurpose development agent, the village-level worker (VLW). He was responsible to a Deputy Project Executive Officer (DPEO) at the Project headquarters in Deoband, which was staffed by Assistant Project Officers (APO's) for various development spheres – agriculture, cooperatives, and panchayats; social education and village participation; women's welfare; and statistics and information. The DPEO was responsible to the District Collector, aided by the District Planning Officer in the headquarters at Saharanpur. They reported to a regional state officer, the Deputy Development Commissioner for U.P., and he in turn reported to the state Development Commissioner in Lucknow, aided by heads of development departments in the state government. At the top was the Community Development Administrator (later called the Minister of Community Development) in New Delhi. This organization, which sought to comprehend and coordinate the main spheres of village development within a single hierarchy, was integrated into the Planning Commission under the Prime Minister.

The organization was supposed to operate in a manner uncommon in the Indian administrative service. It was above all to work according to extension-service principles of cooperation with existing local institutions such as panchayats and cooperatives, and to seek the maximum public participation on the basis of "felt needs" among villagers. It sought, in brief, not only to accomplish immediate village improvement but also to create the conditions for long-term "self-generating and self-sustaining growth" in the village. It provided for extensive programs of orientation and training for personnel in the organization, especially the VLW's; and it sought to establish within the organization a democratic spirit, especially in relations between the VLW at the village level and the technical experts (APO's) at the project level. These latter officers were supposed not to be desk-bound but rather to spend about three-quarters of their time in the field in close collaboration with the VLW's, who as generalists needed constant specialist assistance.

The area covered in this Community Development Block was almost entirely rural; the district headquarters town was excluded from it, and of a total population of 78,337 in the Block only 1,024 were industrial workers, many of them temporary. The primary emphasis was of course on agriculture and related fields. The original plan encompassed measures for reclamation of land, improvement of irrigation facilities, electrification, provision of improved fertilizers and seeds, techniques, implements, and marketing and credit facilities, and the development of animal husbandry and inland fisheries, fruit and vegetable cultivation, and arboriculture and reforestation. Also to be undertaken were measures for improvement of roads and transport facilities, rural housing, education, including vocational and adult education and library services, and health facilities, including medical aid, drinking-water supplies, maternity aid, village sanitation, and disease control (especially against malaria). The plan aimed to reduce rural underemployment by means of supplementary employment, through encouragement of cottage industries and crafts, medium and small-scale industry, and local facilities such as brick kilns and saw mills. Finally, the plan contained a commitment to social welfare, with provision for organization of entertainment facilities, sports activities, fairs, and cooperative and self-help groups.

It is the comprehensiveness of this program rather than the novelty of its specific features that is striking. Indeed, in Khalapur most of the aspects of the program were not novel at all, at least to some of the villagers, for new ideas and techniques had been propagated for some time by field agents of the government, both before and after 1947. The VLW in Khalapur found, for example, that there was already widespread appreciation of improved varieties of seed for the two main crops of the area, sugar cane and wheat. Villagers often expressed a preference for the taste of older varieties of sugar cane, but they knew that the sugar mills offered a higher price for the improved variety because of its higher sugar content.

THE PROGRAM: AGRICULTURAL DEVELOPMENT. In the field of agriculture the program had its most marked successes. According to Dube's survey of the first 18 months of the program in Khalapur, some important improvements were registered in the village.[10] The acreage sown with wheat of improved variety doubled, the amount of ammonium sulphate fertilizer bought by villagers increased by almost one-quarter each year, the trench method of cultivation of sugar cane was introduced on about 15 acres, orchards were improved with the planting of 635 mango trees and of 2,500 other trees for fuel, 228 kitchen gardens were planted, acreage in fodder was expanded by about 50 per cent, cattle breeding was improved with the introduction of two pedigreed animals and the inoculation of 2,683 cattle, and irrigation was extended through the construction of four additional wells (including two of the modern type) and about four miles of irrigation channels. The Khalapur Cooperative Society expanded its membership from 88 to 222, and made loans to 149 members for farming improvements such as the purchase of implements; in Khalapur farmers bought in this period 22 iron cultivators, 11 improved hand hoes, 15 modern ploughs, 16 inflated-tire carts, and one tractor.

But alongside these successes, which depended primarily on the demonstration of visible economic advantage to the villagers, there were failures in other attempts at innovation. Although the VLW explained and demonstrated them extensively, the Japanese method of rice cultivation, the dibbling method of seed multiplication, and the line-sowing of wheat and rice were resisted by the villagers. Less familiar forms of land fertilization such as the use of green manure crops were tried tentatively but abandoned. Resistance to innovation in the village was aggravated by the fact that many landowning farmers took little interest in agricultural matters and left them to their laborers, who were naturally less concerned and receptive to change.

Moreover, a mere listing of the successes of the project in its initial period conceals many persistent problems. The kitchen gardens planted, for example, were mainly the work of children and were generally not taken seriously by adults. Expansion of the use of artificial fertil-

[10] S. C. Dube, *India's Changing Villages: Human Factors in Community Development* (Ithaca: Cornell University Press, 1958), Chapter III. In place of "Khalapur," Dube calls the village "Rajput Village."

izers, sometimes without proper instruction in their use, resulted in some damage to crops. New implements and especially machines were introduced in the village without proper provision for maintenance, which did little to reduce village distrust of mechanization. The introduction of improved breeds of cattle did not alter the religious prohibition against the elimination of weak and defective animals and could do little by itself to improve the overall quality of livestock. The growth of the Cooperative Society did not make it an integral part of the community, for the majority of the villagers continued to regard it as alien, complex, and potentially corrupt. Many illiterates feared to put their marks on the papers required for membership because of suspicion that they might thus become involved in dreaded legal complications. Similarly, they declined to participate in crop competitions organized by the VLW simply because of the requirement that they sign entrance papers. The construction of more wells in the village was welcome, according to Dube, but the operator of the main motor-pump well was "high-handed and corrupt."

Yet a superficial listing of achievements was too often taken as an adequate index of effectiveness in the operation of the Project in Khalapur. Officers of the program at all levels tended to concentrate on and rest content with campaigns producing immediate results which were statistically measurable, in place of the more profound result of creating and enabling an indigenous process of change in the village.

It should be noted, also, that the improvements in agriculture in Khalapur did little to disturb the economic position of the landowning Rajputs. Dube estimates that almost 70 per cent of the benefits of agricultural extension work went to the already affluent farmers. No projects were undertaken for the particular benefit of landless laborers or artisans.

THE PROGRAM: SOCIAL WELFARE. In the fields of education, recreation, sanitation, and other aspects of the program, achievements in Khalapur were still more modest, though the benefits were perhaps better distributed than in agricultural extension work. Adult education classes in literacy for men were introduced, but only about 12 persons attended regularly. A social education class for women, with work in reading and writing and also sewing and knitting, was attended regularly by only five or six, mainly because of poor instruction.

A club for young people was organized, with 64 members, and also an auxiliary for small boys; along with sports competition within the village and with other villages, it established a drama club which performed two plays in the village, and it collected a library of 122 books. But although it tried also to engage in constructive activity such as sanitation campaigns and to undertake agricultural projects such as vegetable growing, it got little guidance in these activities and they waned.

The VLW succeeded also in organizing a program of occasional community singing in the village, with accompaniment by an instrumental group. But he failed in the more significant attempt to establish a community center for regular congregation of the villagers to hear the reading of newspapers and discuss local and national affairs. In sum, though it had a somewhat greater impact on youth in the village, the project did little to change existing attitudes toward education or to raise the educational level of the adults. And the failure to institute a community center demonstrates the persistent lack of a sense of community transcending caste and borough lines.

In the field of sanitation and public health, some rudimentary improvements were achieved in the first 18 months in Khalapur. Three soakage pits were dug for more effective drainage of village lanes; these proved to be of an inappropriate construction for the local soil, and they fell into a state of neglect, but the villagers had initially appreciated them and would presumably respond to an improved version. Three sanitation drives for cleaning of the lanes were organized, with the work done for the most part by young people; such clean-up campaigns, according to Dube, are often occasioned by the visit of a state official and are motivated by a simple desire to impress outsiders, with little or no recognition of the intrinsic value of cleanliness.

For cleaner village lanes the VLW sought also to eliminate habits of careless garbage and manure disposal by the villagers. But a campaign for the voluntary construction of compost pits at the edge of the village produced only 64 pits. The principal obstacle was traditional social attitudes regarding upper-caste women. While disposal of garbage and dung is customarily a woman's work, upper-caste women suffered humiliation if they were seen doing it at the edge of the village. Although a visiting official once chided the villagers with the fact that he found Khalapur in the dark from a half-mile away simply by its smell, the practice of dumping garbage and dung near the houses by and large continued.

In the improvement of the water supply for drinking and washing, the VLW concentrated on the untouchable quarter of the village. Here three wells were improved, with higher walls, new pulleys, and better drainage. Other measures for the improvement of health included epidemic control (1,388 vaccinations by the VLW) and especially malaria control (about 500 houses sprayed with DDT and 500 tablets of Paludrine distributed). But mosquito-breeding ponds and ditches were not treated, and the villagers regarded Paludrine simply as a cure for malaria rather than also a preventive, and they stopped taking it when fever subsided.

A trained midwife sent to Khalapur by the Project opened a maternity center in the village. Her services were free, and in the period under consideration she assisted in 235 childbirths. Although supplies were unreliable, she also occasionally distributed free powdered milk to village children (almost 1,000 in all), and she instructed five village midwives in modern methods. But she accomplished little change in attitudes of women in the village; among 70 women interviewed by Dube on the subject only about 10 per cent thought the trained midwife was of any use to the village, and among those in the 70 who had actually received advice and care from the midwife only 5 per cent had comprehended what she told them. Most women thought it comical to substitute powdered milk for mother's milk, and in general they thought that they knew as much about having and caring for children as the midwife could. Even some of the village midwives under training by the Project midwife were sceptical about the validity of her methods; they had agreed to the training reluctantly, for the sake of the small stipend involved, and since the stipend tended to be paid irregularly they attended the instruction meetings irregularly.

But the main health project in Khalapur, in terms of its cost and significance, was one for paving the village lanes with brick. Here as elsewhere the VLW followed the principle of seeking village contributions of cash and labor for the project, but in this case the equitable distribution of such levies constituted a particularly difficult problem. A complex plan was eventually worked out, by which the villagers contributed about two-thirds of the cost. What is especially noteworthy is the fact that in the resolution of the problem the VLW had recourse not to the official panchayat of Khalapur but to an ad hoc committee; it included the village pradhan simply in order not to offend him, but it was presided over by the principal of the village secondary school. Because the villagers were known to be unwilling to entrust their money or the direction of the project to the panchayat, that agency was evidently considered useless as a partner in development in Khalapur.

Apart from the agricultural aspect, then, the Community Development Program in Khalapur had little impact. The VLW was so heavily burdened with agricultural extension work that he was prone to neglect other projects; higher levels of the organization frequently failed to provide services and supplies, and even mere support, to the VLW at the right times and places; projects were often sporadic and unimaginative, and as in the agricultural work they were often designed to achieve immediate and measurable small gains which could be reported to higher authorities, rather than long-term conditions of development. Dube concludes that in Khalapur these programs "were far below the needs of the community, and did not in any appreciable measure change the attitude and outlook of the people towards nutrition, hygiene, and health."[11]

It may be added parenthetically that, as in the political reforms in Khalapur, so also in community development language difficulties proved to be an obstacle to communication. Since the village dialect differed significantly from standard Hindi, messages of various kinds from higher officials in the program frequently failed to achieve comprehension or even attention in the village. Gumperz conducted a test of intelligibility to villagers (literate, semiliterate, and illiterate) of a small pamphlet announcing a community development fair in Khalapur.[12] He found that illiterates got "only the vaguest notion" of its content when it was read to them; literates reading the pamphlet got the "main part" of the message but did not know some of the terms used, and these terms tended to be precisely those used for new concepts which the Project wished to introduce in the village. Some slight indication of the problem of communication is the fact that the statement in the pamphlet, "There will be a show of healthy babies up to the age of three," was commonly misinterpreted to mean, "There will be a wrestling match of three-year-old children."

[11] *Ibid.*, p. 83.

[12] John J. Gumperz, *op. cit.*, pp. 256–257.

NEW LEADERSHIP IN KHALAPUR

As his role on the ad hoc committee for paving village lanes indicates, a new leader emerged in Khalapur at about this time in the person of the principal of the Intercollege. Filling the vacuum left by the decline of the gaon panchayat and its pradhan, the principal exhibited leadership which was markedly different in some of its bases, methods, and objects from that of earlier notables in Khalapur.[13]

Though as a Rajput he possessed the social rank traditionally necessary for leadership, he differed from prior leaders in being from outside the village, though from a place not too remote from it. He was a member of a prominent family of a village in another district, in which lived also relatives of some Khalapur Rajputs. Learning about him through these relatives, a committee formed in Khalapur in 1949 to organize a new secondary school (which was instigated by higher officials) invited him to take the post of principal. He was different also in the nature of his education, for he had a university degree in commerce and law. He was markedly different in his age, for he was in his twenties. Perhaps most important, he was different in being closely associated with not a religious reform movement, but rather the secular authority of government and the Congress party at higher levels.

Some of these qualities he was able soon to turn to positive advantage. Precisely because he was from outside the village, he was not aligned with any of the factions of Khalapur. He was sufficiently familiar with village life in general to appreciate the importance of this, and after a period of careful study of the intricacies of Khalapur society he was able to step into a role of impartial mediator in village disputes. Because of his association with government and party officials, he was also able effectively to represent the village at higher levels; he interceded, for example, on behalf of landowners wishing consolidation of their holdings and on behalf of sugar-cane growers seeking higher prices. For the same reason he could act effectively as protector of the village; he was able to keep the police from entering the village without his permission and even to secure the removal, through appeal to higher quarters, of several corrupt petty officials in the area. His education in law was of special value to the villagers,

[13] John T. Hitchcock, *op. cit.*, pp. 409–415.

and probably because of this most of them showed respect for rather than suspicion of his intellectual attainments.

In addition to his Rajput status, the principal also possessed or cultivated some of the traditional bases of leadership. He adopted an ascetic mode of life and the demeanor and dress of a simple villager rather than that of an urban intellectual. He worked shrewdly to gain the confidence of key figures in the traditional structure of the village, above all the Rajput faction leaders; in connection with a campaign for village contributions for a new school building, for example, he was careful not to offend the swami teaching in the existing religious school and to mobilize sympathy and support by systematic visits and discussions at the traditional men's sitting-places in the village.

He was not, in any event, highly radical in his proposals for change in the village. While he was in favor of and worked for reforms in the status of women, such as eliminating the practice of seclusion (purdah), he did not attack head-on the traditional caste system. Though he admitted untouchable pupils to his school and did not segregate them in classrooms, he did enforce their segregation in the dining room and kitchen.

But in comparison with the panchayat chairman who led the village in the period 1915 through 1935, the principal was strongly oriented toward development sanctioned by a secular nationalist spirit rather than religious values, and informed by a concept of the village as a part of a larger entity rather than an end in itself. And he was oriented to methods involving positive support and collaboration from higher levels of the system.

Having proven his leadership in the campaign to build a larger school building, which became the pride of the village, the principal engaged more and more actively in village politics and development. In the election of the new village judge in 1954, it was the principal who intervened at an informal village panchayat meeting to propose a selection committee for choice of a compromise candidate. He was confronted daily with requests from villagers, and even from people from neighboring villages, for advice and aid in petty problems. He lent his support and his leadership to development projects such as that for paving the village lanes. In particular, he sought in his school to generate the spirit and practice of development; at the school there were, for example, a model vegetable garden and a fruit orchard planned and managed in collaboration with the Community Development Program. It should be added that these were prompted also by a canny desire on the part of the principal to render the school financially self-sufficient, or, in other words, to render the position of the school independent of his own political fortunes in the village.

Indeed, Hitchcock suggests that one of the brightest aspects of the scene in Khalapur was the growth of a cadre of ex-students of the Intercollege, able to work together and eager to work for development. When in the future they enter informal or formal positions of leadership in the village, including membership in the panchayat, they may give a lasting impetus to a movement for change, so that the village need no longer depend on the sporadic appearance of exceptional individual leaders as it has to date.

THE PANCHAYAT ELECTION OF 1955

Long before the legal expiration of Khalapur's first gaon panchayat, it had effectively expired without accomplishing much more than the exacerbation of village divisions. How pronounced these divisions had become was revealed when new panchayat elections were announced and the villagers' attention focused again on the selection of a pradhan.[14]

The Rajput oligarchy from the outset was agreed on little more than a refusal to consider re-election of the old Brahman pradhan. Though they sought in informal panchayat meetings to choose a single candidate in his place, they were unable to reach a consensus. Even the Rajputs of the two central boroughs, who in coalition had been dominant in the village, were unable to maintain their unity. By the time the deadline for the filing of nomination papers arrived, there were five Rajput candidates officially entered in the race for pradhan, one each from the two central boroughs and three of the lesser boroughs.

There was also an untouchable candidate from the Chamar subcaste. While this was a sign that the untouchables were growing in boldness and in understanding of the new political order, it did not mean that they already constituted a serious threat to the Rajputs; it was unlikely that the intermediate "clean" castes, not to mention the

[14] Ralph H. Retzlaff, *op. cit.*, pp. 90–114.

Brahmans, would vote for a Chamar, and the absence of a candidate from these other castes betrayed the failure of the non-Rajput strata of the village to combine against the status quo. Like the Rajputs, the other strata were more than ever divided. Later in the election campaign it became evident that the Chamars had put forward a candidate in part simply as a defensive maneuver, in order to be able to resist Rajput electioneering, including likely threats, with a plea that they must vote for their own candidate out of caste loyalty.

Yet the non-Rajputs found themselves the objects of an extensive appeal from the Rajput candidates. Each of these candidates could count with fair assurance on the lower-caste votes in his own borough, with the exception of the Chamars' votes; but to win on a village-wide basis he had to achieve the withdrawal of other candidates and the support of their boroughs or, alternatively, to win away from the Rajput candidates of other boroughs their lower-caste supporters.

Both of these tactics were intensively pursued in the weeks preceding the election. The appeal to a lower-caste audience took, significantly, the form of campaign promises related to community development – more and better wells, improved sanitation, and the like. It resulted also in the adoption by one Rajput candidate of the name mazdur (labor) party for his faction; sometimes the English words were used in place of the Hindi, and at least on one occasion this candidate referred to his opposition as the "Churchill party."

But even in an advanced state of disunity the village tended as always to seek consensus, and much activity in the election campaign focused on an attempt to secure the withdrawal of the announced candidates and a compromise among them. At this point the principal, evidently believing that this was the sense of the village or at least of the non-Rajput element, chose to intervene as he had in the 1954 election. In thus involving himself directly in this most important contest among Khalapur factions, he took a great risk with his power, and as it turned out, a miscalculated risk.

Already there had been several informal village panchayat meetings to seek a compromise; although many present urged the avoidance of a direct contest, these meetings ended in bitter failure. Three days before the election the principal announced that he would seek from all the candidates for pradhan an agreement to withdraw, so that a candidate acceptable to all could be chosen. Later he promised that the final candidate would be selected from among the original ones.

He was successful in getting agreement from most, but one Rajput candidate held out despite arguments and entreaties by the principal's representatives through the entire night and early morning before the election. This candidate had been urged on and supported by the largest Rajput landowner of the village, who held a grudge against the principal, blaming him for the loss of some land through action of the gaon panchayat several years earlier. Hostility toward the principal now grew in other quarters. Rajputs confident of the victory of their candidates resented direct interference in the contest; others in the village began to suspect that the principal was secretly trying to secure the re-election of the old Brahman pradhan, whom he had been able to influence; some suspected – and these turned out to be correct – that the principal privately was supporting one of the Rajput candidates. Had the principal succeeded in his effort to secure the withdrawal of all candidates and had then appealed for consensus in a general panchayat meeting, he might have erased the growing resentment against him; but he failed.

On the morning of the election several of the candidates sought unsuccessfully to withdraw their names from the official list. Among them was the Rajput from one of the two central boroughs, and his withdrawal represented a desperate attempt to re-form the coalition between these boroughs; he tried to urge his supporters to vote for the candidate of the other borough, but there was not time to carry out the plan effectively.

The election resolved itself into a close contest among the remaining four Rajput candidates. When the Returning Officers from the state government arrived in Khalapur to conduct the election, they assembled the voting population in four separate groups, according to wards which had recently been designated for the village. Electioneering continued frantically even in these assemblies, up to the moment of voting. A certain atmosphere of confusion developed, with many persons arriving and departing and many children adding to the noise. Only about one in five of the voters assembled were women, and many of these seemed frightened and uncertain about the procedure.

The Returning Officers read off the list of official candidates for pradhan, taking the vote for each by an open show of hands or standing up by the voters. The results showed that in most boroughs the Rajputs and their lower-caste retainers for the most part voted loyally for their borough candidates, but there were significant numbers of defections. The results showed also that the Chamars voted loyally for their candidate, who received the second highest vote in the village as a whole.

The winner was the Rajput candidate, from one of the lesser boroughs, supported by the principal. Like the principal, he was an active member of the Congress party. His election was ensured in part by votes from defectors from the other lesser boroughs who hoped thereby to throw off the domination of the central boroughs; but according to Hitchcock, "Polling irregularities on the part of officials and Rajputs who favored the principal's candidate were a deciding factor in the outcome."[15]

The election of the gaon panchayat members was conducted according to wards, and votes were not totaled for the village as a whole. Each ward was allotted a number of members proportionate to its population, and in each the untouchables were allotted an appropriate number of seats. Voting was, as in the election of the pradhan, by an open show of support, and followed a complex method of multiple voting.

In the aftermath of the election intense bitterness was engendered by suspicion of foul play in the conduct of the voting. Some of the defeated candidates decided to petition for a new election to the state Panchayat Raj Department and to the member of the state legislative assembly for the village (also a member of the Congress party), but their efforts were in vain. The legislator disavowed support of the pradhan-elect, but in Khalapur the feeling grew that the Congress party had conspired to interfere in village affairs.

The legislator had been popular in the village and had risen high in the state government, but in the state election two years later he received only about two-thirds of the vote in Khalapur instead of almost all of it as in the election of 1951. He was defeated for re-election in the constituency as a whole by an independent candidate.

The principal also suffered a serious decline in his prestige and power in the village and this, combined with the divisive effects of the village election, meant that Khalapur was at least temporarily without a leader who commanded respect throughout the community. The result was demonstrated several weeks after the election, on the

[15] John T. Hitchcock, "The Rajputs," *op. cit.*, pp. 298–299.

occasion of the annual short campaign organized by the state government for constructive work (*shramdan*) for village improvement. By and large each borough worked only for itself and quarreled with the others, and much less was accomplished than in previous years. Not even the visit to the village at this time of Lady Mountbatten, the popular wife of the last Viceroy, could arouse enthusiasm for a united contribution to development.

POSTSCRIPT

The gaon panchayat and Community Development Program in Khalapur soon gave way to a new system of local government and development. Following in the main the recommendations of the Balvantray Mehta Report of 1957, the state governments of India enacted in 1959 and 1960 "panchayati-raj" legislation, which had the effect of shifting development powers and responsibilities downward from the state and district levels and upward from the village level to an intermediate level where a combination of general coordination and local participation might more effectively be achieved. According to the report, the new system should rest on popular initiative at the village level; a small cluster of villages should elect a local panchayat, and this in turn should elect representatives to a higher body (called a *Panchayat Samiti*) for a larger area. The pradhans of these area panchayats then would form with other officials a district council (a *Zila Parishad*). But it should be in the area panchayats that most power is concentrated.

Early evaluations of the new system in various parts of India have noted that generally it results in intensified partisanship in local politics. The indirect election of area panchayats, along with the new allocation of power, prompts competing political parties to penetrate to the village base. As it had already begun to do in Khalapur, the Congress party must increasingly intervene and align itself in village factional rivalries, and so also, presumably, must the Communist, Socialist, Swatantra, and other parties. As one aspect of the increasing contact between national and village politics, this will lend impetus to change in both spheres.

It remains to be seen how in the long run this and other features of the new system will affect patterns of politics and development in Indian villages. The earlier history of Khalapur suggests at least that modest ambitions are in order in any attempt to create a sense of community and a will to change at this level. Yet it must be noted that while to outside observers the progress of Khalapur may seem disappointing and disturbing, to the villager the prospects may well appear more promising. In any case Khalapur has been bestirred, and in it some of the conditions for a more dynamic and purposeful interaction and leadership have come into being.

PART V PHILIPPINES

Superficially the Philippines is not very typical of Southeast Asia. It is the one Christian country in Asia, it blends Spanish and American traditions, and in many of its rural traditions seems closer to Latin America than to Asia. The spirit of its mass media and the political language of its spokesmen have a decidedly American accent.

Yet on deeper analysis the country is faced with many, perhaps all, the common problems of Southeast Asian societies. It has long been confronted with a fundamental difficulty: bridging a wide gap between its Westernized elites and its rural masses. This basic bifurcation runs through all the Southeast Asian countries. The cleavages between urban and rural, modern and traditional, and rich and poor are the main impediments to nation building in all countries in the region. In some of the countries the elites have sought to evade the disparities by simply pretending that they do not exist and talking as though their people were fully united.

Other governments have honestly confronted the problem and initiated programs that would bring the rural masses into the modern world and improve their standards of life. Such attempts, however, have not always been successful; in part because the effort was not great enough, in part because the elite could not effectively communicate their ambitions for the masses to the very ones they would help, and finally and above all such efforts have floundered because the Southeast Asian governments have lacked the administrative ability to implement the necessary policies.

In the early 1950's the Philippines seemed about to disintegrate under its burdensome problems, disaffection among its rural peoples and its incompetent governmental agencies. In 1953, however, an extraordinary man swept the elections and brought new hope to the country. Ramon Magsaysay was a truly charismatic leader who could speak the language of the common folk and who insisted that the government should belong to the masses. Years before John F. Kennedy, Magsaysay evoked the vital image of dynamic youth seeking imaginatively to make government care and act to support the less fortunate.

Tragically, before his untimely death in an airplane crash, Magsaysay was having profound difficulties in establishing the necessary machinery for effectively implementing his chosen policies. It has been said frequently that Magsaysay lacked administrative ability, that he was essentially an inspirational leader, not a routine implementer of programs. From Jose Veloso Abueva's case study we learn, however, that Magsaysay's difficulties in many ways were those inherent in ruling according to essentially American institutions of government. The story of Magsaysay's effort at building a community development program closely foreshadows the problems President Lyndon B. Johnson had in seeking to implement his War on Poverty. This case study is thus a bridge from the world of American politics to that of Southeast Asian politics.

JOSE VELOSO ABUEVA

7 Bureaucratic Politics in the Philippines

Ramon Magsaysay was elected president of the Philippines in November 1953, defeating the incumbent with the greatest electoral margin in postwar presidential history. He had waged a far-ranging campaign that revolutionized Filipino national politics in its grass-roots penetration and appeal. As the third president of the Republic, Magsaysay's sustained emphasis on uplifting the "common man" was intended to fulfill a rousing campaign promise, which he confirmed in his Inaugural address: "My administration shall take positive energetic measures to improve the living conditions of our fellow citizens in the *barrios*[1] and neglected rural areas and of laborers in our urban and industrial centers." Undoubtedly, it was also in his continued political interest to consolidate his national leadership by providing the expectant people in the barrios with new opportunities for improving their lives.

The president's off-and-on search for a dynamic and integrated overall program of rural development — even as he augmented all

This case study is based on the author's book, *Focus on the Barrio* (Manila: Institute of Public Administration, University of the Philippines, 1959).

[1] *Barrios* are the smallest political units, usually made up of one or more villages.

government rural services and expanded public works – followed the general pattern of policy making on the economic front. In rural development the competition and interplay among the many protagonists were even more spirited, if more diffuse and less bitter. Here the policy stage would show even more foreign actors and agencies as the scenes shifted from Manila to the provinces, to Washington and New York, and back to the country.

Top administrators under Magsaysay straddled the economic and the rural development fronts by holding concurrent and interlocking positions. Filemon Rodriguez was Magsaysay's first choice for Chairman of the National Economic Council (NEC), formally the highest economic advisory body to the president. At the same time Rodriguez was board chairman of the government's National Power Corporation (NPC) and was to become the first chairman of an interagency Community Development Planning Council (CDPC). Salvador Araneta was Magsaysay's Secretary of Agriculture and Natural Resources. He was appointed an ex-officio member of the NEC, and, later on, a member of the CDPC. Businessman Alfredo Montelibano was appointed Administrator of the Office of Economic Coordination (OEC), which gave him supervision over all government corporations, including the National Power Corporation headed by Rodriguez. Like Araneta, Montelibano was appointed an NEC member. Thus in the NEC Rodriguez was senior to Montelibano, whereas the two reversed their roles in the OEC and the NPC. Rodriguez would soon have policy differences with Montelibano and Araneta, which flared up in public debate and personal animosities. Without resolving these differences between two of his highest aides, President Magsaysay would appoint Montelibano as NEC, and, concurrently, CDPC chairman upon Rodriguez's resignation. But we will set aside the latter events for now, to make our story unfold chronologically.

BURGEONING PROPOSALS

In enthusiastic response to Magsaysay's rallying call to the barrios, several government agencies and voluntary organizations improved and expanded their rural services. The Bureau of Public Schools and three voluntary organizations – the Philippine Rural Reconstruction Movement (PRRM), the Community Centers of the National Movement for Free Elections (NAMFREL), and the Philippine

Rural Improvement Society (PRUCIS) – whose rural development projects antedated the Magsaysay administration, found the new climate much more hospitable to their intensified efforts. Other technical agencies, like the Bureau of Agricultural Extension, the Social Welfare Administration, and the Bureau of Health, enlarged their field services to embrace new aspects of rural community life and organization.

The urge for empire and the political ambitions of some administrators led to lively and, at times, bruising competition for primacy in the government's booming but rather uncoordinated program for rural development. As early as ten days after becoming president, Magsaysay received from Secretary Salvador Araneta and Social Welfare Administrator Pacita Madrigal Warns a joint plan for a grant-in-aid program for voluntary agencies, to be administered either by the Cabinet, by the National Economic Council, or by an interdepartmental committee. The next month Department of Agriculture and Natural Resources (DANR) Under-Secretary Jaime N. Ferrer proposed to the president that a consultative council be established. By the middle of 1954, NEC Chairman Felimon Rodriguez had received four proposals – from Secretary of Health Paulino Garcia, from Mr. Isabelo Tupas of the Bureau of Public Schools, jointly from Dr. Edward R. Chadwick, community development expert of the UN Bureau of Social Affairs, and Colonel Harry A. Brenn, director of the local operations mission of the United States Foreign Operations Administration (USOM/FOA), and from Dr. Generoso F. Rivera of the Philippine Council for United States Aid.

On August 16, 1954, the president created by executive order an eleven member Community Development Planning Council (CDPC). Under the NEC chairman as concurrent CDPC head were seven cabinet members and three private citizens representing voluntary agencies. Unfortunately, the executive order had been prematurely processed by the Malacañang[2] staff for the president's signature. The draft, based on the Chadwick-Brenn plan, had been submitted by Filemon Rodriguez merely as a working paper to be considered by all those who were to compose the proposed council. The president had assumed "completed staff work" when he signed the document. Considering the rivalry brewing among some of the CDPC members for leadership in Magsaysay's overall rural development program,

[2] The popular name given to the Office of the President of the Philippines.

and the conflict between Rodriguez and Araneta over economic policies, imposing the CDPC on the unknowing cabinet members vitiated the organization from the start.

Upon Rodriguez's advice, the president appointed Ramon P. Binamira as CDPC Executive Secretary. At 27, the lanky, bemoustached lawyer had been executive secretary of the NAMFREL community centers. The year before he had campaigned for Magsaysay in Cebu while ostensibly a neutral NAMFREL coordinator for ensuring free elections. Because of bureaucratic intricacies, it took Binamira, the neophyte official, four months to finally obtain his funds and get the president to administer the oath to the CDPC members. He had to make an impassioned plea to the president to help him cut the red tape that had snarled his organizational work. On this occasion, Binamira told the president, with a little youthful exaggeration:

> Mr. President, the people in the barrios are now confused with so many organizations ostensibly for their good. They are asked to organize themselves into "barrio councils" by the Bureau of Agricultural Extension, and before their second meeting they are asked again to organize a "rural council" according to the Administrative Code. Before they can gather their bearings, they are herded by school teachers into a "purok" [neighborhood association]. Meanwhile, their wives are not spared the ordeal: they, too, are being formed into "Rural Improvement Clubs" by the Bureau of Agricultural Extension. The children do not escape: they are drafted into 4-H clubs. After this, the PRRM, the PRUCIS, the NAMFREL, and other civic organizations join the melee with their own barrio teams. Net result – confusion, duplication, waste, and jealousies.

If the government agencies had overextended their resources and in some ways worked at cross-purposes, their common avowed objective was to rally to Magsaysay's call to the barrios. On the whole the results were in fact substantial. Reviewing his first year, Magsaysay devoted almost half of his report to Congress to the subject "Rural Reconstruction." The exodus of farmers from areas of high tenancy to government settlements was reflected by 33,000 applications for public land and the issuance by the Bureau of Lands of 28,000 land patents to qualified settlers – three times the number issued in 1953. The Agricultural Credit and Cooperative Financing Administration had released 18.9 million pesos in loans and organized 232 farmers' cooperative marketing associations (FACOMA's) with an aggregate of

105,943 members. In operation or nearing completion were seven irrigation projects covering more than 50,000 hectares. Ninety communal irrigation systems had been constructed in 27 provinces at a cost of nearly 1 million pesos. Already begun were seven bond-financed irrigation projects estimated to cost 22 million pesos. Fifteen waterworks systems had been completed, and 80 spring development projects were in progress. Whereas 256 artesian wells had been dug the year before, 1,300 were installed in 1954 – with the assistance of the Liberty Wells Association, a civic organization. Road and bridge construction had been stepped up considerably under the administration's 200 million peso, five-year highway program, for which a new Bureau of Public Highways was created by Congress on Magsaysay's initiative. In addition to more than a hundred road projects, 430 barrio feeder roads serving 80 communities were built.

Although claiming that food production had increased appreciably, the president admitted insufficiency in rice and other critical items. He justified anew his controversial early ban on the slaughter of working carabaos by citing a 9 per cent increase in this livestock and a decrease in the price of carabao meat. Without offering figures, the president announced that the steady flow to the barrios of prefabricated schoolhouses, at half the cost of the conventional structure, would start in 1955.

As Magsaysay's second year commenced, it looked as if serious implementation of the legally promulgated "community development" approach to rural problems would soon begin. National policy had been formally set by the chief executive. An interdepartmental CDPC had been constituted and its technical staff organized. The essential elements of a national program of community development had been outlined at the UN Community Development Conference for South and Southeast Asia, which was hosted by the Philippine Government in Manila in December, 1954. Moreover, in his second address before Congress, the president said:

> The spirit of self-help is sweeping our rural communities . . . the role of the government is simply to tap the creative energies of our people and to provide the means by which their desire for improvement can be translated into permanent benefits.
>
> It is for this purpose that our health, education and social welfare programs are being re-oriented with emphasis on self-help.
>
> These varied social measures – for better health, wider opportu-

nities for education, and more gainful employment – are now being carried out with the use of more efficient techniques of community development. Coordination and integration on a national scale will be effected through the newly created national Community Development Planning Council.

In reality, the president was expressing more of an intention and a hope than reporting actual accomplishments – when tested against the authoritative UN definition of "community development" as "the participation by the people themselves in efforts to improve their level of living with reliance as much as possible on their own initiative; and the provision of technical and other services in ways which encourage initiative, self-help and mutual help and make them more effective." The dominant spirit in governmental rural projects was still paternalistic. A national program based on the "spirit of self-help" was yet to be evolved – by the CDPC, one might hope.

But from the beginning the CDPC seemed doomed to fail. It was true that despite his primary duties as NEC chairman, Rodriguez personally led the CDPC meetings until his illness and resignation. However, neither he nor his equally attentive successor, Alfredo Montelibano, could get the department secretaries to attend the CDPC meetings. These busy VIP members merely sent their alternates, some of whom in turn sent their proxies. Despite Binamira's appeals to the president, the latter never made the cabinet-CDPC members account to him for their absenteeism in the CDPC. They were anxiously pushing their individual departmental programs to produce the tangible results the president expected of them. Strangely, the president did not make them feel collectively responsible for the coordinated prosecution of the administration's total rural development program. Members' representatives attended CDPC meetings more to protect the interests of their respective agencies than to plan an integrated community development program or to coordinate their activities in the field. In fact, the Social Welfare Administration and the Bureau of Public Schools aspired to presidential designation as *the* national coordinating agency for community development.

The president's tendency to take administrative shortcuts also complicated the organizational life of the CDPC. Even before it began to meet, he had instructed Binamira to formulate a national plan for community development. This was about the time when, under legislative attack, the president bypassed the cumbersome NEC and created the interim Cuaderno Economic Planning Board (named after its chairman, Central Bank Governor Miguel Cuaderno). As directed, Binamira drafted a plan, with the help of Dr. Edward Chadwick, UN expert, and Dr. Robert McMillan of USOM/FOA. He secured approval of the plan by the CDPC representatives, and submitted it to the president with a memorandum summary. However, just as the president had formed the Cabinet Committee on Employment and Production in April (under Salvador Araneta), he entrusted the CDPC "National Plan" to another Cabinet Committee mostly made up of the absentee CDPC members.

The Committee met in June, supposedly to deliberate on the "National Plan," which proposed a Community Development Authority be established. The designated chairman, Presidential Complaints and Action Committee (PCAC) Commissioner Manuel P. Manahan, came late. In his place Araneta presided over the meeting, which brought the cabinet-CDPC members together for the first time in the six months since they took their oath before the president. All the ills that had plagued the CDPC from the start – the members' absenteeism, the president's indifference to the body, faulty communication between the members and their alter egos, and the jealousies, prejudices, and lack of coordination of the rival agencies represented – resulted in the suspension of the "National Plan" and the arbitrary assignment of the CDPC's coordinating function to the Social Welfare Administration.

Varying concepts and language confused the tense discussions held in Malacañang. No real consensus could have come out of this belated meeting. Binamira did not have a chance in the lopsided confrontation with his prestigious elders. The combined pressures on him prevented his coherent and uninterrupted presentation of the "National Plan," which was not carefully analyzed by the Committee members. The fact that the president made the Manahan Cabinet Committee – and then, casually, the cabinet as a whole – act upon the "National Plan," and the fact that the president acquiesced to its unceremonious shelving, confirmed the feeling of the absentee CDPC members that the Council was of no consequence as a policy-making body.

Two other influential groups helped, in effect, to downgrade the CDPC to a mere competitor for the president's acceptance and support, instead of becoming *the* national agency for community development that its well meaning architects had intended. One of them was the Philippine Rural Reconstruction Movement, in the person of its Chinese founder, Dr. Y. C. James Yen, and of its trustee and political strategist, Senator Tomas Cabili. While the CDPC was muddling through in its tormented existence, Cabili and Yen had obtained Magsaysay's endorsement of their plan to set up a joint Philippine-American Presidential Action Committee on Rural Reconstruction, patterned after China's belated Joint Commission on Rural Reconstruction, which Yen had organized in 1949 with funds from the United States Government. The freezing of the CDPC "National Plan" by the Cabinet Committee coincided with vigorous efforts by Cabili and Yen to secure the needed funds directly from the United States Congress — with Magsaysay's blessings!

The other powerful "competitor" of the CDPC was the Government Survey and Reorganization Commission, under Budget Commissioner Dominador R. Aytona. The GSRC had a statutory mandate to reorganize practically the entire executive department, including of course the NEC, the CDPC, and whatever national organization for community development the CDPC would recommend to the president. Thus, from its birth the CDPC was constantly threatened with absorption, change of leadership, or total extinction, by external fiat — not to mention its internal hemorrhage in mid-1955, brought about by the neglect of its members, the president's disuse, Rodriguez's illness and resignation, and by the wounds inflicted during the "Great Economic Debate" between Rodriguez and Cuaderno on the one hand and Araneta and Montelibano on the other.

The success of Cabili and Yen in getting the United States House of Representatives to support a Joint Commission on Rural Development (JCRD) finally aroused the otherwise passive and divided United States aid mission in the Philippines (now called the USOM/ICA) to fully support the painfully sought national program of community development. Fearful that the JCRD would divert aid funds away from the established channels and aggravate current charges of American meddling in Filipino politics, Director Harry A. Brenn and Ambassador Homer Ferguson appealed to Magsaysay. As they had hoped, the president readily agreed to stop the Cabili-Yen mission in the belief that the membership of two Americans in the JCRD would indeed be unconscionable foreign intervention in a program politically vital to his people. Magsaysay did not consult Cabili or the Philippine Embassy in Washington on his change of heart, just as he had not officially endorsed his two personal envoys through the usual diplomatic channels. The informality of the Cabili-Yen plan and mission had prevented consultations with the many officials and planning agencies in the Philippines involved in rural development. In his improvisations and casual, simultaneous quests for organizational and financial means, Magsaysay was at his best, or worst, depending on how pragmatic or systematic the observer.

The search by the many competing planners for a workable community development formula was now aimed solely at getting Magsaysay's approval and United States financing through the USOM/ICA. For the first time Colonel Brenn and Dr. McMillan of the USOM/ICA, Cabili and his PRRM associates, the CDPC as represented by Binamira, the UN Bureau of Social Affairs through Dr. Chadwick, and the GSRC, under Aytona, were now being brought together to search for a common denominator. At one point the president was bent on appointing Cabili as head of a Philippine Rural Development Authority, but this did not prosper. In the meantime, the technicians of the USOM/ICA, the CDRC and the GSRC were feverishly working toward a common plan amid increasing assurance of United States financing. In December, 1955, ICA/Washington accepted a "compromise" plan that had been jointly presented by NEC-CDPC Chairman Montelibano and Director Brenn. With the prior approval of Aytona and the president, the plan would commit $4.2 million over five years to be administered by a reconstituted CDPC. But, unaware of these developments, a "task force" in the GSRC was now pushing the idea of a brand new Department of Community Development and Welfare.

A PROGRAM AT LAST

It took all of 1955 for the president to realize that if he did not personally and resolutely attend to the organizing and financing of *his* community development program, nothing would happen to it. Nevertheless, his official approval of the plan submitted to Washington – for the practical purpose of getting something finally working – did not carry his conviction that the program to be launched under it would be guided strictly by the accepted theory and techniques of community development. He remained opposed to the idea of training multipurpose community development workers who would act as agents of social change in the barrios: to train barrio leaders and help them organize the villagers for self-help community projects, to stimulate other projects with grants-in-aid and technical advice, and to aid the provincial governor or municipal mayor in coordinating the technical agencies in the area. However, through a common friend, Fernando de los Santos, the president made known to Binamira his firm decision to scrap the obsolete CDPC, to veto the department proposed by the GSRC, and to appoint Binamira as his direct assistant in charge of the entire "Philippine Community Development Program" — as the plan submitted to Washington was called.

Binamira was in a quandary. As CDPC executive secretary, he was under obligation to execute the official plan to reinforce the CDPC, not to abolish it. To play safe with Chairman Montelibano, Binamira decided to follow the plan. On December 24, he saw the president, who was then with a group of officers led by General Jesus Vargas, chief of staff.

> BINAMIRA: Mr. President, here is the draft of the executive order which you requested me to make. Judge Esguerra and I went over it yesterday afternoon, and the Judge feels it is now ready for your signature.
>
> THE PRESIDENT: Let's see. No! This is not what I want. This is still too weak and will not permit you to act. It is too complicated and too long. Never mind this Council [the reorganized CDPC]. What I want is that you have the power to act for me. You issue orders and sign for me, just furnishing me a copy of your directives. For example, you want to build a road fast. You issue the order direct to the district engineer, furnishing the Secretary of Public Works a copy of your order. . . .
>
> BINAMIRA: That would be ideal, Mr. President, but department secretaries are very jealous of their prerogatives, and I would be in trouble if I undercut them by issuing orders to their subordinates. . . .
>
> THE PRESIDENT: But you issue the orders on behalf of the President. Thus you will say, "By order of the President." If they do not comply, and the Department Secretary will not follow, you tell me and I will fire him out [*sic*].

General Vargas nodded in assent and the rest of those present smiled.

THE PRESIDENT: For example, you need the Army to help you to build roads. You call on General Vargas here. I'm sure he will help you, because you are acting for and on behalf of the President.

Again, General Vargas nodded in agreement.

BINAMIRA: That is the very root of the present problem, Mr. President. We have a Council that cannot act. Our requests for assistance addressed to the different departments are ignored. What we need is some coercive power to ensure that our requests are really followed.

THE PRESIDENT: That is why you should throw this executive order away. It does not give you any power. You make another one appointing you as special presidential representative to act for and on behalf of the President in all matters of rural development.

Then, you can go ahead and issue directives, just furnishing me a copy. If you find difficulty, you tell me so I can straighten things out. If nobody believes you, tell me so I can fire him out [*sic*].

If I want you to do something fast, I will just tell you and you can start immediately without this goddam red tape. Thus, your work will mainly be to issue directives to provincial offices, then you go there and follow it [*sic*] up and see that it is complied with.

The president leafed through the draft again. Then he asked:

Did you study this thoroughly? How about Brenn, did he see this?

BINAMIRA: Yes, Sir, this was shown to Colonel Brenn.

THE PRESIDENT: You know, these American advisers still think they are in metropolitan New York. When I met Brenn last, he was talking about training 2,000 teachers in Central Luzon for so many months, spending thousands of pesos, so that after the training they will go out all over the Philippines, spread the gospel and do things.

This is not practical. What we need is action! Our people need roads, irrigation systems, artesian wells, right now. We cannot go to school and have them wait.

These American experts are not practical and do not know the conditions prevailing in the rural areas. Imagine, I read a plan of Moreno [Secretary Florencio Moreno, Department of Public Works and Communications], prepared with the advice of American experts, calling for 30-meter-wide roads. I told Moreno to throw it away.

Why, 30 meters is three times the size of this dining hall. This is a six-lane highway. It's too big for us to handle. Barrios do not need a six-lane highway, they need a one-lane highway big enough for a jeep to pass. You know, a jeep is about as wide as a bull cart and the barrio people will need only a one-lane highway.

BINAMIRA: That's right, Mr. President. As a matter of fact, I am trying to work with ICA and the Department of Public Works in drafting a practical program of building roads. The ICA expects to receive 59 bulldozers by the middle of January [1956] and we are trying to plan how to use them immediately upon arrival, building barrio roads.

THE PRESIDENT: Good. What is your plan – will you use them as teams?

BINAMIRA: Tentatively, we plan to distribute the machineries to the different regions in the Philippines and form teams for such regions. Then we will set up a system of priorities so that a schedule of their work can be set up. . . .

THE PRESIDENT: Priorities – that is theoretical and hard to follow. You must have a more practical plan on using the equipment.

BINAMIRA: Yes, we're trying to draft that, Mr. President. The use of the equipment, of course, will be subject to weather conditions prevailing in each of such areas. . . .

THE PRESIDENT: Weather, that is good . . . you have to consider that. . . . We have to be practical.

This is why you should be careful about advice from American experts. That plan of Brenn to train workers and conduct community development using the PRRM technique will not work. We start with those things needed most by our people – roads, wells, irrigation. . . . Our people are not yet ready for the PRRM approach.

This system of asking the people to donate labor in building roads will not work. You use machinery to build roads fast. If machinery is used, there will be no need for human labor.

However, I believe in the self-help principle with respect to irrigation systems. Here the people can furnish the sand, gravel and other materials, and also labor. As a matter of fact, I have already issued cash from my funds here on condition that people will provide a counterpart in materials and labor in constructing irrigation systems.

The president leafed through the draft executive order once again.

BINAMIRA: You remember attorney de los Santos of Cebu, Mr. President? I have thought that if the Council [CDPC] would continue, he might be a good man to fill a vacant Council seat, since it does not carry any remuneration, and de los Santos is hesitant to receive pay from the government.

THE PRESIDENT: Yes, de los Santos is practical, I like him. But I don't like that Council to continue. If you like you can have de los Santos under you, and both of you can handle the rural program, with de los Santos flying around the country to check progress. Both of you will come from Cebu [the president smiled], but that is all right – I like that boy . . . maybe you can balance de los Santos with another person, and form some kind of a commission. . . .

But I think it's better if you alone are appointed my assistant so that you can act for me. You revise that executive order.

BINAMIRA: Yes, Mr. President. I will be back this afternoon.

In his next meeting with the president, on December 29, Binamira asked Director Harry Brenn to accompany him.

BINAMIRA: In accordance with your instructions, Mr. President, I have revised the executive order. I have checked it with Judge Esguerra. It is O.K. with him as this note will show. It is ready for your signature.

The president glanced at Esguerra's note and read the new draft executive order that Binamira had prepared.

THE PRESIDENT: Very good! This is what I like. No more Council [CDPC].

Harry, have you seen this?

COLONEL BRENN: Yes, I have.

THE PRESIDENT: Is it O.K. with you?

COLONEL BRENN: Yes . . . we have $4 million for it. And, Mr. President, who will be the Presidential Assistant?

Pointing to Binamira, the president replied:

There, Ramon.

Ramon, you prepare your appointment. You bring Harry here so I can ask him how much salary we can agree on.

The president signed the document, which became Executive Order No. 156, establishing the official and agency known as the Presidential Assistant on Community Development (PACD).

A few days later Binamira and Brenn were joined by de los Santos when they again saw the president. As instructed, Binamira presented his appointment paper with the salary omitted.

THE PRESIDENT: Now, what is the salary of Ramon?

COLONEL BRENN: The PPA [Project Proposal and Agreement] says 14,532 pesos per year.

De los Santos: That is what the PPA says but Ramon does not want to put it there.

The president: Well, if that is what you agree on, that is nice; but if Ramon will work with department secretaries and he receives more salary, they will get jealous. So you just get 12,000 pesos huh? Like the Department Secretary. We'll see later what I can do.

The president then wrote "12,000 pesos" on the blank space and signed the appointment. Thus, at 28, Binamira became presidential assistant on Community Development, having demonstrated to the president his leadership and loyalty. Other things must also have influenced the decision. Compared with Senator Tomas Cabili, who was a politician in his own right, Binamira's youth and lack of political support made him an expendable administrator. If he should fail, he could be junked with impunity. But should Cabili fail as an administrator, or become a threat politically, he could not be discarded without loss to Magsaysay.

The last critical hurdle was to gain the president's consent to the formal training of the PACD field workers. For moral support, Binamira requested de los Santos and Senator Emmanuel Pelaez to come with him to Malacañang. When they entered the president's bedroom, the president had just gotten up and Mrs. Magsaysay was serving breakfast on a small table. The conversation opened with Binamira reporting on the progress of the barrio roads program. In a short while he and de los Santos informed the president of the scheduled start of the training course for the applicants who had just passed the examination.

Visibly irked by the report, the president said that it was unnecessary to train for community development work.

The president: Training, that is all theory! Never mind training. Hire the people you want and send them out to the field.

Binamira: Mr. President, it is very important to train our barrio workers, because their job is new.

De los Santos: Yes, Mr. President, it is very necessary to train these young men. . . .

The president's temper was near the breaking point when he interrupted them. He insisted that high school graduates could be immediately assigned in the field and that college trained people were afraid to do manual work. Then, after an ominous silence, the president started shouting in anger. He pounded on the breakfast table with his fist, making the dishes and silver shake and clatter.

Senator Pelaez slowly walked away to the far end of the room. Binamira and de los Santos did not say a word. The president was still seething with anger and berating Binamira when, suddenly, Mrs. Magsaysay said softly to her husband:

> Please lend them an ear, Monching.

Just as suddenly, the president calmed down, and Mrs. Magsaysay served him breakfast. At this time Senator Pelaez came around. Calmly, he suggested to his friend:

> Well, I think you are right in your fears about the delay and these college graduates who will be trained. It could happen. But, why don't you give it a try? They can start in a few provinces. There would be no harm. Let the boys try.

The president silently considered Pelaez's suggestion.

Then Binamira said:

> You appointed me Presidential Assistant, Mr. President. And, frankly, I do not think I can do the job without trained workers. As Senator Pelaez suggests, why don't you let us try? I assume full responsibility for the training and for the entire program.
>
> THE PRESIDENT: All right, go ahead and try. If anything happens, I'll hang you. I don't like it.

In parting Binamira thanked the president.

Fifteen days later, on April 9, 1956, the training course opened: in attendance were 220 community development trainees, 50 agriculturists, and 67 home demonstrators.

The Philippine Community Development Program had been launched.

The president's decision to replace the CDPC with the office of the Presidential Assistant on Community Development (PACD) was his first deliberate act concerning the administrative organization for community development. Both his approval in August 1954 of the executive order creating the CDPC and his endorsement late in 1955 of the plan to make the reorganized CDPC administer the requested United States aid had carried his mere acquiescence to the proposed organizational structures. Characteristically, like a guerrilla commander with separate combat patrols stalking the enemy in the jungle, Magsaysay had relied simultaneously, almost by trial and error, on several competing planners and organizations.

As in economic planning and policy, it took nearly two years of evolving political awareness and administrative perception for him to realize that the chief executive must personally interest himself not only in program ends and day-by-day management but also in crucial questions of administrative organization and coordination. Otherwise, as hard experience had taught him, the most well-meaning administrators and citizens were likely to engage in costly and frustrating bureaucratic warfare. Having acted decisively on establishing the PACD, all other parties fell in line. But the presidential groping for a suitable organization and administrator had taken all of his first two years!

PART VI

INDONESIA

The problems confronted by the Filipinos in achieving effective governmental organization are known elsewhere in Southeast Asia. Yet some of the other countries have stressed faith in the power of ideological pronouncements. In Burma, first under U Nu and then under Ne Win, the leaders believed that declarations about the "Burmese way to socialism" could change reality, and they showed little sympathy for maintaining the administrative structure of government inherited from colonial days. Similarly, in Indonesia during the years of Sukarno the administrative machinery rusted away as all attention and resources went to symbolic displays and grandiose projects.

Indeed, behind the most radical and militant pronouncements in Southeast Asia we find an extraordinary incapacity for action. In Indonesia under Sukarno, and in other places, vivid language replaced substantive progress, and ideological declarations became a means of pretending to achieve modernization and national development. Conceivably such appeals to the national spirit might have been constructive if they had been followed by substantive policies and programs.

Indonesia was unfortunate in that behind Sukarno's flamboyant performance throughout the 1950's was little development and extensive decay. In spite of pretenses the country was slipping back into precolonial ways. Those with modern skills who were committed to national ways lost all influence. In the meantime those who continued in the bureaucracy more and more often reflected traditional attitudes and practices in their thoughts and deeds.

In Ann Ruth Willner's analysis we find not just a case study but an informed discussion of persisting tradition in Indonesia. It is an appropriate close for this book because, subjected to much propaganda about Asia's efforts to modernize, it is easy for us to overlook the great strength that old cultural patterns still have in most of Asia. Those who are realistic about Asia will continue to recognize that which makes Asian culture unique. Eventually Asian countries will probably reach modernity and improved economics, but it is certain that whatever may be their paths they will never be able to completely part with their traditions. Their traditions may hold them back, as they have been doing in Indonesia, but in time, if progress comes, some traditions will have to be modified so as to perform more constructive functions. In the meantime we must be realistic, understanding that old traditions are profoundly important in the contemporary politics of Asia.

ANN RUTH WILLNER

8 The Neotraditional Accommodation to Political Independence: The Case of Indonesia

In our concern with the process of political modernization in new states, we tend to overlook its converse — the process of political traditionalization that can and frequently does take place in these states. In speaking of traditionalization, I am not merely referring to the frequently mentioned persistence of traditional "residues" and "primordial" attachments[1] or to the revival of traditionalist political movements in transitional societies which so-called modernizing political elites strive to eradicate or contain. Nor am I concerned here with the strategic uses of traditional symbols and practices by political leaders for purposes of legitimation and national integration,[2] although these can be viewed as contributing to a neotraditional syndrome.

This essay is concerned with the process by which traditional, indigenous elements of belief and behavior become reinvigorated within

[1] See Clifford Geertz, "The Integrative Revolution — Primordial Sentiments and Civil Politics in the New States," in Geertz, ed., *Old Societies and New States* (New York: The Free Press, 1963), pp. 105–30.

[2] William H. Friedland, "Some Sources of Traditionalism among Modern African Elites," in William J. Hanna, ed., *Independent Black Africa* (Chicago: Rand, McNally, 1964), pp. 363–369.

the modern organizations inherited by new states from their colonial predecessors. It elaborates some of the features of this renewal in one new state — Indonesia, particularly emphasizing how indigenous values affect the exercise of authority and the functioning of the public bureaucracy. Many features of indigenous repatterning described here might also be traced in other modern or would-be modern organizations, such as commercial and industrial enterprises, labor unions, and political parties.

However, traditionalization within a national bureaucracy and specifically within its elite sector is, I believe, significant, both in enabling us to understand the problems of modernization and to see its implications for the process itself. There has been a tendency to overidentify the impetus (as distinct from the aspiration) to modernization with the skilled and educated elites and to overidentify the resistance to the changes they ostensibly promote with the inert, rural, and parochial masses.[3] Furthermore, either the more easily visible party activities and struggles to attain power or our own emphasis on the importance of organized political and social groups as vehicles of mobilization of and participation by citizens in a modern political system has led to increasing attention to the "input" functions of political change as compared with the "output" functions.[4]

What I take to be most salient in effecting and institutionalizing enduring political and socioeconomic transformations in new states are the agencies of government. Goals and ideologies of national leaders may be admirably articulated; plans, programs, and projects for development may be clearly specified and formally initiated; party members may be mobilized and public demonstrations organized to express popular enthusiasm for policies and programs. But what matters, in the final analysis, is their implementation. And implementation in new states largely hinges, directly or indirectly, on the actions taken or not taken by the various levels of the public bureaucracy.[5]

[3] See, for example, Edward Shils, *Political Development in the New States* (The Hague: Mouton, 1962); and Max F. Millikan and Donald L. M. Blackmer, *The Emerging Nations* (Boston: Little, Brown, 1961).

[4] It is my impression that the volume of empirical studies, as distinct from attempts at theory-construction and model-building, on the behavior within and of political parties and groups in new states exceeds that of studies focused on bureaucracies or their component elements.

[5] It might be argued that the lack of a sense of national identity, of norms of political legitimacy, and of integration between central government and regions are independent factors that limit bureaucratic effectiveness; it might also be argued that effective administration can help to overcome these problems.

CHANGE AS TRADITIONALIZATION

At the microscopic level, the process of traditionalization, as it is described here for Indonesia, increases the influence of indigenous and particularistic rather than modern, rational criteria on the way in which public officials fulfill their prescribed roles, often despite their intellectual awareness of the demands of these roles.[6] On a broader scale, it can decrease the capacity of public institutions to perform a variety of functions customarily expected of them. These functions are not necessarily equated with those expected of governments of older states, but with those performed under colonial rule, from maintaining order and internal security to providing specific services and a minimal standard of material welfare.[7]

The process of traditionalization tends to weaken and dissipate in many respects the institutional modernization begun or intensified during colonial domination. In countries where indigenous repatterning of modern structures has been carried far enough, the resultant political and economic systems may come to resemble more closely, in some important characteristics, their precolonial precursors than they do the Euro-American systems upon which they are formally modeled. Some striking analogues may be seen between Indonesia's "Guided Democracy" and Java's Mataram Empire of the sixteenth to eighteenth centuries.

To call this a process of "political decay"[8] would be to place contemporary new states in a somewhat misleading and limited perspective. The attributes we tend to identify with political development or modernity[9] were not attained by these states as autochthonous

[6] I do not mean to imply that, from the perspective of the individual bureaucrat within his system, indigenous and particularistic behavior may not be more "rational," as judged by his own interests.

[7] The constantly asserted "revolution of rising expectations" may be more a revolution in the minds of the elites of these new states and their well-wishers abroad than for the bulk of their populations.

[8] See Samuel P. Huntington, "Political Development and Political Decay," *World Politics,* XVII (April 1965), pp. 386–430.

[9] For specifications of these attributes, see Rupert Emerson, *Political Modernization: The Single-Party System* (Denver: University of Denver, 1963), pp. 7–8; Robert E. Ward and Dankwart A. Rustow, eds., *Political Modernization in Japan and Turkey* (Princeton: Princeton University Press, 1964); Lucian W. Pye, *Aspects of Political Development* (Boston: Little, Brown, 1966), pp. 31–48.

political entities; so far as these attributes were present in their territories, they had been gained and were maintained by virtue of the colonial power or in response to it. The concept of "political decay" can be more appropriately applied to older or more mature states that have had a history as sovereign political entities. Then some transformation or diminution of qualities already present, and therefore to be equated with political "health" or "normality," may be seen as manifestations of decline or decay. One can refer in such terms to the "disintegration" of a once relatively integrated Austro-Hungarian Empire or the "instability" of a formerly more stable Argentina. But to use these terms for analogous phenomena in new states is to endow these states with a spurious political continuity.

The process of change in new states may rather represent a decolonizing interregnum, an accommodation to the conditions preceding and immediately succeeding the attainment of political independence. Measured against the norms of late colonial status or of older states, some transformations may well appear regressive. In long-range perspective, however, neotraditional accommodation may turn out to be the initial phase of modernization, a type of reequilibration. Particularly if one views modernization as a sequential or evolutionary process, postcolonial traditionalization may be seen as a necessary, if not a sufficient, preparatory state for a "takeoff" to modernization that can be generated and sustained from within.

The likelihood of a reinforcement of indigenous elements resulting from political independence might logically be deduced from two salient structural differences between a colonial system and its newly independent successor. These two differences alone would make it difficult for administrative as well as economic development to proceed from the point at which colonial administrations had left off.

First, a colonial system is a rational bureaucratic system. It is relatively free from the constraints imposed by a domestic political system, even though it is affected by political decisions in the metropolitan country. However, within its own domain, it deals with subjects for whom it is responsible but to whom it need not be responsive. The bureaucracy that supplants the colonial one must function within the framework of a domestic political system, subject to political pressures not only in formulating policy but in nearly all areas of implementation.

Second, the colonial bureaucratic system and its economic counterpart are buttressed by supports from outside the system, for the colonial system is, after all, a partial system, fed from the metropolitan power. Whatever the merits and demerits of various colonial regimes as reflected in the gains and losses of the indigenous inhabitants and apart from conjectures as to alternative outcomes had these territories not been colonized, it nevertheless remains true that the direct inputs for modernization, such as skills and capital, are largely imported.

With the withdrawal of the metropolitan power, the new administration not only loses some of these supports but has no automatic claims upon the external environment for the resources it needs to sustain and augment development. Substitute infusions from outside are sought and provided only to a limited extent through bilateral and international assistance programs. But these are often of limited utility, for reasons that will be discussed below.

These two features that differentiate postcolonial from colonial frameworks, (1) the introduction of a recognized electorate into the political system and (2) the withdrawal of external supports for which substitutes must be found, can impose on postcolonial bureaucracies restrictions with which their predecessors did not have to contend.

Admittedly, these restrictions and their consequences can vary widely, depending upon such factors in each country as (1) the kind of colonial system inherited; (2) the extent to which members of the indigenous population had entered modern organizations, assumed new roles, learned new skills, and internalized new values; (3) the conditions under which transition to political independence took place; (4) the type of new political system; (5) the availability of substitute resources; and (6) the mode of utilizing external aid.

Few, if any, of the new states and their bureaucratic sectors could continue the process of modernization from the point at which it had been at the end of colonial control. For Indonesia, as I shall endeavor to show, the process of traditionalization began with the attainment of political independence, if not earlier, although it was not clearly evident on the surface. Depending upon factors such as those specified above and many others, traditionalization may take place more slowly and take different forms in other new states. The traditionalization syndrome in Indonesia may represent an extreme case; however, the elements that contribute to it are found, to some degree, in other countries.

GUIDED DEMOCRACY AND PRECOLONIAL INDONESIA

At a typically Indonesian pace, Guided Democracy is slowly being dismantled. What will formally take its place remains to be seen. I would hazard the guess that the pendulum is not likely to swing back to anything resembling the preceding period of "constitutional democracy," a constitutional democracy that was never more than embryonic.[10] It is more likely that the succession crisis will ultimately produce another strong leader, who will cap a system not too different in substance, if different in form, from Guided Democracy. In some respects, Guided Democracy was the culmination of trends that began with independence and are not easily reversible.

What I shall be doing in this section is playing a game, one somewhat at variance with the games usually played by political scientists who deal with emerging countries, or what has come to be called the "third world." One such game, both creative and instructive, is to develop conceptual schemes within which to fit these countries' systems of government.[11] Another not uncommon game is to attempt to assess how closely a third-world government or type, such as that of the single party, approximates the classic "democratic" or "totalitarian" model. And it is not difficult to find in many of these governments elements that fit either.

My game runs as follows: Let us superimpose a map of a contemporary new political system upon a map of what is known of the major indigenous political system in that territory before and during the early years of colonialism. In each case, let us look not at the forms – i.e., not at what the system is supposed to be like – but at salient features of how the system functions or functioned, insofar as this is possible. (This is obviously a game best played by teams of

[10] The most impressive history of Indonesian politics of this period is Herbert Feith's *The Decline of Constitutional Democracy in Indonesia* (Ithaca: Cornell University Press, 1962). I agree with Harry Benda (see his review article in *The Journal of Asian Studies*, XVIII (May 1964), pp. 449–56) that its major drawback is in its framework – that of attempting to ascertain the causes for the failure of what Feith perceived to be a functioning democracy.

[11] For two examples, see David E. Apter, *The Politics of Modernization* (Chicago: University of Chicago Press, 1965), and Fred W. Riggs, *Administration in Developing Countries* (Boston: Houghton Mifflin, 1964), each of which contains the fruits of years of model building.

historians and political scientists.) What kind of analogues will be found between now and then?

Not impossibly, current presidents, prime ministers, or military heads of state might exhibit a style of leadership closer to that of precolonial rulers than their titles suggest. And might not their goals appear similar – primarily the expansion and consolidation of their personal power and effective control? Do not current ideologies serve mainly instrumentally as the secular myth replacing the attenuated precolonial, sacred myth to validate and support their leadership?

What about relations between the capital and regional areas, especially those differing ethnically from the area of the center of government? Is the effective control by central governments over outlying areas much greater today, despite the use of modern technology and transport, than that of past monarchs and tribal chiefs over areas where they claimed hegemony and tribute? It might well be argued that, or at least might well be worth investigating whether, regional and local components of states that are not yet nations exhibit about the same relative autonomy today as they had before colonizers imposed themselves on the scene. Central governments today cannot impose their mandates as they will, but must often negotiate the terms of acceptance and compliance. How different are they from paramount chiefs negotiating with recalcitrant subject chieftains, or emperors with petty monarchs?

How many of the effectively and efficiently operating modern industrial and commerical installations are (1) maintained and run by foreign personnel, (2) administered or advised by them, or (3) in the hands of one or two ethnic groups that have traditionally been noted for entrepreneurial activity? If the proportion is indeed substantial, do we not see another parallel here with foreign resident merchant groups or the so-called "factories" of European trading companies in Asia and Africa before the European governments assumed political and administrative control?

Playing this game more specifically with Indonesia, we note the following outstanding characteristics of its governmental system under Guided Democracy:

1. A president who appeared to be the sole source of legitimate political authority, which he exercised both symbolically and in fact in semi-monarchical fashion.

President Sukarno successfully assumed lifetime tenure, an impressive array of titles, and a style of life that included the entourage, regalia, and rituals customarily maintained by traditional Javanese monarchs. Not only was he formally accorded deference, but important national measures, even if not necessarily initiated by him, were promulgated in his name or with his approval. Political opposition to and dissatisfactions with many aspects of the regime were rife, but he was not the explicit target of any of them. On the contrary, he was both formally and informally appealed to as the final arbiter in conflicts, and rival leaders and factions contended for his influence and support for their objectives. Significantly, he did not maintain his position of supremacy by direct control of a tightly organized and disciplined political, bureaucratic, or military apparatus, commanding either overt or implicit instruments of coercive pressure at his direction. Rather, his strength derived from his adroit command of various strategies of manipulation, negotiation, and bargaining; from bestowal and withdrawal of approval; from appointments and emoluments; and from psychological exploitation of his knowledge of the probable responses of his chief lieutenants and subordinates, their lieutenants and subordinates, and other leaders and contenders for power and position. Again significantly, there was the absence of concrete and specific provisions for succession, which served to heighten the jockeying among the contenders for his favor.

2. A multiplicity and continued proliferation and substitution of formal legislative and administrative bodies with diffuse and overlapping jurisdictions and no clear-cut division or allocation of power and responsibilities among them.

During the period of Guided Democracy, the following were among the organs nominally charged with policy formulation and execution: formally representative bodies, such as the Gotong Rojong Parliament and a rarely convened 616-member People's Consultative Assembly; a number of national advisory councils with some combination of legislative and executive functions, such as the Supreme Advisory Council (DPA), the National Planning Council (DPN), the State Leadership Consultative Council (MPN), a quasi-cabinet superimposed upon and comprised of various members of the official Cabinet and others, and the Council of Assistants to the Leadership of the Revolution

(MPPR); the official Cabinet, which was several times reorganized, and whose total membership ranged from over forty to nearly one hundred portfolios, including an Inner Cabinet or Praesidium of ten, eight, or three members; a number of other agencies and committees, some subordinate to the ministries, others autonomous, such as a committee for "retooling" and an agency for education and indoctrination.

During the periods when the country was officially in a state of military emergency and under martial law, the massive civil bureaucracy had a parallel and competitive counterpart, both national and local, in the Supreme War Authority and its regional war administrators. At the same time, bodies were created to arouse and organize popular support from so-called "functional groups" of peasants, workers, women, youth, and so on, such as the National Front and its military counterpart, the Body to Mobilize the Potential of Functional Groups (BPPK). Later, there were established administrative "commands": the West Irian Supreme Command (KOTI), the Supreme Economic Operations Command (KOTOE), the Self-Reliance Command (KOTARI). The original retooling apparatus (PARAN) was itself "retooled" into the Command for Retooling of the Revolution.

While some agencies were superseded by or absorbed into others, many continued to exist with lesser or greater authority, duplicating the functions and tasks of others and remaining in competition with each other. At the same time, a number of the top posts of these organs were distributed and redistributed among a few chief figures, deputy ministers (such as Subandrio, Chaerul Saleh, and Leimena) who simultaneously wore a number of caps. Sukarno himself also served as the head of many of these bodies. The creation, manipulation, and "retooling" of posts and personnel formed one prong of his "balancing" or "juggling" strategy for retaining the reins of power while permitting the semblance of widespread participation in the mechanisms of government.

3. The interpenetration of the spheres of politics and administration. In a civil-military, bureaucracy-dominated political arena, policy was made and enforced (or not) and political conflicts were conducted within and among the various sectors of the large and amorphous bureaucracy.

Although party activity was less pronounced in later than in earlier years of the Guided Democracy period, political groupings, or *alirans,* by no means disappeared. Sometimes overt but more often thinly veiled, the orientations and preferences of the various Islamic, nationalist, Socialist, and Communist groups were expressed in pressures upon Sukarno and upon their supporters or sympathizers in the various segments of the bureaucracy. The higher echelons of the civil and military bureaucracies contained, often within the same organ, officials representing opposing political views, as well as sectors dominated by one or another political faction. This was the context in which ensued struggles to promote or undermine one or another set of policy objectives as well as personal struggles for power. What we term "political demands" and "political struggles" were expressed and conducted either obliquely, in an atmosphere of subsurface intrigue, probe and withdrawal, alliance, counteralliance, and cross-alliance, or in the form of mass protests and demonstrations, often stage-managed.

Five characteristics of the governmental system can almost be deduced from the preceding three and are closely interrelated:

4. The development of many agencies or their regional branches into what were in effect the personal and political domains or fiefdoms of their chief officials.

5. The relative autonomy of regional administration and the tenuousness of central government control over many localities, with relations between the center and the regions characterized by negotiation rather than by command and compliance.

6. Official government ownership and control of large sectors of the economy, combined with inability to implement government economic programs or to prevent large-scale evasion of regulations.

7. A proliferation of frequently contradictory regulations, resulting in ineffective and inefficient administration, with administrative discretion often exercised arbitrarily, nepotistically, and for personal and political aggrandizement or reprisal.

8. Frequent changes and transfers of personnel contributing to a much looser, more decentralized, and in many ways more flexible and responsive governmental system than the formal structure and apparent policies would indicate.[12]

[12] For details on the politics of Guided Democracy, see Herbert Feith, "Dynamics of Guided Democracy," in Ruth T. McVey, ed., *Indonesia* (New Haven: Yale University Press, 1963), pp. 309–409.

Let us now look at some of the outstanding features of indigenous precolonial government in Indonesia, as exemplified by its last major empire in Java, Mataram, which was gradually dismembered and incorporated by the Dutch.[13] At its peak and center, residing in often precarious splendor in a palace and court city built to represent a microcosm of the universe, was a semidivine monarch in whom was nominally vested supreme power over subjects and land. He was both buttressed and circumscribed by elaborate and aesthetically intricate ceremonials, court regalia endowed with mystical significance and supernatural power, and deferential courtiers who plotted with and against him and each other. His titles were many and impressive, testifying to his assumed descent from the rulers of all previous dynasties and through them from the gods of the Hindu pantheon. The titles also reflected the special sanction derived from adherence to Islam and proclaimed the ruler's hegemony over many areas whose local rulers had at one or another time formally recognized (by dispatching missions, tribute, or hostages to his court) the overlordship of Mataram, gained through conquest, alliance, or marriage.

But the control any monarch exerted extended only as far and as deep as he could exercise it effectively. There was no fixed and narrowly circumscribed rule of succession. As a result, wars of succession among rival claimants for the throne were frequent. Periods preceding and succeeding accession of a new ruler were marked by intensification of intrigue, alliances, and counteralliances close to the court and by increased efforts of remoter vassals to attain greater autonomy. The successful claimant then would seek to counteract centrifugal tendencies and reconstitute or augment the hold of Mataram upon the more distant parts of the realm.

At the apex of Mataram's formal administrative structure, it appears, was a council of ministers, generally five, headed by a *patih* or chief minister, although occasionally the ruler served as his own prime minister. A "left of the throne" and a "right of the throne" minister divided between them certain state tasks; similarly, responsibility for the ruler's warehouses and treasury was assigned to "left" and "right" ministers. A triumvirate of royal princes managed the royal household. Beyond the circle of these "inside" councilors were the "outside" ministers, supervising the "inner realm," or royal ter-

[13] B. Schrieke, *Indonesian Sociological Studies,* I and II (The Hague and Bandung: Hoeve, 1957).

ritories surrounding the capital. Extant charters from the earlier Madjapahit Empire suggest a long tradition of an inner council of five, with functions equivalent to prime minister, military and/or naval commander, treasurer, and so on, as does evidence of a similar basic structure in some of the outer islands. Madjapahit also seems to have had an equivalent triumvirate of royal dignitaries.

It appears that in practice, however, both the men who held the highest offices and the powers and responsibilities conferred on the individuals or the offices changed frequently, depending upon whom the ruler trusted or distrusted or whom he needed to favor at any particular time. Thus records show that in the 1660's a certain Wirajaya not only was the *tumenggung,* or commander of the capital, but also supervised the seaports, the "foreign relations" with Dutch-held Batavia, and foreign trade; oversaw the trial of criminal cases; and took charge of preparations for a naval attack on Bali and a military expedition against Bantam in the west. Sometimes high officials retained their titles or were given other honorific titles, but were withdrawn from active service to be retained as confidential councilors, only to be restored to service later, if it became advantageous to the ruler.

There were varied arrangements for control over the outer realm. It seems that the earlier Madjapahit rulers tried to consolidate their power by assigning the government of distant areas to their close kin or by establishing matrimonial alliances. Later Mataram monarchs, to stave off threats from more ambitious princes, called these princes to court and farmed out their territories to nonroyal officials, who retained part of the revenues while forwarding specified amounts to the court. In many instances, the lands or people assigned to a governor or regent were not contiguous, an arrangement intended to prevent ambitious officials from consolidating power enough to become dangerously autonomous. Jurisdictions were often shifted and a single area might be subject to the authority of several different officials.

There was of course competition among aspirants for and holders of such appanages for the favor of the ruler and for increases in such assignments and the benefits derived therefrom. The ruler could utilize this competition to build and retain loyalty. And villagers who found too onerous the taxes and labor imposed upon them by greedy governors or by those intent upon improving their position at court, by presenting to the ruler more munificent gifts than those of their rivals could and did remove themselves from one regent's jurisdiction to another's.

The institution of such grants and rights of tax-collecting tended to create a semihereditary nobility, but one with a different base of power and therefore a different type of relationship to the ruler from that typical of European feudalism, for such benefices were not technically hereditary and could be recalled and redistributed at the ruler's will. In effect, this resulted in vague demarcation between the administrative and the political orders and in considerable fluidity underlying the formal organization.

Officially, much of the internal and external trade, especially the collection and distribution of the basic staple, rice, was a state monopoly. Mataram rulers attempted to channel most of the sea trade through the port of Japara as a means of controlling tolls, prices, and levies. But such regulations were often honored more in the breach, especially since many of the eastern and northern seaports had been independent principalities before their conquest by Mataram rulers. Smuggling and independent barter arrangements were far from uncommon; attempts to enforce regulations produced threatened or actual revolts.

Thus, despite the veneer of royal absolutism, in the indigenous system royal charisma required constant maintenance by psychological and military weapons. Central power was not firmly institutionalized but waxed and waned. The bureaucracy was fluid and highly politicized. Relations between and among rulers, their immediate subordinates, and the underlings of the latter were characterized on all sides by the employment of intricate and subtle strategies of negotiation, manipulation, guile, and evasion. If we read the *Babads,* the Javanese chronicle histories, whether or not we accept their historical authenticity, we cannot help but be struck by the parallels between the political behavior recounted and the intricacy, subtlety, and elaborateness of traditional Javanese art forms as evinced in architecture, music, dance, and drama.

Certainly, many changes have occurred in the archipelago of Indonesia, particularly in the last century and particularly in Java and other areas where the Dutch colonial system penetrated deeply and powerfully. Technology, economic organization, and social structure have changed, although not evenly and in some salient respects not profoundly. But if one were to superimpose a map of the Indonesian bureaucratic polity of Guided Democracy upon a map of its Mataram or Madjapahit predecessor, I suggest that the congruities would be more pronounced than the disparities.

THE PROCESS OF ACCOMMODATION TO TRADITION

Indonesia in the early 1950's undoubtedly presented a different political surface than it did a decade later and than it does today. It then boasted an impressive array of competitive political parties, factions, and interest groups organized along familiar lines; a parliament that debated and legislated programs and policies proposed by cabinets; a record of several elections — in short, the usual paraphernalia of a "modern" polity.

The explanation, by now conventional, for the "failure" of this "system" and for the apparently dramatic changes that followed barely a decade of independence is that between two elites arose a struggle that paralleled and reinforced a struggle between Java and the outer islands. An "administrative" or "problem-solving" elite, largely composed of leaders of the Masjumi and Socialist parties, allied with and sympathetic to the more dynamic entrepreneurial elements of the outer islands, lost power and influence to the more Javanese-oriented, radical "mass-solidarity-builders" and "symbol-wielders."[14] The first group could be seen as the direct inheritors of what the Dutch had developed in Indonesia, for during the early years of the new state they held many leading posts in the cabinets and upper echelons of the civil service, and their goals were articulated as not merely assuming political control of the "modern" sector but building upon, expanding, and diffusing it.

We can take issue with the overfacile designation of a group as "westernized," "modernizing," or "problem-solving" largely because the social and intellectual backgrounds of its members have enabled them to communicate with us sympathetically and to espouse, with varying degrees of conviction, familiar goals in familiar terms. Such deceptively simple categorization not only blurs the differences between the kind and depth of adaptation to externally derived values; it also fails to take sufficiently into account the situations in which people

[14] See Feith, *Decline of Constitutional Democracy;* and Leslie Palmier, *Indonesia and the Dutch* (London: Oxford University Press, 1962).

act, which often provide more valid indicators of basic orientations or of the directions in which value conflicts may be resolved.

Even if we assume the doubtful proposition that this group was as instrumentally dedicated to development as their statements suggest, the resultant state of Indonesian affairs cannot be attributed mainly to their inability to implement the policies they espoused or to their consequent exclusion (or the exclusion of many of them) from positions of leadership. Such an interpretation, though not incorrect on one level of analysis, does not take into account the more fundamental aspects of the decolonization process.

This process, which I term "accommodation to tradition" or "indigenous repatterning," began, certainly in the administrative and economic sectors, with the advent of independence. Most of the features of Guided Democracy were not major departures in type from similar elements existing before 1959, often considered the year of the great transition. They were merely more intensified and overt manifestations of a trend that was discernible during the early 1950's by those not unwilling to recognize it.

Admittedly, the traditionalization, or "erosion," of the administrative system, if evaluated by Western administrative criteria, was partially disguised during that period by two factors:

1. The high visibility at the upper echelons of the government hierarchy of the so-called "modern elite" members.
2. The presence of their relatively invisible "silent partners," the Dutch and Chinese advisers and business interests with whom the elite maintained a symbiotic relationship, which paradoxically supported the colonially induced modern superstructure while inhibiting its actual development by Indonesians.

The constraints and consequences of decolonization leading to traditionalization may be analytically classified into three types: structural factors, as mentioned above, political-situational factors, and cultural orientations, or value factors. The latter two are closely related. Modes of perceiving, evaluating, and responding to situations are also culturally conditioned. One kind of cultural predisposition may result in a perception of a situation different from that formed by another. And although individual decision-makers from different cultural backgrounds may analyze a situation similarly, their responses may differ, since each is partly influenced by the psychological constraints he has absorbed from his cultural environment.

Before reviewing the factors contributing to the process of traditionalization, I shall briefly describe some of the traditional Javanese core values.

A SUMMARY OF SOME TRADITIONAL CULTURAL VALUES

The values described here are perhaps most characteristic of the dominant Indonesian ethnic group, the Javanese. They are sufficiently shared by other major ethnic groups, however, to constitute part of the wider Indonesian culture. At any rate, *contextual adaptability,* or responsiveness to the pressures of the particular environment in which one happens to be, is characteristic of Indonesians generally. Thus, since the Javanese have tended to dominate the public arena in Indonesia and much of government has radiated from Java, the tendency has been for members of other groups (especially when they are in Java) to take cognizance of, come to terms with, or adapt to Javanese values that might conflict with their own.

These values are "traditional" in the sense that they have been elicited from the traditional literature and the literature on the traditions of Indonesia and also they have been inferred from statements made by and the observed behavior of Indonesians in the "traditional" contexts, i.e., rural villagers, farmers, artisans, aristocrats.[15]

It should be emphasized that these are not necessarily uniquely Indonesian values. To some degree, any of them can probably be found in almost any culture, including our own. It is the combination of values, rather than any particular value, that is unique to a culture.

[15] For additional and more detailed descriptions of these values and their content, see the following: Donald R. Fagg, "Authority and Social Structure: A Study in Javanese Bureaucracy" (Ph.D. dissertation, Harvard, 1958); Clifford Geertz, "Ethos, World View and the Analysis of Sacred Symbols," *Antioch Review* (Winter 1957–58), pp. 421–437; Clifford Geertz, *The Religion of Java* (New York: The Free Press, 1960); Hildred Geertz, *The Javanese Family: A Study of Kinship and Socialization* (New York: 1961); Robert R. Jay, *Religion and Politics in Rural Central Java* (New Haven: Cultural Report Series No. 12, Southeast Asia Studies, Yale University, 1963); and Ann. R. Willner, "From Rice-Field to Factory: The Industrialization of a Rural Labor Force in Java" (Ph.D. dissertation, Chicago, 1961). Major sources of data for this and other sections were my own observations during four years of work with the Indonesian government.

Control and minimization of conflict. A number of values can be subsumed under the concept that has generally been termed the *maintenance of harmony or unity,* but that I prefer to consider *a theory of conflict control.* The world of men, like the natural and the supernatural worlds, is viewed as one of potentially diverse and therefore potentially destructive forces that must somehow be reconciled and adjusted to coexistence or balance. To achieve and sustain an equilibrium that is always at best precarious requires the constant efforts of individuals to conduct themselves calmly with each other and to subdue elements of potential discord and dissonance.

Since ends and means are perceived as a continuum, rather than distinct, and the ritual of behaving "as if" is a mode of bringing about the desired end, the tone, style, or prevailing mood of any interpersonal or group situation or interaction becomes nearly as important as its purpose or direction. The *manner* in which something is said or done is of no less importance than what is actually said or done.

Foreigners first exposed to the smiling countenances and friendly gregariousness of Indonesians tend to consider them a naturally euphoric people, not realizing how important external appearances are to them. Indonesians do not find it any easier to live with, agree with, or approve of each other than do people in other societies. But their own cultural stereotype of themselves is that of "one happy family" whose members are cooperative and mutually helpful. Therefore, personal inclinations, motives, and antipathies that might disturb the atmosphere of ease they strive to maintain are often kept carefully concealed behind bland smiles.

They attach a positive value to the avoidance of overt conflict. Disagreement may well exist, but it should be expressed with discretion and not brought to the point of embarrassment or open conflict. If signs of discord cannot be averted, they should be rapidly dissipated.

Similarly, one should not completely alienate one's opponents or leave them no lines of retreat. Since one never knows when one might need them in the future, one should leave the door open for the possibility of future reconciliation and rapport. This is especially important since one cannot predict that one's current opponents may not be needed as future allies against other opponents.

The maintenance of such external behavior requires of an individual considerable *control and restraint of emotions,* another quality particularly prized by Javanese. In particular, the code of the Javanese aristocrats, which many government officials inherited and others have sought to emulate, stresses the necessity of keeping one's feelings *dalam*, or inside. According to this code, to exhibit enthusiasm, vehemence, excitement, or anger is crude or uncouth, appropriate only to the lower class. That which is forceful, vigorous, or insistent is frowned upon unless deliberately or instrumentally assumed for effect. Even children are permitted only a brief period of spontaneous expression and freedom from constraint. They are trained early to contain their feelings and curb their impulses.

Emotional detachment is not only carefully cultivated to ease social intercourse and inhibit possible friction; it is also valued as a means of achieving spiritual force and moral strength. He who can be unswayed by feeling gains not merely power over self but potential power over others. Detachment is also a form of psychological self-protection. In the traditional view of causality, the individual is at the mercy of luck or fortune, and his destiny is determined largely by forces outside himself. Therefore, the less he permits himself emotional involvement, the less he is likely to be hurt by the vicissitudes of life.

Yet controls are difficult to maintain, especially in the face of major frustration or grave provocation. Therefore, the converse of minimizing conflict, of inhibiting impulses to aggression, and of limiting the legitimate outlets for aggressive expression can be sudden and severe violence. Extremes may produce extremes; what is constantly repressed may unexpectedly explode; one's darkest fears become fantasies that take on the fascination of the forbidden; what is buried then rises up to possess one. *Amok* may ensue.

STATUS AND ORDER. This value can be summarized by stating that every encounter, between two Javanese especially, involves a mutual recognition in language, gesture, and attitude of their relative place in an elaborately and subtly stratified social order. The proper observance of the niceties of etiquette, with recognition of the precise degrees of deference and condescension, is of utmost importance.

FIT AND PLACE. Closely related to the concept of status and order is the notion of fit or congruence, or the appropriateness of elements or individuals in a pleasing or proper pattern in their placement or relation to each other. This notion is applied to colors, arrangement of houses, dress, marriage, timing of activities, and particularly behavior in a wide range of situations for which the proper patterns have been established. Randomness and spontaneity have little place; aesthetic correctness and stylization predominate.

INTERDEPENDENCE OF COMMUNITY AND RECIPROCAL OBLIGATION. *Gotong rojong,* or mutual cooperation, is not a vague ideal of cooperation but a generic term for a number of fairly concrete and calculated practices of economic and social exchange among kin and neighbors.[16] The types and varieties of interchange, of rights or claims by virtue of kinship, clanship, or residence are too numerous to be detailed here. Suffice it to state that individuals in more fortunate circumstances are expected to support the aged and indigent, distribute as widely as possible opportunities for work or office or other favors they are in a position to bestow, and, in general, share as widely as possible whatever windfalls they may receive. These forms of assistance are not necessarily felt as the burden or drain that they are in fact. Nor are they given to obtain virtue or satisfaction with self. Rather, provision of assistance confers upon those who receive it reciprocal obligations toward those who give it although not necessarily in the same form. The donor or even potential donor creates rights to call upon recipients or potential recipients for whatever type of help, support, or loyalty he may in turn need and that they are or will be in a position to provide. Concern for the welfare of one's group and action on behalf of any of its members are investments in one's own future and are thus seen as forms of social and economic insurance. Conversely, to deny the claims of one's group is to forfeit one's future claims to the resources of the group and its members. This is a risk that few who are brought up in an atmosphere of interdependence dare to take.

One consequence of this system of interlocking rights and obligations beyond the immediate family is that individuals need not feel isolated and completely dependent upon their own resources for survival and advantage. Among many, there develops less need for and motivation toward personal striving and economic self-sufficiency than are found in our society. For those who achieve prominent public position, the pressures to distribute its fruits within the circles of private claims are great. And it is difficult to subordinate private loyalties and personal obligations, whose returns are familiar, to abstractions of public loyalty and obligation.

[16] Koentjaraningrat, *Some Social-Anthropological Observations on Gotong Rojong Practices in Two Villages of Central Java* (Ithaca: Cornell University Southeast Asia Program, 1961).

A related value to which Indonesians have been conditioned from early childhood is the importance of *conformity to group norms and expectations.* Although an infant in this society is reared with love and affection and an absolute minimum of physical chastisement, he is early made conscious that he is but one, and the least important, member of a large group. He is soon made aware that approval, acceptance, and affection are contingent upon subordinating his impulses and urges to what is regarded by those around him as proper. The learning pattern stresses observation, absorption, and imitation. Experimentation is not encouraged. Acquiescence to instructions and opinions of elders brings praise and rewards. To demand attention, to assert oneself, or to strike out in a different direction brings reprimands and similar negative responses.

A common word in Indonesian is *malu,* translated variously as "shyness," "hesitancy," or "shame" and frequently used to convey reluctance. It is really more than a word. It is a concept connoting states of feeling ranging from discomfort to a deep sense of humiliation. These states are produced at the prospect of entering a situation or taking an action — or as the result of a situation or action — in some way beyond the range of the expected, the conventional, the approved. The sense of malu, the fear of being shamed or ridiculed, is indoctrinated in children early and not easily overcome. It transforms the need to act into a need to *act with* or *in conformity to* a group. It expresses an unconscious fear that individual action might result in isolation, apartness, social ostracism.

STYLE AND STRATEGY OF ACTION. It can easily be inferred from the preceding discussion that the Indonesian style and strategy of communication and action are, to put it mildly, oblique and circuitous. Disagreement, dissent, and threat are often conveyed by indirection and innuendo. Indonesians indicate to each other in many subtle and tenuous ways the meanings behind the words they employ. A request is very seldom refused outright. But the tone of voice in which someone agrees to a request provides a clue as to whether he has a real intention of complying with it. The words selected may also convey whether the assent is merely a polite affirmative or signifies actual intention to fulfill what is asked of one.

In traditional work contexts, for example, discontent with the performance of a subordinate is rarely expressed by outspoken reprimand, nor is it given as a reason for dismissal. A dissatisfied employer is likely to dispense with the services of an unsatisfactory worker with a face-saving pretext, such as saying that he has not enough work in the near future or that some relative has suddenly turned up whom he is obliged to hire in his place. Or he might, without being in any way sharply critical, convey sufficient lack of appreciation for the worker's efforts to induce the latter to decide to seek a living elsewhere. Similarly, a discontented subordinate does not complain of his conditions of work, payment, or treatment, or announce that he can do better elsewhere. He finds that some urgent situation in his family forces him to sever the connection temporarily. These pretexts do not of course deceive anyone about underlying motives but are appreciated and expected as part of the ritual of face-saving.

A BRIEF NOTE ON DUTCH COLONIALISM

Although Weber did not, as far as I am aware, discuss colonial systems, in many respects the Dutch colonial order, especially in its later stages, might be considered a fair approximation of the Weberian model of legal-rational authority. A bureaucracy — elaborately hierarchical in structure, functionally differentiated, recruited on the basis of education and skills — formulated and applied relatively uniform systems of rules and procedures, in accordance with what it took to be rational criteria.

Perhaps more significant, the regulatory activities of this bureaucracy in its last flowering were extremely extensive and intensive. When, as the result of investigations indicating the declining welfare of the inhabitants of Java and Madura, the so-called "ethical" policy was instituted and when serious development of the "subsistence" sector was undertaken during the depression years, the Dutch went at development with Calvinistic zeal.

If the early Dutch colonial policies, as many historians suggest, had destroyed much of Indonesian initiative and enterprise, later attempts to redress the balance may have discouraged much of what remained. The excessive paternalism has been illustrated by two jokes, one to the effect that an official engaged in uplift would begin with "Let me show you," continue with "Let me help you," and conclude with "Let me do it for you," and the other to the effect that a villager could not scratch his head without first getting permission from the subdistrict officer and without an expert to show him how.[17]

Much has been made of the seemingly differential response of some of the outer island peoples and the Javanese to the economic changes instituted by the Dutch. The Javanese response has been termed "involutional,"[18] i.e., turning upon itself, in contrast to the more dynamic adaptation of, for example, Sumatra. Javanese lack of economic interest and comparative Outer Island economic acquisitiveness may well reflect the more predominant Islamic world view in the latter contrasted with the Hindu-Buddhist world view of the Javanese. These qualities also may reflect the effects of several centuries of penetration and control in depth and breadth by foreigners in Java, contrasted with several decades of relatively light penetration of the outer islands, except in coastal areas.

THE POLITICIZATION OF THE BUREAUCRACY

It will be recalled that in the traditional milieu of colonial Indonesia, competition was frowned upon, and the members of units such as the family, the neighborhood, the village, and the indigenous work organization tended toward cooperative, reciprocal interdependence, at least as a norm if not always in practice. If there is introduced into such a society a system of organization, i.e., political parties, whose basic rationale is competition, almost unbounded competition will arise, unlike societies in which competitiveness is an acceptable norm and its limits tend to be institutionalized. Indonesian political life became one of almost unbounded political competition. In such a situation, almost all other objectives can be sacrificed upon the altar of the party's competitive position.

Furthermore, conscious efforts to maintain surface harmony often conceal subsurface frustrations and hostilities. If the more traditional forms of organization cannot easily serve as legitimate outlets for their expression, parties can. Political parties in Indonesia therefore not only have served as vehicles for the attainment of power and

[17] See J. S. Furnivall, *Netherlands India: A Study of Plural Economy* (Cambridge: Cambridge University Press, 1944), pp. 381–393, esp. p. 389.

[18] See Clifford Geertz, *Agricultural Involution: The Process of Agricultural Change in Indonesia* (Berkeley: University of California Press, 1963).

prestige and as avenues of social mobility; they also have served as outlets for the expression of displaced hostilities transferred from other arenas.

The political climate therefore became one of almost unbounded party competition that neither cabinets nor policies could long survive. One immediate effect was politicization of the bureaucracy.

One of the means by which a party could mobilize and retain support was by providing rewards to its members in the form of civil service posts and promotion. In addition to the more traditional forms of nepotism involving family and ethnic-group preference, party affiliation and party loyalty often became more important criteria for higher bureaucratic preference than skill, education, or performance. Certain ministries or certain parts of certain ministries became known as the domains of certain political parties.

This produced a kind of vicious circle in which bureaucratic preference as the result of party affiliation led to intensified loyalty and often to primary loyalty to the party and its positions on various policies or programs. Not only in cases where the ministries had responsibility to help formulate policies and programs, but also where their task was mainly to execute them, officials would often be more responsive to covert party directives than to those from their superiors in the service. This impaired the morale of officials who were originally task-oriented. Party infiltration of the civil service was intensified before the national elections in 1955, especially on the provincial and local levels. There was a turnover of many regional officials at this time and there was strong utilization of their official posts to proselytize for the parties.

Another factor, affecting both the staffing and performance of the bureaucracy as well as its effectiveness in attempting to cope with developmental problems, was the need to reward those with revolutionary records over those with expertise derived from backgrounds in the colonial service. Though the latter were retained, some of their power to make and enforce decisions was effectively weakened.

Politicization also produced a transformation in the sociological makeup of the bureaucracy. The need to provide employment and to satisfy the aspirations of semieducated young people also brought in more officials with subnational traditional orientations as well as those with the revolutionary egalitarian outlook.

THE REINFORCEMENT OF INDIGENOUS VALUES

As I mentioned earlier, I should like to take issue with the distinction drawn by Herbert Feith, and followed by others, between two groups of leaders, the "solidarity makers" and the "administrators" — a distinction in the Lasswell tradition.[19] Useful though this heuristic device may be as an ideal-type characterization of two analytically discrete orientations or skills, it suffers from the weaknesses of many such devices when applied to real people in the real world. I disagree with the inference that the group whom Feith designated as "administrators" were as dedicated to problem-solving and instrumental activity on the levels of decision and action as they seemed to be on the level of rhetoric. Elsewhere I have characterized them as "Janus-faced."[20] The majority of elite officials whom I knew and worked with in Indonesia could talk and write as intellectually sophisticated a game of proposals, prerequisites, and priorities as could any of their Western counterparts, and they did so, especially to Western counterparts, advisers, observers, and scholars.

But in one part of reality, especially in making and implementating crucial decisions, these same officials tended to act out of several analytically distinct sets of values, alternatively and even simultaneously. Their behavior in many instances reflected adherence to a fundamentally Indonesian orientation. A familiar example of the role of traditional values in administrative behavior is that of the official who agreed, with little or no protest, to undertake a course of action urged upon him, despite his conviction that it was undesirable or unfeasible. His formal assent was his most positive contribution to the project. Subsequently he either made no attempt to begin the action to which he had verbally committed himself or delayed interminably all but an initial step or two. In the traditional context, verbal agreement is not necessarily a commitment. It merely reflects the cultural reluctance to reject an explicit demand or express opposition in a face-to-face or group situation. Delay or neglect in performance communicates in a more tactful way disapproval of a request or order or inability to carry it into effect.

[19] See footnote 14.

[20] A. R. Willner, "The Foreign Expert in Indonesia: Problems of Adjustment and Contribution," *Economic Development and Social Change,* II (April 1953), pp. 71–80.

One traditional attitude, which was reinforced by exposure to and participation in the Dutch system of administration, was respect, almost bordering on veneration, for the appearance of legality and correctness of form. Despite the antipathy of many of the younger people to what was conceived to be "Dutch," this respect remained, especially among the Javanese, because it accorded with their traditional notions of symbolism and ritual. Thus rules and regulations, by their very existence, achieved a sacrosanct existence of their own, regardless of their applicability to a specific situation, the need for regulation in that situation, or the possibility of handling the situation by regulation. Especially among middle-level bureaucrats, a ritual of proliferating elaborate sets of rules developed, especially in procedural matters. Regulations on a matter were frequently internally inconsistent, contradicting other regulations on the same subject, irrelevant to the issue at hand and impossible to enforce. Yet the time and effort spent in seeking them out or in seeking ways to circumvent them hampered the performance of work perceived even by these same bureaucrats to be more vital. But the concern with regulations did not diminish, for the paper work they imposed provided a sense of security.[21] And government apparently proceeded despite the paucity or ambiguities of policy.

What I am suggesting here is that the problems of achieving policy consensus in the political arena with its almost unbounded competition among political parties, the problems of party loyalties and factionalism within the bureaucracy, of scarcity of resources, and of lack of skilled personnel on lower levels may well have constituted strong constraints on effective administration. But these problems were not necessarily the determining factors in the failure of the so-called "problem-solvers" to execute many of their policies. Perhaps as strong an impediment — although admittedly it is difficult to estimate relative weights — was this element of dysfunctional traditional behavior and response that characterized the so-called modernizers.

However much many of the "modernizers" derided and deplored many of their traditional cultural patterns and the values these reflected, they could not free themselves from these cultural influences and were often psychologically inhibited from acting in accordance

[21] A similar phenomenon, termed "rituals in place of rationality," in the performance of the Burmese administrative service, has been described by Lucian Pye in *Politics, Personality, and Nation Building* (New Haven: Yale University Press, 1962), pp. 215–216.

with the utilitarian standards they intellectually perceived to be required by a particular situation if these standards conflicted with those traditional values.

The low level of performance of the Indonesian civil service, characterized by one sympathetic student of Indonesian affairs as "the weakest by far of any major state,"[22] has too often been attributed to such factors as the low levels of education, the lack of prior training and experience of much of its personnel and the reluctance of politicized bureaucrats to implement policies with which their parties did not agree or which threatened to arouse political opposition. I do not deny that in the period of Guided Democracy lack of requisite skills was a contributory factor, although perhaps more among the regional and local bureaucrats than in the higher echelons of the central government. Political considerations did contribute to the gap between policy directives and their implementation, although from one perspective it can be argued that assessments of political risks were colored by indigenous values related to risk-taking.

However, in the course of three years of direct participant observation of three national ministries during the middle 1950's, I could not help but be impressed by the number of instances in which delays and failures in the performance of even routine tasks could be attributed neither to the absence of skills nor to the intervention of political factors. Many officials possessed a sophisticated grasp of the functions and responsibilities of their offices and of the means and procedures that "rational administrative criteria" would prescribe as appropriate to their effective and efficient execution.

But between their awareness of the formal role prescriptions and their assumption of these roles in day-to-day operations, traditional values intervened. For example, upper-echelon officials might postpone consideration of important issues for days or weeks because the relevant documents were not available. The file clerks in charge of these documents were ill and absent, and it was not appropriate to the status of those above to have knowledge of or direct access to files. Or the "processing" of a decision might be delayed because by some oversight the necessary papers had been left in the office of the chief of the division instead of being forwarded through channels. His subordinates could not be guilty of disrespect for his status by initiating

[22] George McT. Kahin, *Major Governments of Asia* (Ithaca: Cornell University Press, 1958), p. 522.

action for return of the material. Among officials of different ministries or departments who were working at the same level on issues of interministerial or interdepartmental concern, direct cooperation or exchange of information rarely took place, unless the officials had informal access to each other outside of the bureaucratic context. There was only slight cross-cutting of the elaborately hierarchical vertical structures of communication of parallel units. Instead, these formal channels were constantly overloaded, as the necessity for urgency failed to overcome the standards of propriety, etiquette, rank, and ritual.[23]

Sometimes well-trained officials refused assignments to agencies or divisions that urgently needed their talents or, if these assignments could no longer be avoided or delayed, refused in oblique fashion to cooperate with their new superior, not because they did not respect his abilities or politics but because they disapproved of his manners, which lacked the refinement of the Javanese aristocrats.

After spending several months preparing proposals for technical aid from an American foundation, a minister of "Westernized" background and "pro-Western" orientations changed his mind, ostensibly on the basis of critical American press views of a policy he supported. How could he, he argued, take the risk of accepting a "favor" and therefore incurring an obligation to an American source that might in turn ultimately expect him to reciprocate by modifying his policies in other areas in order to accord with American expectations. Early resistance of Indonesians to American aid was not easily overcome by the assurances of American officials that technical and economic aid did not entail political "strings," for the Indonesian concept of reciprocal obligation incorporates the possibility that assistance that cannot be returned in kind can become a claim upon the recipient by the donor for future returns in a form needed by or pleasing to the donor. And since segments of the American Congress and people apparently share this view, Indonesian skepticism concerning the proclaimed motives of American aid seems not to have been unwarranted.

The influence of indigenous value orientations could be noted not merely in the narrow context of routine bureaucratic activities (whose cumulative effects on government administration were far from negli-

[23] Lucian Pye describes a similar phenomenon in the Burmese civil service under the rubric "formalism and imperfect communication," *Politics, Personality, and Nation Building*, pp. 216–217.

gible), but also in the broader aspects of policy implementation. One example will illustrate the parallels between the mode of handling problems in the traditional milieu and in the national government, especially where the means appropriate to one goal would appear to conflict with or minimize the satisfaction or achievement of another goal. In Indonesia overapportionment of labor in village agrarian activities and in cottage and small-scale industry has been uneconomic and costly. The land-holding farmer and small-scale entrepreneur have not been unaware, as is too often assumed, of alternative methods of organizing production more efficiently and at more profit to themselves. However, they have rationalized their current practices in terms of their responsibilities to the less fortunate members of their immediate communities and because of their fears of arousing disapproval, enmity, and reprisals among the latter.[24] On the national scene, the analogue to this was the abandonment by several cabinets of their original goals of reducing and rationalizing the swollen ranks of the civil and military services in order to utilize government funds for more directly developmental objectives; they succumbed to fears of the consequences of unemployment.

THE EROSION OF AUTHORITY AND THE PARADOX OF DECISION AND RISK

The resurgence of traditional values as partial determinants of decision and action — or of indecision and inaction — can perhaps best be discussed in terms of the erosion of authority, whether microcosmically in the small unit of a government department or macrocosmically on the level of implementation of national government policies. The difficulties of those in formally authoritative posts in exerting their authority effectively can be seen as resulting from the tensions caused by overlapping and conflicting notions of authority and of its exercise in the environment of decolonization.

On the microcosmic level, the problem is illustrated by Sudjarwo, a department head who had requested and obtained the services of an American expert to help him "rationalize" the operations of his department. Sudjarwo had been educated and trained in three European countries. His problem was that he had a dozen or so profes-

[24] Ann R. Willner, "Management and Authority in a Transitional Society," *Human Organization*, XXII (Summer 1963), pp. 133–141.

sional subordinates, most of whom either did not do the work assigned them in the prescribed period or did not do it at all. It did not take long to ascertain that he was not exaggerating: several subordinates seemed to find the cafeteria more inviting than their desks; others allocated their time somewhat unevenly between official tasks and catching up on their magazine reading; two were quite openly engaged in translating film titles for extra income.

Naively eager to contribute vaunted American efficiency in organization and management, the American suggested that perhaps some of the subordinates did not know the nature of the tasks appropriate to their titles (which in some departments was the case) — a suggestion that would have necessitated detailed job descriptions. Investigation disclosed that this was not the problem. The second possibility was that the assignments were understood, but the officials were not familiar with the techniques of carrying them out, so that an on-the-job training program was called for. This proved to be the case in several instances in which subordinate officials had been inhibited by shame or embarrassment (the aforementioned concept of "malu") from admitting their ignorance. Despite the training program, however, the department was still left with several officials who showed small inclination toward performance, although they were obviously qualified and knowledgeable. There was no sharp improvement in the productivity of his subordinates and Sudjarwo exhaustedly struggled to do much of their work as well as his own.

The American then suggested that if Sudjarwo could obtain no plausible reasons for nonperformance, he might enforce compliance by threats of demotion, dismissal, or other sanctions. He was astonished. In the first place, he patiently explained, his departmental blueprint called for fifteen high-level subordinates; he had only twelve, so how could he even consider reducing the number. With what might be regarded as typical American arrogance, the expert pointed out that a dozen men not doing much of anything were no great asset; perhaps if one or two were disciplined as examples, the others might start producing. Sudjarwo retorted that Americans might think in such fashion, but his subordinates had large families to support and needed these jobs. Besides, they didn't earn enough anyhow.

Trying another tack, the American asked whether his subordinates did not perceive his requests as they were obviously intended — a polite way of giving an order. Naturally they did, he affirmed, but they were just as polite in their excuses and evasions. And he could not be rude and crude by calling their bluff. The American then pointed out to Sudjarwo that his post by definition carried with it some presumption of authority which he ought at least to try to exercise. And Sudjarwo responded that he was as well aware as Americans of the "proper" exercise of authority and the enforcement of discipline from his years in the Dutch colonial service. But the Dutch were no longer there to back him up. And should he now try to act as suggested, he would only arouse resentment, be labeled "colonial," and further undermine his position.

Having assumed that the transition from a "colonial" to a "national" environment by definition implied the preference for indigenous over external authority, the American suggested that Sudjarwo's subordinates should, on the contrary, be more amenable to his instructions. He felt that this distinction was irrelevant, since a Dutchman would be expected to act in an arbitrary fashion whereas he would not be.

Sudjarwo had here put his finger on one of the major dilemmas confronting the nationalist Indonesian administrators in managing the system they had inherited from the Dutch. For in discrediting their colonial rulers, they had also undermined the system and procedures that had been legitimized by the Dutch and had strengthened what we might call the "semilegitimate," or traditional, system, which had continued to exist beneath and in the interstices of the colonial system.

The traditional system of authority, as observed in families, small groups, and villages, might be called "nonauthoritarian paternalism." It is neither specifically authoritarian nor specifically democratic, as we would tend to perceive these mutually exclusive categories, but rather a fluid admixture of both authoritarian and democratic elements.

The traditional authority figure, whose status is legitimized by ascriptive or charismatic criteria, is hopefully perceived by his subjects as benevolently paternal, or is so treated in the expectation that he will so respond to their perceptions of him. Legitimacy also rests on the way in which he exerts his authority, which can best be described as "manifestly" authoritarian with "latently" democratic features. Thus the flow of directives appears to proceed downward from the authority figure, matched by the upward flow of assent and obedience. The latent process, however, is one of continual probing and testing, as the authority figure communicates his wishes by innuendo and by stages, constantly sounding out the responses and estimating the type and extent of compliance he can command, without appearing to enforce it.

Conversely, his "family" or subjects make their "voices" felt by the oblique ways in which they indicate agreement or dissent, whether verbally or through a series of acts, half-acts, or nonaction. And the dissenters are also constantly engaged in testing out the risks and limits of discreet or overt opposition. Implicit bargaining, negotiation and counternegotiation, communication by parable, veiled threats of sanctions, subtle methods of shaming into compliance or into retreat from attempting to coerce compliance may mark the process at every step.

In the traditional context, authority figures rarely find it necessary to exert overt force to exact compliance, attempt to avoid doing so, and do so only as a final and drastic measure. Paradoxically, exerting overt force tends to diminish presumptive authority in constituting a tacit admission that it can no longer be taken for granted. Challenges to authority are also rarely direct, but take the form of withdrawal, evasion, token compliance, or noncompliance.

In this process of anticipating and testing the limits of potential command or resistance, intermediaries are frequently resorted to. By communicating between the parties they help to arrive at the terms of trade, so to speak, between the maximum desires and the minimum conditions for settlement of both parties. The intermediary also serves the function of sparing the players in this game the humiliation of either one's having publicly to give way to the other.

Mediators are often used in the traditional context in conflicts between parties arising out of different interpretations of customary law or where custom has not created a clear precedent. And whether claims are referred to some higher authority or are resolved through the intercession of mediators, the resolution of conflict is generally based upon considering more factors than those bearing directly on the issue. Mutual concessions are pressed on the contestants rather than an impersonal norm being applied to assess the guilt or support the claims of one party to the exclusion of those of the other. The ultimate resolution often favors neither party completely but tends toward some compromise in which all parties obtain a modicum of satisfaction. Tensions are thereby diminished, and sustained bitterness is at least temporarily averted.

In its ideal form, this system allows for considerable flexibility. From its perspective, the ideal form of the impersonal rule of law imposed by the Dutch in Indonesia appears relatively rigid. Whether Indonesian or Dutch paternalism proved either more benevolent or more exacting in practice depended on particular practices of particular administrators in particular circumstances. While many Indonesians adapted themselves to the Dutch framework, many Dutch officials learned to work within and manipulate Indonesian traditions. In some respects acculturation worked both ways.

In the sphere of authority, this often meant that in their modes of communication and methods of applying and enforcing regulations, Dutch administrators could and sometimes did play the game by Indonesian rules of circumlocution. They might first try to shame the Javanese into compliance or apply tactics of "gentle pressure." However, they had the choice of dropping this game and applying stronger sanctions should their objectives be endangered.

But for several reasons, postrevolutionary Indonesian administrators had no such choice of rules to play by. Unlike their predecessors, they could not pretend ignorance of the "signs" or "cues" of the traditional Indonesian game. Nor could they resort to the final Dutch game of crude coercion without the alien overlord upon whom to deflect the resentment aroused by this alien mode. Not only were they barred from this game by their own convictions; they had fought it in the name of egalitarian democracy. And egalitarian democracy, as adopted and adapted in some quarters with touching and painful literalness, became a boomerang.

An administrator might find his claim to authority recognized by one group of subordinates provided he exerted it in the traditional mode; but this mode might earn him the quiet contempt of another group for his inability to be as "hard" as the Dutch. One group might resent his occupancy of that status if his formal educational qualifications were less than theirs; another, disregarding his superior professional attainments, would deplore his social origins as insufficient to command respect and obedience.

But hardest for administrators to cope with were those individuals whose conception of democracy entailed the notion that valid leadership over any group, including a work group, is derived solely from selection by and voluntary agreement of the members of that group. Similarly, the interpretation of equality of representation did not easily permit delegation. In some administrative contexts, a "voice" in decision-making was taken to mean that everyone with any responsibility for implementing any phase of a decision ought to participate equally in its formulation. And freedom included the right of a minority or dissenting group to refuse to implement a decision that it had opposed.

This repudiation, in whole or in part, of the previous norms of authority and the consequent inability of those in authority to assume compliance with their directives by virtue of their possession of formally authoritative posts had significant consequences for the process of decision-making. Traditional indigenous values surrounding this process, such as the importance of resolving latent or overt differences to maintain or restore the appearance of group harmony and unanimity, were reinforced by the practical necessity to obtain consensus on decisions in order to strengthen the possibility of their implementation. More than ever, a satisfactory decision came to be seen as one affording concessions to all parties involved.

In effect, this meant that the urgency of solving problems was subordinated to achieving their resolution at the least possible cost in residual opposition and enmity. Time was less important than were procedures permitting participation and discussion until some general accord was reached by all who wished to participate or whose role was seen as relevant. Furthermore, the content of a decision, i.e., its instrumental relevance to the problem at issue, might be considered subordinate to reaching accord.

This gave rise to the *musjawarah-mufakat* (joint deliberation-decision) syndrome, which I suspect to be less the traditional institution it is reputed to be than a postcolonial syncretic repatterning of elements from several distinct institutions. In the hands of a relatively firm and politically skillful leader, such a deliberative process could achieve its purpose. A quotation from my field notes describes the process as observed on several occasions:

> There appears to be little in the nature of a debate, characterized by sharply drawn lines of opposition and clear-cut exposition or by support of distinct points of view, in working toward a decision on an issue. Each speaker ranges over the issue, may recapitulate its history, describes in detail the course of his thinking about it and how he has arrived at his convictions, and reiterates his feelings about it and what he thinks should be done — all in several different ways. A

subsequent speaker can begin with no direct reference to what preceded him and introduce completely extraneous matter. The chairman makes little attempt to keep a speaker on the subject at hand; and discussion and interchange tend to be rambling, diffuse, and often nonspecific.

Objections are not often raised to another's argument but are preferably expressed by elaborating one's own views. It is considered unseemly to attack another or belittle his point of view in his presence. The most acceptable means of rebuttal involves first accepting as legitimate the views at variance with one's own and then proceeding to suggest that their adoption would entail undesirable consequences. The consequences pictured may seem to have no logical relation to the action proposed, but their being advanced as imminent possibilities reveals the intensity of the speaker's opposition to such a line of action.

This is probably one of the most effective tactics by which the chairman himself can cast doubts on views at variance with his own without injuring the self-esteem of their proponents or losing the support of the latter. For, given the presence . . . of members who have acquired sufficient awareness of democratic debate to want to make their voices "felt," he must encourage the expression of all possibilities of choice. At the same time, he cannot allow what to him may represent an absurd alternative to gather with repetition a snowball sort of momentum. Nor can he cut short its presentation by sharp criticism, for that would produce an atmosphere of acrimony and cleavage with a residue of tension, which members with a traditional psychological orientation cannot tolerate and would hold against him. Therefore his object is neither to inhibit opposition nor to overwhelm it but to dissipate it. And one of the more disarming means of doing so is to give opponents a respectful hearing, compliment their sincerity, and imply that they have not completely thought the issue through.

This illustrates the latent ambiguities of the leadership role in a decision-making process that resembles nothing so much as a game in which some players use one set of rules and others a different set. Thus, in what might be called the winding-up phase of discussion, when modification of initial positions appears, some members line themselves up unmistakably behind one alternative or its most active advocate in what in our context would be the preliminary to a vote. Others, however, while withdrawing from an earlier position, now announce themselves in favor of one of the remaining choices for one group of reasons and simultaneously in favor of still another for

> a different group of reasons. Yet this is the stage at which, however much in flux opinion still appears, the impetus toward reconciliation and resolution has set in. Perceiving this, the chairman, riding the current, then brings his best rhetorical weapons to bear. And ultimately — whether because the process of attrition has been completed or because a type of catharsis has taken place — he senses a flow of support, briefly recapitulates what he takes to be the decision, asks whether all are not agreed, and receives signs of assent from all.

This is obviously a long, drawn-out process; meetings observed lasted for hours or were temporarily suspended after hours to be resumed again the following day or week.

Under the direction of a weak or politically inept leader, such discussions might result in an impasse or in a resolution that had obtained the snowball sort of momentum referred to above but was considered logically absurd by the leader or by the more astute members of the group. The effort to gain unanimity, perhaps strengthened by the syncretic approach to many areas of life particularly characteristic of the Javanese, sometimes produced a compromise resolution that incorporated elements of several logically distinct proposals while containing no single internally coherent proposal. It might be, for example, that course A, requiring certain prerequisites in the use of resources, offered some advantages, whereas proposal B had another set of advantages but was based upon a different pattern of resource utilization. Either course, if adopted and pursued wholeheartedly, might conceivably go far toward solving the problem. But the A-B amalgam finally decided upon, juxtaposing the steps envisaged by A with the resource pattern appropriate to B, would not be viable and would ultimately have only symbolic value. It might be noted, in passing, that this is a not uncommon policy outcome contributing to failures of policy in countries other than Indonesia.

Both the process of decision-making and the exercise of authority were colored by a particular attitude toward taking risks. On the surface, this appeared as a reluctance and even a fear of embarking upon a course of action of which some of the possible outcomes initially envisaged might be undesirable. It was an approach to problems quite at variance with the calculated-risk approach that is more familiar to us. Thus, future possibilities or consequences of alternative courses of action which to us might appear so remote as not to justify inclusion in present calculations would be perceived and weighed as if they were imminent probabilities. This would entail not merely avoiding a step, one of whose two possible results might be unfortunate, or even avoiding a step with four possible outcomes, one of which could be viewed as disastrous, one positive, and the other two mixed. Rather, the range of possible outcomes four or five degrees removed from the initial move would be envisaged; should one or two turn out to be objectionable, the decision might well be made not to take the first step lest the ensuing sequences of action and response should generate the least favorable outcomes rather than those most desired.

This explains the frequency of the phenomenon of *nondecision,* or *impasse,* in situations that an outside observer might perceive as calling for immediate action. In an American context, it is more likely that if all the alternatives perceived as means of coping with an urgent problem held some disadvantages or risks, the course of action selected would be that which, on the whole, appeared to offer the maximum advantage with the minimum of risk. But some action would probably be taken on the assumption that any action is better than none. By and large, our dominant or modal cultural orientation is toward action; nonaction in the face of provocation or problems tends to be disvalued. Objections on the grounds that a course offering specific advantages might in some contingencies entail negative consequences tend to be met with such statements as "We can tackle that difficulty if and when we come to it."

Indonesians and especially Javanese I have known have tended to view such an orientation to action as somewhat hazardous. In their opinion it implied either a naive obliviousness of chance factors or overconfidence in the possibility of controlling or reversing the momentum of events and responses.

My observations of decisional situations in Indonesian contexts in the 1950's suggest an almost opposite modal orientation to a situation in which all alternatives that could be envisaged seemed for one reason or another unpalatable. Then the most desirable course was nonaction or postponement of action, in the hope that (1) some factors in the situation would change, rendering one of the presently unacceptable alternatives acceptable, (2) a previously unconsidered choice, less risky, might present itself, or (3), best of all, the situation might in time somehow clear up by itself — time being a great solvent — completely removing the necessity of making risky and therefore unpleasant decisions. Within this framework, *abeyance of action* or *nonaction* were not defaults or negatives but rather positive categories of action.

The orientations to authority, risk, decision, and action, roughly sketched out in the preceding pages, can themselves be constraints on the exercise of authority. For those in nominal posts of authority, these orientations color the perceptions of the limits of action in the face of conventional political constraints. The inability of Indonesian governments during the early and middle 1950's to implement many of their policies can be and has been attributed to the constraints of interparty and intraparty competition, intramilitary conflicts, regional cleavages, ideological differences, and the like. Yet one might question to what extent these were constraints only because they were viewed as such.

Sudjarwo and his peers illustrated on a microcosmic level in their offices an approach characteristic of cabinets on the macrocosmic level. During 1956–1957, regional groups, in cooperation with local military commanders, engaged in large-scale smuggling activities and conducted their fiscal and export activities autonomously and in contravention of central government regulations. Central government response to these challenges generally took the form of sending intermediaries, often natives of the areas involved, to negotiate with the dissident elements. Then the government tacitly recognized the de facto situation: when negotiation proved fruitless it resorted to unenforced legal formulas that on the surface seemed to preserve nominal authority. Yet two years later, an open regional insurrection was effectively quelled.

Sukarno's past successes in situations in which the odds seemed stacked against him can be accounted for partly by his willingness to take long risks while his antagonists were, in traditional fashion, carefully calculating the possibilities and hesitating to move without assurances of success.

THE LIMITED INFLUENCE OF FOREIGN AID

As I have earlier stated, one of the consequences of decolonization was the withdrawal from former colonies of some inputs that had formerly flowed in from the metropolitan power to sustain and develop the "modern" sectors of industry, commerce, and the public bureaucracy. Foreign technical and economic public assistance and foreign private investment can be considered as attempts to fill these gaps as well as to catalyze indigenous replacements. Much has been written and much more remains to be said on the problems and limitations of international and bilateral programs of aid for development and the limitations, both self-imposed and imposed by the recipient countries, on the developmental role of private foreign investment. Here I shall confine myself to a few observations on the limited influence of foreign aid in public administration.

Broadly speaking, the development or decline (depending upon one's perspective and criteria of evaluation) of Indonesian public administration during the years preceding Guided Democracy was relatively uninfluenced by programs of foreign aid, despite the fact that Indonesia, far more than such countries as India, suffered from a scarcity of trained and skilled administrators. There were many reasons for this, only a few of which will be touched upon here.

As all those directly involved in the process of providing or receiving aid know, the need for reforms and for training programs aimed at facilitating some kinds of improvements is often more apparent to would-be donors than to officials of recipient countries. And the former often have to exert considerable effort to convince the latter of the desirability of some types of aid, as contrasted with others, and to induce them to undertake the formalities of requesting such assistance.

One of the fields in which influential Indonesians at this period were long reluctant to act upon offers of aid was that of public administration. Suggestions for a public-administration institute sponsored and administered by the UN several times failed to gain approval by an interministerial advisory coordinating committee on foreign aid. Objections were raised that foreign experts would be least useful in this area, knowing neither the language nor the local conditions and the *modus operandi.* Suspicions were voiced that some foreign experts might abuse their positions to the advantage of their own governments. One public administration expert was in the first Indonesian Planning Bureau, which was staffed at the senior level by a number of foreign experts whose services were recruited and subsidized by the UN but who had been nominally hired by, and were responsible to, the Indonesian government. Compared with his colleagues in other fields, he received less cooperation from and his advice was less frequently sought by other government agencies. When a new director of the Bureau dropped the "social" as distinct from the "technical economic" posts for foreign experts, this expert's was among the first to be discarded.

This was in contrast to the relative ease with which training programs were at least accepted and initiated in such fields as transportation, health, and agriculture. For obvious reasons, interest in training and advice on the part of potential recipients tends to vary directly with the distance of the sphere of activity from what is felt to be the heart of government. On the surface, it might appear that overt admission of inexperience and therefore limited capacity in the area of activity formerly least open to them should not pose a problem for those newly freed from colonialism. But nationalism has a logic of its own. And it is understandable that to many Indonesians a request for training in public administration would seem tantamount to a public admission that they were incapable of administering the apparatus of government they had just obtained after so great a struggle. In the more narrowly technological and industrial spheres, the problem was less severe. Here the Indonesians could freely claim that the Dutch had hindered their development, such hindrance having provided one of the stimuli to self-government.

Even the more defensive attitude, however, did not prove to be a complete stumbling block to providing some kinds of training in administration. About six years after the initial discussions, public administration training centers did become established. And meanwhile the UN, Colombo Plan, and United States programs for overseas training and observation did send abroad Indonesian officials in the fields of public administration.

As with a number of other implicit assumptions underlying the concept of foreign aid, several concerning the anticipated effect of overseas training can be recognized in retrospect as rather overoptimistic. It was assumed that the process of assimilating "modern" principles and techniques would be both accelerated and intensified by direct observation and training in the "developed" contexts in which such principles and techniques were already institutionalized. It was further assumed that, upon their return, the trainees would be reassigned to responsible posts in which they would serve as catalysts, diffusing their newly acquired expertise throughout their respective organizations, or at least in their immediate sectors of activity.

One might overlook the small proportion of trainees who by some vagaries of the local selection procedures were less equipped to take advantage of their training than they should have been and those whose time abroad was largely spent in absorbing knowledge of foreign cultures not relevant to their assignments. More significant in assessing the direct results of such programs is the fact that those selected for such training did not generally include the more senior bureaucrats or their immediate subordinates. These could not easily be spared. And this played no small part in what happened to numbers of trainees who returned to ministries and agencies and their regional branches eager to proselytize and put into operation the principles and procedures acquired in Australia, the United States, Belgium, and other countries.

Unfortunately, the trainees were unable to bring these contexts home with them. The enthusiasm of some was rapidly dissipated upon their return. Overwhelmed by the contrasts between what they had seen and the situation at home, they became convinced of the uselessness of even beginning to apply, if only in modified form, what they had learned. As was the case with many foreign technical assistance experts, they tended to view principles and methods as almost entirely dependent upon the equipment with which these were linked abroad. Without such equipment, they felt helpless.

Another, and at a rough estimate the largest, group among the returned trainees initially attempted to improve and innovate. However, in place of the receptivity they had anticipated, they often encountered apathy, resistance, and suspicion. Frequently they were seen as threats to their status superiors and peers who became even more defensively conscious of their inadequacies and clung even more assertively to the practices to which they had been socialized.

The returning prodigal sons were often seen as embarrassments rather than assets. Their initiative became blunted as they found the atmosphere unreceptive to their attempted innovations. They would tactfully be told, often not without cause, that their ideas might be eminently suited to Canberra, Washington, or Geneva but were inappropriate to Indonesia. This was generally enough, especially for the Javanese among them who, as already mentioned, are highly susceptible and responsive to social environmental pressures. They rapidly subsided into silence and readapted to prevalent norms. More intrepid would-be innovators took somewhat longer to succumb to subtle forms of disapproval and ostracism.

Some of the returnees found that their foreign training retarded rather than advanced their careers in the bureaucracy. As with those in political disfavor, they were shunted off to posts where they could not threaten the vested interests of their colleagues. Others, unable or unwilling to readapt, left government service entirely to devote their newly acquired managerial skills to private entrepreneurship.

Finally, there could be discerned the group whose training has produced and may continue to yield slow and perhaps initially barely detectable results. These were the ones who externally readapted to the pressures or confined their attempts to innovate to those associates and those areas in which receptivity was evident or resistance minimal. They expressed their determination to renew or increase their efforts at some future period, either when they might attain posts of greater authority or when their numbers would be sufficiently augmented for them to feel reasonably secure of some success.

Obviously, resistance to innovation and the discouragement and effective emasculation of innovators are not unique to Indonesia but can be found to some extent in organizations everywhere. One distinction may be made, however, between the relative strengths in different societies of values favorable to innovation and those favorable to conformity and accommodation and the effects of these upon the behavior of those in potentially innovative roles. Another distinction might be made between (1) societies that have a highly developed business sector that can stimulate innovation in the public bureaucracy and supply it with personnel, and (2) societies in which innovation must be generated, if at all, from within the government. And though in some parts of the outer islands indigenous entrepreneurial activity survived and even prospered under later Dutch colonial domination (unlike Javanese entrepreneurial activity, which was submerged in the earlier years of colonialism), the business sector characterized by large-scale organization and administration was nevertheless mostly a foreign sector. That the erosion of administration was less visible in the early years of independence is partially attributable, as I shall show in the following section, to the "silent partner" role of many members of this sector.

SURFACE EMULATION AND THE SILENT PARTNERS

Here I should like to utilize several examples to indicate three other related factors that tended to inhibit development: (1) the dysfunctionalism resulting from overinternalization of imported values, (2) the problem of surface emulation, and (3) excessive dependence upon what I term "silent partners."

Although earlier I have stressed the indigenous values within the value framework of the Europeanized Indonesian elite, it is also true that some individuals had fairly thoroughly absorbed and internalized the values commonly associated with industrialized, urbanized, and bureaucratized societies. So thoroughly had these individuals absorbed such values that they would undoubtedly have been far more operationally effective in Western Europe than in their own country, if we include as an important component of operational effectiveness the ability to predict with fair accuracy the consequences of actions contemplated or taken. It was an open question as to who understood less of the outlook of other Indonesians and mispredicted their possible responses to programs instituted to aid them, these gentlemen or some of their American, Canadian, or Australian advisers.

Perhaps it was that their knowledge of social processes had been derived mainly from textbook study in and about industrialized societies. Or perhaps in the process of psychological dissociation from their traditions and as a result of nationalist pride, they were unconsciously forced to commit the fallacy of projecting upon much of their society the values they had acquired. For example, the so-called "Benteng" fiasco was primarily the brainchild of a brilliant Dutch-trained Indonesian economist who, not illogically, concluded that the quickest way to create an Indonesian entrepreneurial class was to give a group of Indonesians a monopoly on licenses for some classes of essential imports and government loans to enable them to commence their activities. It was assumed not only that this would result in Indonesians' expanding their commercial activities, but that some of the profits from trading would soon be reinvested in productive enterprises within the country, resulting in a spiral of local industrial entrepreneurship.

Some Indonesians so aided were either fearful of or understandably confused by the complexities of foreign trading. Consequently they unofficially combined with a local Chinese partner, who undertook the complexities of the work and often provided the necessary working capital while they skimmed a percentage of the profits in return for their contribution to the joint venture – the name of their firm and the import licenses. These were the so-called "Ali-Baba" firms. Others of the group solved their problems even more simply by in effect selling the licenses, for a flat cut, to Dutch firms with licensing problems, an arrangement that solved the problems of the Dutch firms also. The effects of the added costs on the consumers of these imports need not be spelled out.

The immediate results of the loan to the typical businessman who attempted his own operations were visible. He rapidly acquired an impressive office, a large desk surrounded by modern office equipment, a staff of subordinates, many of them kinsmen, and a salaried board of directors composed of friends and government officials who had assisted him in obtaining the loan. He purchased a house in the most fashionable residential suburb, a car, and perhaps even a weekend house in one of the mountain resorts. He was seen at business conferences in the restaurants and lounges of the leading hotels. And he soon found himself short of working capital to pay for the goods consigned to him when they finally arrived. He was therefore forced to scurry around to his friends and relatives in the leading political parties and requisite ministries to try to raise an additional loan to stay in business.

To what can we attribute such unanticipated consequences? Degrees in law and philosophy or experience as a school teacher or petty bureaucrat do not necessarily equip one for the intricacies of the international market, a risky business indeed. Risk-taking, as we have seen, is not a major attribute of the Indonesian, especially not of the Javanese. It was especially risky to attempt to compete with the Dutch and Chinese whose expertise was obviously superior to one's own (or was assumed to be, which had the same effect). What was more "rational," from the point of view of the individual entrepreneur who wished to ensure his survival, than to combine with them in a mutually fruitful partnership?

As to those entrepreneurs whose enterprises seemed more conspicuously "consumptive" than productive – many of them were prime examples of the phenomenon of surface emulation. They tended to confuse the external or visible attributes of organization, its "surface," so to speak, for its substance. Modernization is, after all, a form of emulation. And what did the aspiring Indonesian businessman have to emulate? By and large, he had been exposed, often at a distance, to what could be called the "fringe benefit" stage of development of the foreign firms. These firms provided their executive personnel with houses, cars, mountain retreats, and expense accounts. He had not observed the firms themselves closely or worked with them in their initial stages. Besides, as I have already mentioned, the observance of external forms, the appearances of things, is an important attribute of the culture.

Admittedly, our entrepreneur might have used as his model the Chinese trader who had made his first million from a dark hole of an office somewhere in the rabbit-warren of the Chinese quarter before branching out. But that would not have given him the social prestige of his Dutch and other European models and counterparts.

There were indeed Indonesians who attempted to emulate the "Chinese model," starting with low overhead and a modest style of living. This was also not easy, as exemplified by the experiences of two who worked full time as engineers in Dutch companies, while they spent most of the rest of their waking hours trying to develop in one instance a machine shop and in the other a motorized fishing fleet. The time came when they needed additional financing to enlarge their operations. Unfortunately, both had been relatively apolitical. One was completely unsuccessful in gaining any assistance from government banks and ministries. The second put his scruples in his pocket and decided to join the party that he felt would be most useful to his needs. However, when he was given the unofficial terms of the loan agreement, it appeared that the salaries of his new board of directors or "sleeping partners" would account for a good 50 per cent of it.

The graduates of middle-level technical training institutes also often suffered from similar misconceptions of surface emulation concerning "career building." Anticipating or responding to the demand for "Indonesianization" of their staffs, many foreign companies offered technical management-training programs to young men from these schools. Some of those taken on were appalled to discover that the programs required them to spend several months being rotated among different departments, including the workshops and production lines. This did not accord with their expectations that their educational certificates would *ipso facto* give them executive status and exemption from any appearance of manual labor. The voluntary casualty rates in the training programs reportedly were high.

The confusion of form with substance also characterized much of the functioning of the public bureaucracy, as I have mentioned. "Paper and *pangkat*" — the precise and ritualistic handling of documents and concern for the niceties of their position in the bureaucratic hierarchy and what was due them by virtue of it — typified the approach of many civil servants, as it does in bureaucracies throughout the world and especially, I would assert, in those of the Netherlands which served as the models for Indonesians. This suggests one of the many limitations of bureaucracies as catalytic agents for economic and social development.

To return to the phenomenon of the "silent partner," the symbiotic relationship between entrepreneurial Indonesians and their Dutch and Chinese counterparts was partly replicated in the public sector, whose high level officials also had their private and unofficial advisers, often Dutch, though the majority of the Dutch members of the civil service retired or were withdrawn from the Indonesian government in relatively short order. In some instances, the relationship was semitutorial, as the Indonesian gradually gained confidence in his abilities and judgment; in others, the use of the adviser became a labor-saving device.

It was not unusual for foreign experts provided by the various UN missions to wait for weeks for more than social recognition of their existence and for a call for their expertise from the head of the department to which they were assigned or for some response to suggestions they had made in memoranda. Meanwhile, the inaccessible Indonesian official would be consulting his unofficial Dutch adviser. The reasons most often given for this were the ease of communication in a common language and the fact that the Dutchman was more familiar with the local environment, the procedures, and the political obstacles to be faced and overcome. The difficulties and embarrassments of communicating these to the Scandinavian or Canadian expert often appeared considerable. Another reason, rarely admitted but nonetheless important, was the invisibility of the Dutch expert, whose position was not such that he or his organization need gain publicity or claim public credit for whatever plan emerged from their consultations.

The political climate of the 1950's was characterized by increasingly acrid public pillorying of the Dutch and their presence. The covert antithesis was the symbiotic relationship described above. A similar relationship existed with the indigenous Chinese, especially on the regional and local levels. This type of relationship served both to preserve certain levels of bureaucratic and economic performance and at the same time prevented these levels from being attained autonomously by Indonesians.

The campaigns that resulted in the withdrawal of the Dutch community and the circumscribing of the Chinese community were politically inspired. In many ways their consequences were unpremeditated and unanticipated. Many Indonesians opposed the manner in which they were undertaken. The destructiveness to the economy in the short run was immediately visible.

The impetus for these campaigns, which were primarily supported by Sukarno and groups allied with him at that time, was associated with the desire to eradicate economic dualism and to remove the rivals thought to be stifling indigenous development, such as the Dutch "Big Five" companies and the network of Chinese middlemen. However, I suggest that the motives underlying the efforts to curb and expel the Dutch and Chinese economic interests were somewhat more complex and subtle than the obvious ones of taking over their properties and activities and presumably the benefits to be derived from them and removing the rivals against whom Indonesians found it difficult to compete. There was also the desire to learn to run the machine of economic and administrative modernity. And in view of the too easy temptation to leave the wheel in the hands of the partner upon whom one has come to rely excessively, perhaps the only solution to continued overdependence was to thrust out the silent partners and somehow learn to go it alone. That these campaigns were pursued with more fervor in Java than in the outer islands reflected the longer Javanese subjugation to, more intense interaction with, greater resultant dependence upon, and stronger ambivalence toward the alien elements in their midst.

Indonesia has a long history of exposure to, partial rejection, partial absorption, and partial repatterning of exogenous elements. Some of the elements imposed from without during the colonial period may have had to be regurgitated in order to achieve sufficient reintegration to accommodate further modernization.

THE NEW ORDER – A NEOMODERNIST REVIVAL

During the three years since the preceding was written, the system officially called Indonesia's "New Order" has gradually assumed discernible, if still somewhat fluid, shape.[25] The correctness of that term – what is significantly new, what remains the same, what is basically old wine in new bottles or even in old bottles disguised by new labels – forms the substance of serious and open debate among Indonesia's intellectuals and press, of more covert comments and some bitter humor among its urban masses, and of disagreement among informed foreign observers of the past and present Indonesian scene.[26] Obviously, judgments on changes and continuities vary according to (1) the time perspectives employed for comparison, (2) the elements selected for comparison, and (3) the relative importance attributed to any of these elements.

If one takes as the base line the later years of Sukarno's Guided Democracy, the differences are undeniable. The composition of government leadership has changed at the national and regional levels. Sukarno and his chief aides and supporters, with some notable exceptions, are out; Suharto and some formerly little known military figures, with some notable exceptions,[27] are clearly directing the country's course. The constellation of political groupings and their relative significance has been dramatically altered, most notably by eliminating Communists and their allies and sympathizers as a potent political and ideological force. Moreover, the kinds and extent of political activity engaged in by other groups are primarily determined or bounded

[25] The following analysis is based in part upon personal observations in Indonesia during 1967–68.

[26] See J. R. Angel, "Indonesia Since the Coup," and H. W. Arndt's dissenting comments in *Australian Outlook,* Vol. 22, No. 1 (April 1968), pp. 81–95.

[27] As in all cases of the survival in high posts of figures who had held leading posts in the previous discredited regime, the reasons are complex and involve idiosyncratic factors. Ties of kinship, obligations incurred in the past, an actual or presumed hold over an important ethnic or religious group and its potential usefulness, the type of role played in the previous regime are among the considerations that explain such survival.

by decisions arrived at in conferences of military leaders or by negotiations with them.[28] The bureaucracy, more pervasively military than before, reflects these alterations in its internal shifts and readjustments in staffing that began in the first phase of the period generally referred to as "transitional."

The very phrase "transitional period" symbolizes the self-identification of the new regime on the basis of sources distinct from those of the old one. The official stance of the New Order is derived from a composite model of some of the recent Western social science literature on modernization. The regime presents itself as a partnership between a modernizing elite corps of military organizers and one of civilian intellectuals and technocrats steering the country through the "stage" of economic and political stabilization to the "stage of take-off" to "development" and "democracy" for which the "blueprints" are being drawn up.

In its goals and policies and in the language in which they are enunciated, the current government strives to distinguish itself sharply from that of its predecessor. The emphasis on ideology, the romanticizing of the permanent revolution, and the activities designed to project Indonesia as a major actor on the world stage that were most characteristic of Sukarno in his later period have been abandoned. His policies of recent years have been repudiated and some have been reversed. The Suharto regime officially defines itself as anti-ideological, program-oriented, and primarily concerned with solving concrete problems by a pragmatic approach to them.

[28] Thus, the formerly strong Nationalist Party has been weakened, forced to purge itself of its old leadership, temporarily banned by military commanders in several parts of the country, and riven by factional disputes over accommodation to the terms for survival set by the military. In contrast, religious parties and groups appear to have gained in strength and influence, especially outside of Java. However, the new reformist Moslem Party, the replacement for the Masjumi which was banned by Sukarno, encountered numerous delays and obstacles in its emergence, mainly over the issue of the composition of its top leadership. The quasi-independent action fronts of intellectuals and students, overtly responsible for precipitating the removal of Sukarno, showed signs of becoming a major political force. They were quasi-independent in the sense of having been initially stimulated or sponsored by factions of submerged political parties or military groups opposed to Sukarno or soon used and coopted by them. Some developed internal and independent leadership and momentum of their own and a critical approach to the current regime. Internal and inter-front factionalism over a variety of issues led to increased fragmentation and military action to curb their criticism weakened them further. Their initial potential for emergence as a cohesive and significant political grouping has been greatly vitiated.

This definition itself carries overtones of the dominant characterization of a "modernizing orientation" found in the conventional literature on development. Moreover, a new vocabulary is in vogue in cabinet meetings, seminars, "briefing sessions," and in the various "upgrading courses" conducted by the intellectuals for military and civilian bureaucrats and by the latter for their lower-echelon subordinates. Economists refer to "infrastructure factors" and "cost-effectiveness calculations." Discussions of the "social role" of the military are sprinkled with such phrases as "engineering the dynamics of social change," "mobilizing target population support," "integration and synchronization." "Coordination" between "line and staff functions" and "effective utilization of skills" are spelled out as part of the process of overhauling the "administrative apparatus." In brief, the jargon of the behavioral and military sciences has become the official mystique. It has been disseminated down the line and echoed by many who neither understand it nor, when they do, agree with its implications.

The complications of the protracted succession crisis that followed the coup and counter-coup of 1965 are too intricate to elaborate upon here. They are relevant, however, in that they account in part for the emergence of the doctrine of modernization or development that has become the keynote of the new regime and the rationalization for many of its activities. Three factors are responsible for the emergence of this doctrine: (1) internal maintenance of some semblance of order, (2) the need to fill the ideological gap, and (3) the dependence upon external aid to cope with economic chaos.

The military leaders who almost inadvertently inherited the reins of government found support within their own ranks and throughout a broad spectrum of the population for a defensive and punitive campaign against the Communists and the military and civilian groups allied with or deemed sympathetic to the latter. On the basis of opposition to an internal enemy, a loose coalition of other groups was formed in the first stage of the succession crisis. These were more diversified than unified on a host of other issues. There was no sharp break with a previous regime of the type in which a cohesive and organized "out-group" of aspirants for power deliberately seize control of the government from an "in-group." Included in the shifting coalition were major power holders of the old regime as well as those formerly excluded from power. Aligned against the Communists were such divergent elements as secular Socialists who had been consigned to political limbo, exile, or internment and orthodox religious Islamic groups. Moreover, many military and civilian political leaders and their followers were anti-Communist but pro-Sukarno in accordance with their interpretations of Sukarnoist doctrine.

More than shared opposition to a common and rapidly decimated enemy was needed to continue a minimal working coalition among such diverse groups. It was clearly necessary to repudiate many policies of the recent past, especially those which had contributed to the economic and physical deterioration of the country. Yet the repudiation itself required a mode of doing so that would incorporate and not further fragment the still powerful leaders and groups who had collaborated or acquiesced in such policies. To accommodate groups with differing perspectives on the past and potentially conflicting ones on the future demanded an affirmation broad enough to gain general adherence. In brief, merely to restore order and consolidate power the new regime needed self-definition and legitimacy with a positive content.

Providing this was a task somewhat beyond the skills of the military leaders themselves. So was that of coming to grips with the economic chaos of the country. Nor were the military leaders certain that they alone could gain the confidence of the Western world, which Sukarno had alienated, and succeed in attracting its assistance.

Into the breach were called or stepped academicians and other intellectuals. Some of these had maintained close contact, in some cases covert, with some of the members of the new military leadership. Many had received their academic training in Western countries and had kept up, despite difficulties, with the dominant ideas in their fields produced in these countries. They were able to provide a ready-made and flexible framework to fill the ideological vacuum.

Apart from those committed to the doctrine of modernization, others could conveniently find in it a rough scenario for improvisation, roles and dialogues in shaping the new order. Since modernization is a theme with many variations on the means to attain ultimate ends, specific measures can easily be justified in its name. A military interregnum could be defended by the emphasis in some of the modernization literature on the role of the military as the organizational core and primary agent of modernization. The sequence which stresses national identity as a prerequisite for other aspects of modernization and allows for xenophobic nationalism as one of its components could provide an explanation for "Sukarnoist excesses" and at the same time supply permissible past roles to members of the new regime who had gone along with them. Finally, the very flexibility of contemporary Western theorizing on modernization could make it palatable as a doctrine to the intellectual leaders in nearly all camps. No specific formula has been devised as yet for the process of modernization but various alternative formulations are available. Whether and what kinds of economic development goals and programs should take precedence over and possibly prevent or delay achieving the goals of political democracy and its various institutional arrangements, or vice-versa, is open to question. There are no easy formulas prescribing the optimal combination of each at any stage. There is little consensus among theorists as to which elements of any indigenous tradition may be functional or dysfunctional to ultimate modernity. Thus there is ample room for dialogue and debate among many groups in Indonesia interested in advancing, preserving, or defending their interests under the general notion of modernization. Such an open-ended doctrine can help to stabilize a country so recently rent by cleavage and violence.

I do not argue that all these considerations entered into the calculations of the architects of what serves as the ideology of the New Order. A far more immediate and conscious element may have been the need to proclaim adherence to the general standards set by those who control the aid and investment sectors of the foreign governments, international agencies and private corporations whose assistance was sought in efforts to deal with Indonesia's desperate economic situation. I do suggest, however, that the conditions under which modernization or development became the official doctrine leave room for doubt as to how much of the new look is surface and how much can be transformed into substance.

In considering this transitional period a neomodernist revival, I may admittedly be overinfluenced by the similarities between the present scene and that of the pre-Guided Democracy period of the early 1950's. The problems are seen as substantially the same, although magnified, namely: restoring internal security, then challenged by Islamic guerrilla elements and now by Communist ones; reconstructing basic facilities that in the earlier period had been damaged by years of occupation and revolution and recently by years of neglect;

stabilizing the economy by controlling inflation and increasing production; rationalizing and reducing the civil bureaucracy and the military establishment, then considered too large and now considerably augmented; formulating a system for democratic representation and national and local elections.

The policies and programs officially promulgated for dealing with these problems are also broadly similar. Moreover, on the national level the younger and more sophisticated architects and planners of modernization are in the direct line of descent from their predecessors of the 1950's. Not only are they by and large protégés of the latter, but some of their forebears have returned to prominent posts and others act as influential advisers behind the scenes.

The handicaps faced by the first generation of would-be modernizers, described earlier in this study, make it useful to suggest some of the requisites for a genuinely modernizing "breakthrough" and to estimate whether these have been approximated under current conditions. Special attention is given here to the bureaucracy as the focus of implementation.

One requirement seems to be that members of an elite with a commitment to innovation and the skills to effect changes be strategically placed in formal posts of authority or sufficiently influential with those so placed that their plans and advice are acted upon. Second, in view of the easy discouragement and emasculation of the isolated innovator, it seems desirable that enough skilled and innovative officials be placed together within the same organization in order to reinforce each other. Suggested here is an administrative analogue to the concept of "critical mass," i.e., the point at which an accumulation of talent in a particular working unit can trigger an explosive effect upon the unit that will be reflected in its performance as a whole.

The continued overseas training provided for many Indonesians, often in groups at particular academic centers, suggests that there is a greater reservoir of skilled personnel with shared backgrounds and experiences to provide such nuclei as suggested above. A further advantage of shared training, especially if the trainees are of diverse ethnic and religious origins, is that it develops among them a commitment to professional norms that can transcend parochial loyalties.

In a few sectors of the public bureaucracy there can be observed the emergence of such nuclei of innovators. Thus a group of economists, many of them trained at the University of California at Berkeley, constituted the economic advisory team and form the core group of the National Planning Bureau. Two national ministries seem heavily staffed at the upper echelons with graduates of overseas public administration programs. The West Java division of the army seems to contain a number of upper-level officers with identical or similar overseas training.[29]

Several factors, however, seem to militate against the effective utilization of such nuclei and of the greater reservoir of available talent. One, already mentioned, is that the New Order was an improvised response to circumstances rather than a concerted takeover. This meant that such skilled groups were placed mostly in advisory or "staff" posts in administrative hierarchies rather than assuming authoritative or "line" posts. Another factor has been the test of political loyalty, applied either overtly or indirectly.[30] Just as in the early post-independence period, many skilled individuals trained in the colonial service were not considered politically acceptable for high posts, the "screening" processes under the new regime resulted in the removal, retirement, or transfer to minor posts of well trained non-Communist as well as pro-Communist bureaucrats. As a consequence, the expertise of those retained as sufficiently loyal and of the newer appointees is spread too thinly and they have little time to concentrate on their major tasks.[31]

As, in the early 1950's, the bureaucracy was politicized, it has more recently been increasingly militarized. I do not suggest that the assignment of military men to nominally civilian posts is in all cases harmful to administrative performance. Some, indeed, may add a dimension of authoritativeness where it has been lacking. However, the tacit assumption by many officials with a background in one of the armed forces that such a background somehow endows them with leadership ability applicable to any context can be doubted. Assignments

[29] Since data are not readily available on the composition and backgrounds of even upper-level officialdom, which government agencies interested in administrative reform had difficulty in obtaining, the above is based upon scattered data and impressions.

[30] This occurs to some extent in nearly every country in the course of changes in an administration or a regime. It can be harmful where high-level skills are scarce and negligible where they can be found throughout the political spectrum.

[31] Two other factors also diminish their working time and effectiveness, the acceptance of other forms of employment simultaneously in order to augment low incomes and the involvement of many in political activities.

of military men were made for many reasons, one of the least of these being expertise in the area or post to which they were assigned.[32]

If the notion of a consciously modernizing or innovating elite has any validity, we should expect to find among its members considerable agreement on the goals they wish to achieve in a specified period, on the means available, and on the strategies that are likely to be effective. The would-be modernizers among the civilian intellectuals and bureaucrats I encountered expressed divergent rather than shared views, particularly on basic issues that had split them and their predecessors formerly such as the preferred structure of government, electoral arrangements, and the preferred political party system.[33] On the immediate issue of the role of the military, for example, three distinct orientations were evident. The first favored returning military men to the barracks as soon as security would be firmly established and argued for a concerted effort by civilian forces, whatever their other differences, to promote this. The second can be called the "make-the-best-of-the-inevitable" stance. On the assumption that the military was likely to remain in the saddle for the foreseeable future, the argument stressed the necessity for the intellectuals to assume a cooperative and tutorial role to "prevent excesses" of military rule. The third point of view was an enthusiastic endorsement of the military as a modernizing force with superior organizational skills and sufficient authority to command compliance with government policies that might be initially deprivational but ultimately beneficial.

The blanket assumption that military administrators are relatively immune from the paradoxes of decision and risk and from the outcome of impasse earlier described is open to question, as will be indicated. No more than their civilian counterparts did the self-styled military modernizers I interviewed agree on a blueprint for the future or on a preferred pattern of civil-military relations in politics or government. All echoed the official line of their interim caretaker role until a viable democratic system can be formulated and some drew

[32] Among the reasons for assignments noted were: (1) the need to find a "place" for a field commander whose loyalty might be doubted; (2) the desire of military politicians to have one of their men overseeing or controlling the activities of a civilian agency; (3) the request of the agency itself for a military man in the hope that he could provide greater access to the top or a greater flow of resources.

[33] On the details of the debates, differences, alignments, and realignments on such issues over the last two years, see Herbert Feith, "Suharto's Search for a Political Format," *Australia's Neighbours* (May-June, 1968), pp. 1-7.

on the examples of Burma and Pakistan as outcomes to be avoided. It was clear, however, that for some this was merely a *pro forma* and ritualistic defense against allegations of "militarism," especially with an eye to foreign critics and foreign aid. Others may have enjoyed the perquisites of power but recognized and feared its responsibilities and their own limitations. A third orientation was the narrowly professionalist one of a genuine reluctance to live in the political arena.

Such differences on the current and future role of the military are mentioned here because uncertainties on this, as well as on other basic issues, seem to affect the process of making and implementing decisions all down the line. Unless he is reasonably certain that his directives will be backed by his superiors, are acceptable to his subordinates, will not be undermined by civilians with their own channels to higher military authorities, and will not arouse popular criticism, a military man in a nonmilitary bureaucratic post more often than not seems to exhibit some of the same insecurities in exerting authority that have characterized civilian bureaucrats. Moreover, the fear of the military among many of the population appears to limit the information feedback that policy makers can obtain in order to estimate the consequences of their policies, the reasons for failures, and the types of adjustments that might ensure greater success.[34]

CONTINUITIES, CONTRADICTIONS, AND CONSTRAINTS

Despite the current emphasis on organizational efficiency and pragmatic problem solving in accordance with "modern, rational, impersonal" criteria, many problems are resolved or their resolution is evaded in the same traditional indigenous modes that have been described earlier. These are employed by administrators and military leaders who can and do expound at length the principles and techniques of management they have learned abroad and the teaching of

[34] One of the major complaints of the economic policy makers during late 1967 and early 1968 was that their policies and regulations were formulated on the basis of what they took to be built-in incentives. However, when the anticipated results did not occur, e.g., with respect to rice production and exports, they had no way of ascertaining the reasons for the failures, particularly in regions remote from the capital. In this respect, it might be noted that the further a region from the national capital the greater the autonomy of its military officials from military as well as civilian authorities in Djakarta.

which to their subordinates they define as one of their major functions.

If confronted with the contradictions between principles and practices, however, they do not react with embarrassment or withdrawal, as did their predecessors. Nor do they take refuge in extolling "our Indonesian way." For the manuals they have memorized have also provided them with such justificatory concepts as "environmental adaptability" and the "human relations approach." Traditional modes of response may be quite rational, if they are viewed in the perspective of the current environment and from the point of view of the individual who faces a problem. Paradoxically, a particular decision in accordance with such modes may be a pragmatic approach to the dilemmas posed by the problem, even though it is at odds with an official policy.

When traditionalization has progressed so far that traditional practices are strongly reinstitutionalized on several levels of a society, the environment itself tends to reinforce traditional values in determining decisions and actions. However much a "modernized" man may wish to utilize a "modern principle," its application in a particular context can produce some socially harmful as well as remedial consequences. Moreover, its application may jeopardize his position in such a way as to endanger what he perceives to be his future effectiveness in a larger context.

This can be illustrated by the case of the general, known for his modernist orientations and exhortations, who was faced with the problem of combatting corruption within his ranks. There had come to his attention complaints, too numerous to ignore, of increasing extortionate practices by some of his soldiers on the citizenry. Local entrepreneurs particularly suffered from enforced exactions and "contributions." In the traditional context, the commander was the *bapak* or father of his men, responsible for their welfare. The rising costs of living and the far from adequate pay of those in the lower ranks made their temptations understandable. To institute penalties would cause resentment and would lower morale. Nor could he press for increases in military pay because of the austerity budget insisted upon by his "modernizing" allies at the economic helm of government. Yet as the military commander of an area he, no less than its civilian governor, had civic as well as defense responsibilities for its inhabitants. Moreover, the persistence and increase of such practices by his men would damage the "image" of the military as the protector of society.

He therefore devised what he felt to be a "pragmatic" solution. He encouraged his men to pool their resources and form small cooperative producers' and commercial enterprises, initially augmented by funds from his military budget. In this way, they could increase their incomes without depredations on the civilian population. Within a few months, however, complaints arose from local civilian entrepreneurs of "unfair" competition from the military in their traditional domains.

In discussions with this general, I raised the issue of distinguishing between the type of corruption engaged in for survival and that practiced by those on upper echelons for personal enrichment and luxuries. He conceded the distinction and admitted that he suspected some of his own subordinates of the latter. But what to do about the "big corrupters" was also a problem. "We can't stand them up against a wall and shoot them," he declared. "That would be inhuman." Considerations other than inhumanity, however, inhibited him from disciplinary action against his immediate subordinates. Not the least of these may have been the considerable political influence he possessed by virtue of his command of a major military force and his interest in influencing the future political shape of the country. He had succeeded to the command of that important division fairly recently and only after prior informal negotiations between the army high command and the upper echelon officers of that division had revealed that he was the most preferred or the least objected to of the other candidates.[35] Moreover, there are precedents in Indonesian military history for the removal of a commander by disgruntled subordinate officers, either by direct or devious action.

This example and its focus on corruption is used here not only because (1) the pervasiveness of corruption is generally conceded to be one of the major obstacles to Indonesia's economic rehabilitation, (2) the eradication and/or control of corruption is an explicit objective of the current regime, and (3) the implementation of this objective is one of the major demands of the articulate political public and the ap-

[35] This is not an unprecedented procedure in the appointment of high-level field commanders in Indonesia, particularly during crises and in view of some of the problems of authority described in preceding sections. It is more analogous to the procedures involved in appointing administrators in the American academic context than to the "ideal-type" military procedures Indonesian military leaders profess to adhere to.

parent failures of implementation are among the major subjects of criticism. Corruption and the discussions and actions surrounding this issue serve as a paradigm to illuminate the conflicts and contradictions in values and behavior similarly relevant to a range of problems.

Implementing the objective of combatting and penalizing corruption is not easy, given lack of agreement on definitions of what it includes and where lines should be drawn. At one extreme are the all-inclusive apologists who argue in effect that, since hardly anyone is immune from some sort or degree of sin, none dares to cast the first stone. Others attempt to distinguish between defensible practices under current conditions and intolerable practices. An example of the former is the lowly government clerk who pilfers small amounts of office supplies to sell on the local market for rice to feed his family. The latter can be illustrated by the minister who diverts large amounts of public funds to his personal bank account abroad. They would limit the definition of corruption to instances of the second type.

Even among those who subscribe to such a definition, however, differences arise in its application to particular cases. Discrimination is practiced and defended by one or another group on the basis of past as well as anticipated reciprocal obligations and loyalties. Barely had the student groups and action fronts concluded their relatively successful campaigns to remove from office the most notoriously corrupt civilian ministers of the Sukarno regime when they began to attack several military men with similar reputations whose tenure of office continued. One of the favorite targets of students and press was a general who headed one of the major income-producing state enterprises. He continued to survive the attacks, it was privately explained, because in the past he had diverted part of the revenues of the agency he headed to military groups desperately in need of funds, most recently in the later stages of their campaign to remove former President Sukarno.

Spokesmen for student and intellectual groups have expressed impatience and disillusionment with a phenomenon they find unchanged from the old to the new order – the preaching of patience and sacrifice to the general public by personally corrupt and luxury-loving officials. Some generals are repeatedly singled out for criticism, their luxurious new residences and style of life being cited as evidence of their lack of integrity. Other generals with similar homes and modes of living seem immune to attack from these critics. The latter seem to be those known to have provided direct and tacit support and protection for the student demonstrations of 1966.

Combatting corruption is hindered in practice not only by the difficulties of gaining consensus on criteria and by a host of particularistic loyalties and political considerations. It is also hampered by resort to another publicly proclaimed principle: "the rule of law." Arbitrary personal rule, it is argued, may have characterized the Sukarno regime; but in a modern democracy the rights of the individual must be protected by due process. This does not include arrest and detention on mere suspicion without adequate evidence obtained by proper and prior procedures of investigation.

Following criticisms alleging corruption in high places, teams were appointed to assist the Attorney-General's office with the tasks of investigation. Initial delays in working out proper procedures apparently were caused less by lack of knowledge of procedural techniques than by the implications of making awkward decisions, such as the year or period to be taken as the base line for beginning to check on the acquisition of assets by potential suspects. Difficulties in securing documentary evidence or witnesses willing to testify were almost insurmountable. In some instances, it was finally announced that evidence had been obtained, but not before the suspects had fled the country.

Symbolic rather than substantive actions seemed to mark the anticorruption campaign. As critics called for drastic action, government spokesmen stressed the necessity for strict adherence to the "rule of law." Some apologists also pointed out the dangers of drastic measures, such as the possibility that the country's development might be impeded by action against upper-echelon officials with needed skills. Cynics quietly compared the lack of difficulty in formulating criteria for discriminating between different categories of Communist followers and sympathizers and in obtaining evidence in screening procedures.

In elite circles, various types of suggestions for overcoming the impasse on combatting corruption have been privately discussed and publicly promoted. One type is a variation on the "wipe the slate clean and start anew" theme. It calls for something like a moratorium on all suspected or actual past offenses. After a specified and publicized date, offenders are to be investigated and prosecuted in earnest.

At odds with this approach is another that stresses "coming to terms with reality." In effect, it openly endorses traditional modes of coping with transgressions. Its proponents advocate leaving the responsibility for dealing with flagrant cases of corruption to the discretion of presumably trusted high authorities to handle tactfully and discreetly. Suggested are such tactics on their part as the transfer of known or suspected offenders to posts that cannot easily be exploited for personal gain and the use of firm persuasion to see that misappropriated funds are returned to government. In fact, these are among the indirect means currently employed. Others include the toleration and encouragement — to a point — of the innuendo type of press criticism.

There appears to be a curious resemblance between the second approach and that of former President Sukarno, who emphasized the unworkability of Western models and the necessity to return to indigenous traditions. Contemporary supporters of this approach, however, do not consider themselves to be traditionalists but gradualist modernizers. They justify their stance as one of temporary compromise in the interest of maximizing the chances for future modernization. Half-hearted and ineffective attempts to apply "advanced" standards and procedures, they argue, can also serve to discredit these and all that is meant by the "rule of law." Therefore such procedures should be suspended for the duration of the "transitional period."

Examples of "freezing" or temporary abandonment of principles presumably supported in order to preserve them intact and respected for posterity can be found in a number of other contexts. Some upper-echelon public administrators with advanced degrees in public or business administration from outstanding universities abroad instruct their similarly or somewhat less-trained subordinates to avoid writing job descriptions, planning work schedules, and submitting progress reports. They see these as meaningless rituals bearing little relationship to the actual work done or not done in their agencies.

In fact, neither they nor their immediate subordinates attempt to exercise more than token supervision or control over the activities of those below them who are more frequently out of their offices during working hours than within them. Nor do they feel justified in attempting to do so. For they, no less than those they nominally supervise, are engaged in various forms of "moonlighting" on the job. However, they do teach the principles and techniques of administration at local universities, interministerial seminars and "up-grading courses" at their own ministries in preparation for the time when they hope these can be applied.

In a sense they can be described as the "custodians" of modernity, the cells or repositories within which to keep and from which to diffuse the professional ethos of the future. In addition to the paradoxes of decision and risk, involving noncompliance, as described earlier, they are locked into the pattern of neotraditional accommodation by the seemingly intractable realities of economic survival. They fear to bring into disrepute the doctrines they preach by premature attempts to practice them among those they try to convert.

It is as if they hope to avert among their potential cadres of modernizers the kind of cynicism expressed by a regional official in remarks to the parliamentary mission visiting the site of a regional electrification project:

> Frankly, Sir, this project was started many years ago and we have had the honor of being visited by many government officials from the capital. With your present visit, this project will have been visited approximately 35 times, but, regrettably, we have yet to see concrete results from those observation visits. The necessary equipment never comes and, as you see, the project is still unfinished.[36]

In the political arena there are also some "custodians" of a future democratic political system who would restrict or curtail current manifestations of democracy. They argue that the political party system should be overhauled, or that political parties should liquidate themselves voluntarily or that they should be dissolved by the government. Such proposals contain elements of continuity and irony, continuity in that they echo the suggestions Sukarno made when he first advanced his "conception" that was to culminate in Guided Democracy, irony in that some of the current proponents of such proposals were among Sukarno's staunchest opponents in the name of "liberal democracy."

The current criticisms resemble those of a decade or more ago, mainly that parties, and their leaders especially, favor narrowly competitive, self-seeking, and particularistic positions to the detriment of national objectives. That those who advocate that the present party system be overhauled or dissolved may have their own particular rea-

[36] Reported in *Warta Harian,* January 16, 1969.

sons for doing so[37] does not detract from the validity of such criticism. For in an environment in which the "economic pie" has contracted and economic hardship for all but a few is endemic, political demands and struggles, however phrased, are essentially economic struggles to retain or gain segments of that pie. Thus, ex-Masjumi leaders who once held prominent economic and financial posts in governments prior to Guided Democracy are now publicly critical of the same types of economic policies they promulgated and supported in the past. For they are defending the current interests of their constituencies of local entrepreneurs threatened by many of the current economic measures and fearful of the consequences to them of the return of competitive foreign commercial and productive enterprises.

The "custodial" approach of the would-be modernizers, whether with respect to the exercise of administrative authority or to the search for a viable political system, can possibly be understood by reference to two dilemmas confronting them. The first is that of creating an environment in which the interpenetration and diffuseness of civil bureaucratic, political, and military spheres of authority are diminished. This would permit the formal authorities within agencies the greater possibility of commanding compliance within their organizations rather than having to negotiate it from those below them, with the constant possibility that the latter can exert countervailing pressures by exploiting their own cross-cutting memberships and alliances. To attain even relative segregation of spheres and roles would appear to depend upon restoring an economic environment more conducive to it.

[37] Such support appears to come primarily from three distinct but partially overlapping segments of the current national political elite and their regional coteries and followers: (1) those presently or formerly associated with the Christian parties, the Murba Party and the Socialist Party (now officially nonexistent); (2) partly reconstituted quasi-party and quasi-military functional groups brought into existence and given representation in the legislative organs during Guided Democracy; (3) the more recent and similarly constituted "action fronts" that are also represented in the legislative bodies. The parties made a poor showing in past elections; the other two categories of groups have not undergone the test of a national election. Lacking a mass base but holding formal posts, exercising influence upon those who do so, or being members of the "brain trust" of the current regime, the leaders of such parties and groups and their clienteles have little to gain and much to lose if the existing party structure is retained. Especially if the current controls upon the freedom of party activity were to be relaxed or abandoned before the projected elections, current estimates suggest that the benefactors are likely to be the mass-based parties, i.e., the Nationalist Party, the Orthodox Islamic Party, and the new Moslem Party, reconstituted from the old Masjumi; the latter two favor strengthening Islam as the basis for the state and society.

The second dilemma can be simply summarized as a matter of priorities between economic development or, more realistically, economic reconstruction, and political democracy. Those concerned with working toward modernity are aware that its many attributes and their many combinations in the modernized Western societies and in Japan have not been achieved simultaneously.[38] They are also aware from their own painful experience and that of other new states that over-ambitious attempts to attain too many objectives simultaneously will hinder, if not prevent, the achievement of most of them.

The strategy of giving primacy to economic over sociopolitical aspects of the process of modernization reflects both internal and external constraints and advantages. Despite disagreements over specific measures, a greater degree of internal consensus exists at this time for the general objective of economic improvement than can be gained for any other goal. As the debates in parliament and in the People's Consultative Assembly in March 1968 indicated, issues concerning the doctrinal and structural reorganization of the basis of the state are dangerously divisive. Indeed, in accordance with the now standard procedures of minimizing potential conflict, such issues were shelved. Moreover, external assistance is more likely to be given on the basis of the more familiar, tangible, and measurable dimension of economic development than on the basis of the more nebulous social and political dimensions. A realistic appraisal of the policies of foreign public and private agencies from whom assistance can be gained suggests that the political dimension most likely to concern potential donors and partners is that of stability rather than democracy. Put somewhat differently, as long as there is sufficient provision for the expression and management of dissent to maintain stability, objections from foreign commentators on the grounds of insufficient democracy are largely irrelevant.[39]

In this respect, it might be mentioned that Suharto's leadership has emerged as apparently similar in style, if different in direction, to that of Sukarno. Admittedly, Suharto lacks Sukarno's charisma for both

[38] See Reinhard Bendix, *Nation-Building and Citizenship* (New York: Wiley, 1964), for a detailed study of alternative sequences and combination of factors in different countries at different periods.

[39] Even what can be termed the "liberal-democratic" camp of Western academics and intellectuals is split on the issue of whether and how much Western-type democracy is compatible with other forms of development in formerly colonial states.

the masses and those close to him. Nor does he have Sukarno's oratorical skills and ability to project himself personally as the symbol of the nation. However, he displays many of Sukarno's talents for political manipulation, balancing potentially conflicting groups and individuals against each other, neutralizing opposing forces by giving each in turn concessions at points of maximum pressure and consulting at length with spokesmen and delegations from various groups before throwing his weight in any direction. These have gained him respect and helped him consolidate his control. Since the term "Guided Democracy" is in disgrace, one might substitute "manipulative democracy" for this somewhat similar phenomenon.

There would appear to be a strategy underlying the overt one that stresses economic rehabilitation and development objectives as paramount. The implicit strategy involves regaining the partnership with outsiders that was formerly rejected but giving it a new and more secure basis. Thus, many large-scale enterprises that were taken over by the government have been or are in the process of being returned to their former owners under new arrangements. Some of these involve retiring or dismissing in the immediate or near future excess or inefficient personnel, particularly in the managerial echelons. Other large-scale industrial opportunities are being offered to foreign investors at attractive terms, including a relatively free hand in selecting local partners and managerial talent. Since these involve foreign interests from a number of countries, it is not easy to apply the term "neocolonial" to their economic entry, as it was when so much foreign investment was held by the former metropolitan power.

This might help in solving one major impasse in the vicious circle of interlocking economic and administrative elements of neotraditionalism and aid in reversing the process. For example, the onus of edging out insufficiently skilled military managers of government enterprises is not easy and frequently is impossible for either civilian or military administrators in the central or regional governments to assume. This burden has been shifted to the foreigner, or at least he formally assumes it, as well as some of the direct costs that presumably will be recovered ultimately under reconstructed management. Similarly, to appoint new indigenous personnel to managerial posts according to criteria of skill and competence places extreme strains upon the most "modernized" Indonesian who has accepted these criteria. For the economic situation lends added poignancy to the traditional claims of kin, friendship, ethnic ties, etc. In this dilemma, he may fulfill some obligations by pressing these claims, but he can acquiesce and even participate in decisions to deny them and still be absolved of responsibility for rejection by referring it to the foreigner. Such considerations can operate apart from the renewed foreign private sector or joint enterprise sector. Foreign experts on loans to public agencies can be used not only to supply advice and added skills. They can also be used to provide a necessary authoritative component or "scapegoat mechanism" for sufficiently skilled Indonesian administrators to enforce directives and maintain discipline.

The road to modernity is long and devious with many backward and sideward twistings and turnings. If the subtle Indonesians, with a securer sense of their own identity and less defensive insights into their strengths and weaknesses than previously, have devised devious strategies to overcome their current "hangups" in the realm of authority, these may prove to be effective paths to ultimate arrival. One cannot judge what is effective except in retrospect. Nor is there ever any ultimate arrival, for modernized societies encounter new sets of problems as a consequence of modernization. It is somewhat ironic to confront the current Indonesian elite conversion to rationality — real or assumed — from the perspective of a country in which the impersonal norms of supra-organization are being rejected by much of its youth who seek the bonds of collective empathy that Indonesians have begun to discard.